THE ULTIMATE SAFE MONEY GUIDE

THE ULTIMATE SAFE MONEY GUIDE

HOW EVERYONE 50 AND OVER CAN PROTECT, SAVE, AND GROW THEIR MONEY

MARTIN D. WEISS, Ph.D.
WEISS RATINGS, INC.

John Wiley & Sons, Inc.

For my son, Anthony

ISBN 0-471-15202-1

Printed in the United States of America.

10 9 8 7 6 5 4

CONTENTS

INTRODUCTION

On September 11, 2001, a handful of fanatic terrorists broke America's heart; and even as we grieved for our fallen countrymen and women, the second devastating impact of that contemptible deed was about to be felt—on our economy.

If our stock markets had been stronger, the economy might have held up well under the new strain. But that was not the case. On the day before the attacks, the stocks of America's technology companies had already been slammed 66 percent, wiping out $5 trillion in wealth, nearly half of the value of all the products and services our nation produces in an entire year. By September 2001, millions of investors were already reeling from stock market losses, their life savings destroyed, their retirement plans smashed.

Or, if our corporations had been making good money, our economy might have been okay, too. But that was not the case either. On the day before the attacks, the 4,000-plus companies listed on the Nasdaq exchange had already suffered from a flood of red ink so large, every single penny of their profits made since the summer of 1994 had been washed away. One technology leader, JDS Uniphase, had just reported the largest single loss of all time— $56 billion. The nation's airlines were losing close to $2.5 billion for the year. In almost every American industry, profits were plunging.

At least, if average American families had been saving for a rainy day, they could have gotten by without too much financial trauma. But as fate would have it, most American families had stopped saving months before the attacks. Instead of putting away five, six, or seven cents out of every dollar they made, like they used to in earlier years, they saved nothing–not one penny. The U.S. savings rate had fallen to zero, even *less* than zero. Compounding the problem, millions of families were drowning in credit card debts.

What's most shocking is that many of America's richest corporations were in the same boat. To survive a couple of bad years, I figure the average American company should have about one dollar in cash on hand to cover every dollar of bills or debts coming due within the next 12 months. But in the days before the attacks, many companies were already very low in cash: Delta Airlines had only 38 cents in cash per dollar of debts coming due in a year. Northwest Airlines had only 36 cents; Vanguard Airlines, only 19. No wonder the airlines needed an immediate, massive federal bailout just days after September 11!

Despite all this, if we could only be confident that the attacks of September 2001 were a one-time event, it might not be so serious. But as we have seen, that has not been the case either. The entire world had entered a new, riskier era. The global economy was already in–or soon to enter–a global recession. Now, a worldwide depression was no longer unthinkable.

All this raises serious questions for anyone 50 or over. Will the American economy and stock market fall to even lower levels? Which insurance companies and banks are most likely to fail? Which ones are safe? How can you protect your nest egg? What changes must you make to your retirement plans? If you've already suffered losses, how can you recoup? What steps must you take immediately to safeguard your investment portfolio, your home, your insurance policies? Where can you invest your money safely?

My family began answering questions like these a long time ago–in 1929, just before the Great Stock Market Crash.

That's when my father, J. Irving Weiss, looked at his research, peeked over the horizon, and saw serious trouble ahead. He was probably the only stockbroker on Wall Street that warned his clients ahead of time to get out of stocks and take their money out of the banks, too. He borrowed $500 from his mother and used it to sell the market short.

When the dust settled a few years later, investors had lost over 90 percent of their money, and every bank in America had shut its doors to withdrawals. But there was Dad, a young man in his early 20s, with close to $100,000.

I came along in 1946, in the first wave of baby-boomers. As soon as I was old enough, I helped Dad with his research and writing and continued doing so until he "retired." Then, when I was in *my* early 20s, I founded my own research company. Dad promptly came out of retirement and began helping me, just as I had helped him before. Our main goal—to show you how to invest your money safely.

At the time, everyone thought banks were safe. But in 1974, I issued my first major warning of trouble—about the coming demise of hundreds of S&Ls. A few weeks later, I got a call from a top official of a major S&L industry association, complaining bitterly about our analysis: "How dare you say hundreds of the best savings and loans in this country are going down the tubes?" he shouted "How dare you say that our accountants are cooking the books?" Several years later, a U.S. Congressional committee hauled this same official before a panel and lambasted him for thousands of S&L failures. But at the time, Dad and I didn't know what to say, except: "The facts are the facts."

This experience turned out to be good training for my later run-ins with financial institutions. In the early 1980s, we started rating the nation's banks, and by the end of the decade, we began looking at insurance companies. Although Dad was already in his early 80s at the time, he was still a great resource to have around. He had one of those rare, piercing minds that's capable of instant recall of the distant past, keen awareness of the here-and-now, plus uncanny foresight of what's to come. His office was just a few doors away from mine at our building in Palm Beach County, Florida.

One afternoon I stopped by to see him, announcing that I was going to start rating insurance companies. I can never forget the very first words out of his mouth: "Check out First Executive (the parent of Executive Life Insurance)," he said. They're knee-deep in junk bonds (bonds issued by high-risk companies). Follow the junk and you will find your answers."

I did, and I found quite a few life insurance companies that were loaded with junk bonds, one of which was First Capital Life, which I gave a safety rating of D- (weak). I was generous. The company should have gotten an F. But within days of my widely publicized warnings on First Capital, a gaggle of the company's lawyers and top executives flew down to our office. They ranted. They raved. They swore they'd slap me with a massive lawsuit and put me out of business if I didn't give them a better rating.

"All the Wall Street ratings experts give us high grades," they said. "Who the hell do you think *you* are?"

I politely explained that I never let personal threats affect my Weiss Ratings. And unlike other rating agencies, I don't accept a dime from the companies I rate. "I work for individual investors," I said, "not big corporations."

"Besides," I continued, opening up the company's most recent quarterly report, "your own financial statements prove your company is a disaster waiting to happen." That's when one of them delivered the ultimate threat: "Weiss better shut the @!%# up," he whispered to my associate, "or get a bodyguard."

I did neither. To the contrary, I intensified my warnings. Within weeks, the company went belly-up just as I'd warned—still boasting high ratings from major Wall Street firms *on the very day they failed.* In fact, the leading insurance rating agency, A. M. Best, didn't downgrade First Capital to a warning level until five days *after* it failed. Needless to say, it was too late for policyholders.[1]

It was a grisly sight—not just for policyholders, but for shareholders as well: The company's stock crashed 99 percent, crucifying millions of unwitting investors. Then the stock died, wiped off the face of the earth. Three of the company's closest competitors also bit the dust. Investors—who did not have access to my Weiss Ratings—lost $4 billion, $4.5 billion, and $13 billion, respectively, in the failed companies. Fortunately, investors who had seen my ratings were ready. I warned them long before those household-name companies went bust.

In fact, the contrast between investors who relied on my ratings and those who didn't was so stark, even the U.S. Congress couldn't help but notice. They asked: How was it possible for Weiss—a small firm in Florida—to identify companies that were about to fail, when Wall Street told us they were still "superior" or "excellent" right up to the day they failed?

To find an answer, Congress called all the rating agencies—S&P, Moody's, A. M. Best, Duff & Phelps, and Weiss—to testify. But I was the only one who showed up. So Congress asked its auditing arm, the U.S. General Accounting Office (GAO), to conduct a detailed study on the Weiss ratings in comparison to the ratings of the other major rating agencies.[2]

Three years later, after extensive research and review, the GAO published its conclusion: Weiss beat its leading competitor, A. M. Best, by a factor of three to one in forecasting future financial troubles. The three other Wall Street firms weren't even competition.[3] But the GAO never answered the original question—why?

I can assure you it wasn't because of better access to information than our competitors. Nor are we smarter than they are. The real answer lies in one four-letter word: *bias.* To this day, the other rating agencies are paid huge fees for each rating—the ratings are literally bought and paid for by the companies they rate.[4] Plus, they empower the rated companies to decide when to be rated, how, and by whom. They routinely give the companies a preview of the rating before it's published and some agencies even grant them the right to suppress publication of any rating they don't agree with.[5]

I don't do business that way. I don't accept any money or any deals from the companies I rate. And I always publish their ratings whether they like it or not. In fact, the only income I get from these ratings comes from investors and consumers like you. That means my only loyalty is to you—not to big corporations.

My strict adherence to this principle is why the GAO found our ratings to be the most accurate, and why *Barron's* said the GAO study is "a glowing tribute to Weiss." It's also why the *New York Times* declared Weiss was "the first to see the dangers and say so unambiguously." And why *Esquire* magazine wrote "only Weiss . . . provides financial grades free of any possible conflict of interest." They recognized the importance of taking the bias out of safety ratings for financial institutions.[6]

Unfortunately, they didn't recognize there was an even more pressing need to take the bias out of the "buy," "sell," and "hold" ratings Wall Street was issuing on thousands of stocks bought by millions of investors. So a year before the Nasdaq began to fall, we introduced our first Weiss Stock Ratings, showing that nearly every tech stock in America was high-risk and vulnerable to a great plunge.

Now the tech wreck is history; and today, Dad is gone. But with the help of 160 analysts and support staff, I continue his work, and this book is the culmination of our collective efforts. In it, I help you learn from my experiences—and from yours as well. I warn of more dangers to come. And I guide you, step by step, on a path to safety and profits.

At 55, I know I cannot afford to make a serious financial mistake, or I may have no chance to recover before retirement. I want to build my wealth safely and protect my future, especially in this new era of uncertainty. If you're 50+ like me, I believe you should do the same.

To help prepare you, I show you how to avoid the pitfalls of so-called free advice and to arm yourself with powerful, independent information that is not biased by any conflicts of interest (Chapters 1 and 2).

If you've been burned by the disasters on Wall Street and the economy, there are some things you may be able to do immediately to get money back. But in the long term, you will find that safety and yield are your best escape, and profits are your best revenge (Chapters 3 through 6).

I show you how to protect your wealth from a decline in value. And I guide you through each of the steps you will need to take to avoid the pitfalls of tax-exempt bonds and insurance—to build toward a comfortable retirement (Chapters 7 through 11).

Good planning to offset the financial burden of medical and health care is your final challenge. But the plethora of plans and permutations you can choose from are both complex and deceptive. Follow the prescriptions I offer in Chapters 12 and 13, and you will be able to sleep nights in the knowledge that you have it entirely under your direct and personal control.

At various times throughout this book, you may find yourself asking the question: "Which programs are right for me? How *much* do I invest in each one? The answers depend a lot on your personal circumstances. But to help you to divvy up your funds appropriately, I have devised a special Risk Self-Test (Appendix A). Before you buy any investments, be sure to take the test. Then, depending on your score, allocate your money according to the recommendations I provide, also in the appendix.

Are you 50+ with no experience in investing whatsoever? Have you suddenly been saddled with the full responsibility of making decisions? If so, Chapter 14 is dedicated to you, giving you an easy-to-understand overview of what to do. But it's also for the veteran investor–to help you put all the recommendations of this book into a single, unified framework.

If you subscribe to my monthly *Safe Money Report,* be aware that the advice I give in this book may differ in some ways. The reason is simple: Each issue of the *Safe Money Report* (www .safemoneyreport.com) is for this month or next; this book is for this year and many years to come.

Moreover, in this book, I assume that you do *not* have regular access to an advisor–that you will be making decisions mostly on your own without additional assistance. I refer you to resources to update a lot of the information contained in these pages, and urge you to stay as current as possible. But you are the decision maker.

Learn now how to avoid any new risks the future might hold by arming yourself with the information and guidance I give you in the pages to follow.

CHAPTER 1

THE GREAT STOCK MARKET SCAM

The stock market decline of the early twenty-first century was caused neither by terrorists nor war. It was the direct consequence of the Great Stock Market Scam—an elaborate system of deceptions that threatened the retirement savings of millions of Americans over age 50.

Back on April 26, 1999, for example, Morgan Stanley Dean Witter plus 18 other Wall Street brokerage firms gave you a recommendation that could have transformed a comfortable retirement into a life on welfare.

They recommended Priceline.com as "a quintessential virtual business model," and gave it a strong buy rating or equivalent. When they made this recommendation, Priceline was selling at $104. Twenty-one months later, it was trading for $1.50 a share. If you listened to Morgan Stanley, or to any of the other 18 firms, and you sank $10,000 into this turkey, you'd be left with a meager $144. That's a whopping 97 percent loss.

Then there's Amazon.com (a.k.a. "Amazon.bomb"), also much beloved on Wall Street. In December of 1999, Merrill Lynch and 32 other Wall Street brokerage firms gave it superlative ratings and told investors like you to scoop it up. If you'd put $10,000 into this company, you'd have lost a whopping $8,761 by year-end 2000.

The battering you'd have taken if you'd followed Wall Street's advice doesn't stop there. If you'd invested in Procter & Gamble (P&G), you'd have lost 56 percent. You'd have lost another 57 percent in Cisco. Investing in Oracle would have cost you 53 percent. Intel, another 60 percent loss. Not to mention the 2,500 other tech stocks that Wall Street brokers kept telling you to scoop up as bargains.

All told, the total market value of the more than 4,300 stocks listed on the Nasdaq plunged from $7.6 trillion on March 10, 2000, to $2.4 trillion on April 6, 2001. Investors lost $5.2 trillion–more money than was lost in the worst crashes of all recorded history, the equivalent of nearly half the entire gross domestic product of the most powerful economy in the world. All in just 13 months.

A key cause was the companies' earnings, which turned out to be far lower than most everyone expected. Some companies couldn't claim a penny in earnings. Others couldn't even claim a penny in *sales*. But nearly all continued to brag about great results and get Wall Street's best ratings until virtually the bitter end.

What happened? How could the earnings information and investment advice given to so many investors have been so far off from the truth? How was it possible for so many investors to lose so much money so quickly?

Many investors blame themselves, regretting their susceptibility to greed or fear. And certainly, those emotions did play a role. But if you lost money in the debacle, you should know that it's mostly not your fault. You probably were the victim of a massive, elaborate scam, which, by sheer virtue of its enormity, is more sophisticated than even the savviest of investors.

This great scam was not planned in a conspiracy; it evolved naturally in an environment of complacency. It is not perpetrated by one, two, or even a dozen exceptional institutions; it envelops almost everyone–chief financial officers at major corporations, the most respected research analysts on Wall Street, and tens of thousands of individual brokers.

Their ubiquitous tool: *misinformation*. Indeed, the critical information you need to make sound investment decisions was–and is–passed through a series of filters, each removing some piece of bad news, each adding a new layer of hype, distortion, and even outright lies.

To protect yourself, you must understand how they misinform you, when, and where. So follow the trail of information–from its source (the corporation), to the Wall Street research analysts, and finally to the brokers who serve individual investors . . . .

THIRTY-ONE PERCENT OF COMPANIES LISTED ON U.S. STOCK EXCHANGES ARE SUSPECTED OF MANIPULATING EARNINGS REPORTS

The single most important piece of fundamental information that you need about a company is its current earnings. It's no coincidence, therefore, that earnings information is often the prime target for manipulation and distortion–by none other than the company officials who are responsible for compiling and issuing the data each quarter.

These company officials come under intense pressure to meet Wall Street's overblown expectations. If they don't, they fear their shares will be severely punished. So when they realize that their actual earnings are falling short, many resort to gimmicks (both legal and illegal) to twist the truth. The consequences for investors are disastrous. Here are just a handful from the recent past:

- When Nine West was investigated by the Securities and Exchange Commission (SEC) for allegedly misrepresenting revenues following its 1995 acquisition of U.S. Shoe Corporation, its stock plunged. The investigation was terminated without enforcement.

- Shareholders in Summit Medical saw their stock slide nearly 90 percent for similar reasons.

- McKesson HBOC, Incorporated, was forced to restate three years' worth of revenues because of accounting improprieties. The stock plunged 82 percent.

- Sunbeam Corporation falsely reported $96 million in income it never earned. Its stock was virtually wiped away—down 93.4 percent.

- Tyco fell 58 percent . . . Informix fell 89 percent . . . and Safety-Kleen lost a whopping 96 percent—all because of allegations that their earnings had been distorted.

In each case, the truth was finally revealed, and by the time most investors found out and sold their shares, it was too late.

How widespread is this problem? To answer that question, my staff and I took a closer look at over 6,000 companies listed on U.S. stock exchanges, and we compared their stated earnings with their *actual cash flow from operations.* Normally, these two measures of performance should be in sync. However, in 1,687 companies, *nearly one out of three,* we found significant discrepancies between earnings and cash flow. These are not proof positive of hanky-panky; they are a red flag, leading us to suspect earnings manipulations, legal or illegal.[1]

This is absolutely shocking to me. Once upon a time, nearly all major U.S. companies followed generally accepted accounting principles (GAAP) to report earnings. They were sticklers for accuracy when reporting key financial information to shareholders. By the late 1990s, though, in their growing desperation to meet Wall Street's expectations, more and more companies resorted to various schemes to massage earnings. That's why, in one typical quarter, the operating income of 665 major companies reviewed by the *Wall Street Journal* rose 9.6 percent. However, when adjusted for all of the costs that would normally be charged under GAAP, actual corporate earnings *fell* 4 percent.

What's the motive? Simple. The officials of America's corporations can get up to 90 percent of their compensation in stock and stock options. So they have everything to gain by putting out information that will boost the value of their own investments in the company.

Consider, for example, AOL's Stephen Case, who was paid a little over $1 million in salary as recently as 1998, but *also* was paid more than $158 million in stock and stock options. Craig Barrett at Intel earned a salary of $2.6 million, plus more than $114 million in stock and stock options. Sanford Weill at Citigroup collected

$10.5 million in salary and about $156 million in stock and options. Henry Silverman at Cendant received $2.9 million in salary and $61 million in stock and options.

Also, let's not forget Disney's Michael Eisner, the all-time income champ among American CEOs. His salary reached about $5.7 million. Additional compensation in the form of stock and stock options totaled a staggering $569 million!

The options portion of the executive compensation package is pivotal. If you hold options to buy your company's shares, known as *call options,* you have the right–but not the obligation–to purchase the shares at a relatively low price and then immediately sell them at a much higher level. If the company's stock fails to go up, the options could be totally worthless; if the stock soars, the options *alone* could be worth more than 10 years' base salary.

It doesn't take a rocket scientist to figure out what happens when the company's stock drops, for instance, by 30 percent: The Big Cheese loses one-third, one-half, or even two-thirds of his or her personal wealth. Depending on the company, that percentage can translate into hundreds of millions of dollars. These corporate CEOs aren't dumb. They know that there's nothing better than a positive earnings report to goose up their stock prices. Hence, once each quarter, unscrupulous CEOs massage the numbers, hide losses any way they can, artificially inflate revenues, and, when all else fails, look you square in the eye and lie their rich, well-tailored fannies off.

It's bad enough when rich corporate fat cats get richer through deceptive practices. When investors like you have to pay the price for corporate greed and deceit it's a disaster. What's most frustrating of all, though, is that the most common methods used to massage earnings are actually legal. Some examples are discussed in the following few pages.

The Goodwill Distortion

A Fortune 500 company buys up a hot, new upstart firm for $10 billion. It's an outrageous price that's 10 times the actual market value of the company's assets. The accountants are then given the job of allocating the purchase price on the company's balance sheet. But they say: "Hey! We can only find assets worth $1 billion. What are we supposed to do with the other $9 billion?"

Management's response: "Create a goodwill account and slap the entire $9 billion into it." This is an asset account, right alongside items like *cash,* or *plant and equipment.* Yet it has no substance. A small amount, to represent the value of the company's good name or customer list, is acceptable. Since when is it normal, though, for 90 percent of a company's assets to be in an intangible, mostly bogus, asset? This is the deception that helped doom the savings and loans. It's the same deception that was routine in the Great Stock Market Scam.

The goodwill scheme doesn't end there, though. Each year thereafter, the accountants are supposed to charge off a portion of that goodwill. For example, if they stretch it out for 10 years, that would equate to $900 million per year in costs. But no—the managers don't want to do that because it would mean their earnings would be *reduced* by $900 million each year. So they stretch it out for 40 years, the absolute maximum allowed, finding various rationalizations for why the goodwill has such an incredibly long lifespan.

The resulting exaggeration of earnings is mind-boggling in its dimensions. If the company had a profit of $1 billion and charged its goodwill over 10 years, at the rate of $900 million per year, its profit would be $100 million. Stretched out over 40 years, however, the charge is only $225 million per year, leaving a profit of $775 million, or nearly *eight times* the actual profit.

Then, guess what! Three or four years down the road, the company has either a great year with windfall profits, or a horrendous year with huge losses. When the company has a great year, they say: "Let's declare the goodwill worthless after all and charge the whole thing off as an expense right now. Since we have such huge profits this year, no one will notice the difference." If the year is horrendous, they say essentially the same thing: "Let's declare the goodwill worthless and charge it off. Our stock has already gotten clobbered because of our huge losses. So who cares if we take an even bigger loss this year?" Either way, the 40-year asset is conveniently transformed into a 3-year asset, past and future earnings are grossly exaggerated, and investors become the losers.[2]

The Pooling-of-Interest Gimmick

With the surge in megamergers in the late 1990s, more and more companies weren't even creating a goodwill account to begin with. Instead, they just "pooled their interests." In other words, they combined their assets into one big account and buried the huge overstatement of values in their balance sheets. This method, called *pooling of interest,* deceived shareholders twice. First, they were led to believe that the company was worth far more than it really was, with no easy way to figure out its true value. Second, because the company didn't have to worry about goodwill charges, it was free to exaggerate earnings to its heart's content.

With this method, instead of reporting $100 million profit or even $775 million profit, the company could report the full $1 billion. Shareholders wouldn't have a clue that it was totally bogus, with no adjustment whatsoever for the fact that the company was valued at 10 times its fair market value.[3]

Sound impossible? Then consider this real-life example: Yahoo! acquired Geocities, paying a whopping $3.6 billion in stock for assets that were worth only $130 million. Under the standard and widely accepted purchase-method accounting, Yahoo! would have had to allocate the difference to goodwill, which it then would have to charge to earnings in future years. Instead, Yahoo! used the pooling-of-interest method, which let it hide the overvaluation and exaggerate its earnings in that year and *every* year for decades to come. Ditto for the megamergers of Lucent Technologies and Ascend Communications, Cisco Systems and Cerent, and Allied Signal and Honeywell. Nearly every major merger was a large investor rip-off—a landmine that was ready to explode at any time. But there's more . . . .

Padded Sales Reports

Top executives aren't the only ones getting fat compensation packages, loaded with stocks and options. Sales managers also get a piece of the pie. Therefore, to boost the value of their own shares and options, they went far beyond just tweaking their financial numbers–they completely perverted and undermined their company's business model.

Tony Sagami, editor of *Stocks on the Move* and a partner in a small but profitable Web-based business, had a personal encounter with this phenomenon in 2000. He and his associates needed to buy a batch of new computer servers and invited bids from various manufacturers.

Manufacturer A came back with an offer to sell the equipment for $2 million, with zero down and payback terms over five years. Tony's reaction: "No money down? Wow! For a small, upstart firm like ours, with very little cash or collateral, this is darn attractive."

However, the reps from Manufacturer B did even better. They offered similar equipment, also for about $2 million, also with zero down and payments over five years. To sweeten the deal, they said: "Look! It's going to cost you money to hire technicians to set up your new servers and workstations. So on top of the $2 million of hardware, we'll write you a check for $100,000 to help you pay for all of the setup expenses."

Tony and his partners were ready to grab this great deal when still a third, big-name manufacturer came along and completely blew their minds with this proposal: "We'll ship you the $2 million in servers. We'll write you a check to cover all the installations and ancillary expenses. And you don't have to pay us a penny–*ever!* Just give us a 5 percent share in your company."

Hard to believe? Maybe. But remarkably common. In each case, no matter how crazy the terms, the sales managers booked the sales immediately, the financial officers boasted to Wall Street analysts about their "wonderful sales growth," and the analysts promptly raised the hype for the company by another octave. Investors ate it all up. They rushed to buy the stock in droves and sent the shares through the roof.

All this continued to snowball until one totally predictable event: Equipment buyers failed to pay up. And the game was over.

I could cite scores of examples. Here's just one: According to a recently filed lawsuit, Lucent offered Winstar a financing arrangement for up to $2 billion, half of which was available at any given time for the purchase of new equipment from Lucent. Less than one year later, Winstar was in bankruptcy, suing Lucent for $10 billion in damages. Result: Lucent's credit rating was reduced to junk status, with huge debts of its own, mountains of unshipped inventory, and a stock in a tailspin.

The Great Options Boondoggle

The biggest payoff for executives is the lucrative stock option deals like the ones I mentioned earlier, and therein lies an even greater deception.

If the stock options are clearly a form of compensation to the managers, they should be deducted from earnings as an expense, right? But they're not deducted. Again, earnings are exaggerated, and investors are the ones who suffer.

To sweeten the deal for themselves even further, if the stock in the company falls, the company may simply replace the old options with new, better options.

Here's how it works: Let's imagine that you're a senior executive at XYZ Corporation, and the stock is selling at $18 per share. To fatten your compensation package, the company has given you options to buy 10,000 shares at $20, only $2 above where it is now. This $20 price is the *strike price*–the price at which your options can be converted into actual shares.

If the shares rise to, for example, $50 per share, the options give you the right to buy the shares for just $20, sell them immediately for $50, and pocket the $30-per-share profit. If you have options to buy 1 million shares, that's $30 million with this one transaction alone. So you see how options can multiply the value of your compensation package by 10 or 20 times, almost overnight.

Instead of going up, let's say the shares fall from $18 a share to $8 a share. You still have the options and you still have the chance to make a bundle if the stock recovers. But you say: "I don't want to wait for the stock to recover before my options are worth something. I want the company to restore the value of my options to what they were *before* the stock fell. Instead of an option to buy XYZ Corporation at $20 per share, I want you to change it to an option to buy at $10 per share."

Unbelievable as it may seem, the board members, who themselves may have a direct interest in the options, typically vote to do just that. This practice, called *rolling down the strike price,* has been widespread during market declines.

Then, if the market recovers, they get to keep the better options. The result is that they have the potential to earn double, triple, even quadruple the profits anticipated in their original compensation packages. All of this happens without deducting one penny of cost from reported earnings.[4]

The effect on the individual investor, once again, is dramatic. According to Smithers & Company, Ltd., a highly respected research institute in London, if U.S. corporations properly accounted for the costs of just the stock options they granted, their profits would have been 56 percent lower in 1997 and 50 percent lower in 1998.[5] The same thing is happening now in many of the stocks whose bubbles have been burst. While the average investor got clobbered by the decline, executives and other insiders rushed in to protect their compensation packages.

Cendant Corporation, for example, repriced 46.3 million options for its CEO, lowering the strike price from as high as $23.88 down to $9.81. This occurred just six days after the share price hit its low. Shareholders ended up paying the full price for this practice.

At Advanced Micro Devices, options were repriced not once, not twice, not even three times. Chairman Jerry Sanders had his options' strike prices ratcheted down *six* times throughout a six-year period. Although the stock was performing well, by lowering the strike price so many times, Sanders virtually guaranteed himself a nice wad of money, regardless of what happened to the stock.

Later, when the cost of these packages is finally booked, investors like you and me wind up picking up the tab in the form of sharply lower share prices caused by surprise drops in earnings. In the meantime, the company's executives, protected from the real world, are cleaning up.

Warren Buffett was so outraged by this all-too common practice that, when he acquired General Re Insurance, he decided to completely do away with stock option programs in the company. He got the managers to convert their options to cash bonuses on the spot and charged the entire expense to earnings. That's admirable. Unfortunately, however, few companies are following Buffett's example. They know that if they report truthfully, they'll have to report a serious drop in corporate earnings. Their shares would be knocked for a loop, and their own riches would be history.

All of these methods that corporations commonly use to manipulate earnings–plus many more–add up to one, gigantic house of cards that is supported by little more than lies and hot air.[6] This helps to explain why so many stocks have crashed and burned: All it takes to knock down the house of cards is a whiff of fresh air–the truth. As soon as the truth comes out, down go the shares.

Most people believe these practices were limited to technology stocks, mostly on the Nasdaq exchange. In reality, they were widespread throughout the stock market.

In an address on the quality of financial reporting in corporate America, former SEC Chairman Arthur Levitt warned:

> Increasingly, I have become concerned that the motivation to meet Wall Street earnings expectations may be overriding common-sense business practices. Too many corporate managers, auditors, and analysts are participants in a game of nods and winks. In the zeal to satisfy consensus earnings estimates and project a smooth earnings path, wishful thinking may be winning the day over faithful representation. . . . As a result, I fear that we are witnessing an erosion in the quality of earnings, and therefore, the quality of financial reporting. Managing may be giving way to manipulation; integrity may be losing out to illusion.[7]

SEC Chief Accountant Lynn E. Turner put it more succinctly:

> These corporate releases are nothing more than "EBS–everything but bad stuff."[8]

Years ago, most Wall Street research analysts would typically pore through all the EBS from the companies, do their best to cull out any lies and inaccuracies, and give the stock a rating based on their own independent opinion. Unfortunately, as I'll show you in the following section, that is not the standard practice today.

HOW WALL STREET STOCK RATINGS ARE BOUGHT AND PAID FOR BY THE COMPANIES THEY RATE

Wall Street's typical pattern today is to take the already-distorted data that are coming from the nation's corporations and *add on a whole new layer of hype and distortion.*[9] What changed? How were supposedly independent research analysts transformed into virtual stock promoters?

It all started when the entire nature of the brokerage business changed radically. You see, back in the old days, brokers made most of their money from commissions (i.e., revenues they earned whether you bought or sold). Starting in the 1980s, however, a whole new crop of brokerage firms (i.e., the discount brokers) began offering cut-rate commissions. Over time, that forced the entire industry to cut nearly all commission rates dramatically.

To continue to grow their profits, most Wall Street firms decided to expand aggressively into another, far more profitable business: helping companies to sell their shares to the public, either in an *initial public offering* (an IPO), or in a secondary offering.

In this business, called *investment banking,* or *underwriting,* the Wall Street firms play a totally different role. Instead of serving investors like you, they cater to big or upcoming corporate clients like Procter & Gamble, Intel, or DrKoop.com. Instead of earning a small commission, they get a share of the proceeds. And instead of making money whether you buy or you sell, they only make money when you *buy.* They have a direct, vested interest in the results. They want to see only good news about the company, only a positive reception from investors, and only a rising price in the shares. They are promoters, not brokers.

Rather than offering objective research and advice, their primary goal is to sell you a bill of goods. That means hyping up the company's performance and touting the stock. It means cherry-picking the best numbers, sugarcoating any difficulties, covering up real problems, and putting out misleading, deceptive, effectively falsified ratings.

For individual research analysts, the incentive to deceive is large, and the penalty for being honest, even larger. According to the *Wall Street Journal,* analysts at Morgan Stanley got bigger bonuses when they made a positive contribution to underwriting revenues. At the same time, the *Wall Street Journal* reported that Morgan Stanley analysts who refused to suppress negative information about underwriting clients find themselves transferred to other, far less remunerated jobs. Still others found themselves out of work and on the street, blackballed in the industry, and their careers destroyed.[10]

A few years ago, an analyst at a brokerage firm wrote a stinging report on Donald Trump's Taj Mahal casino. The report alerted investors to serious problems underlying the hyped-up issue. However, when Trump got wind of the negative analysis, he immediately threatened the brokerage firm with a lawsuit. The analyst was fired and the report was pulled.

In another situation, Merrill Lynch was slated to be the lead underwriter of a major bond issue by Conseco. As usual, it was a lucrative deal, expected to bring Merrill $1 million in fees until, that is, one of Merrill's analysts made the fatal mistake of issuing a negative report on Conseco. Merrill Lynch, to its credit, stood by its report; Conseco, however, reacted by firing Merrill as the lead underwriter and taking its business elsewhere—to none other than Morgan Stanley. The message to Wall Street was clear: Tell investors what we want you to tell them, and you win. Tell them the truth, and you lose.

Pulling away underwriting business isn't the only tactic that corporations use to keep Wall Street's research departments in line. If there is a rating downgrade they don't like, they can close their own brokerage accounts at that firm and take their business elsewhere. This practice is so well known that analysts have a special expression for it: "They put us in the penalty box."

Do these things happen every single time? Of course not. But they don't have to. The threat alone is enough to keep the heat on the analysts and have a chilling effect on objective research.

What is bothersome is not only the shenanigans that reach our attention. It's also the ones we never hear about. We happen to know about Morgan Stanley only because some employees talked to the *Wall Street Journal.* We heard of the incident with Donald

Trump only because the analyst who was fired had the guts to sue the brokerage firm. (He won a $750,000 arbitration award.)

But what about the hundreds of analysts who don't sue or talk? who can't pin down the *real* reasons they were fired? who don't want to be blackballed by Wall Street? or who are simply scared? What happens to them? More important, what happens to you, the investor?

You risk losing a fortune, like the millions of investors who lost over $5 trillion in the tech wreck of 2000 and 2001. Not surprisingly, the analysts themselves continue to make big bucks: In 2000, for example, an analyst at Goldman Sachs issued 11 gloriously positive ratings on stocks that subsequently lost investors three-fourths of their money, or more. One of this guy's best-performing recommendations of the year was down 71 percent; his worst was down 99.8 percent. Yet he was paid $20,000,000 (twenty million dollars!) for his efforts.

How pervasive is the bias in Wall Street's stock ratings? Not long ago, the SEC reported on a study that measured the scope of the problem. It reviewed thousands of buy, sell, or hold stock recommendations issued by Wall Street brokers. You'd expect some kind of a balance among these recommendations, for example, one-third buy, one-third hold, and one-third sell. But that's not what the SEC found. Quite to the contrary, *only a pathetic 1 percent of the recommendations were to sell stocks.* The remaining 99 percent encouraged you to hold or buy more.[11] Moreover, all of this was in a year when only about 32 percent (i.e., less than one-third) of the listed stocks on the major exchanges advanced. A startling 68 percent were losers.

Countless companies with no sales and no revenues are routinely rated as *strong buys.* Companies that are about to be decimated by obvious problems are, at worst, downgraded to *hold* or *market perform.* And when stocks are virtually falling into oblivion, the common response by many analysts is eerie silence: They quietly remove the fallen stocks from their list of rated companies, with no further comment or warning.

The conclusion is clear: Wall Street's stock ratings are effectively bought and paid for by the very companies that are rated. These ratings are then presented to you as objective opinions, but are often nothing more than glorified advertisements for the rated companies.

If you were deciding about which restaurant you should go, or which movie you should see, you'd never dream of relying on a cockamamy rating scheme like this one. Yet, here we have millions of investors betting their life savings on the basis of a rating system that's fatally flawed.

TEN THOUSAND ACTIVE BROKERS CAUGHT SWINDLING THEIR CLIENTS

You've seen how thousands of corporations distort their earnings information at the source. In addition, you've seen how the research departments of many large Wall Street firms add a second layer of distortion in their published ratings and reports. However, it doesn't end there. This information goes through still a third layer of hype: by the thousands of individual brokers who use them to push specific investments to their clients.

It's often difficult to pin down precisely how brokers misuse this information, but it's not hard to pin down even more serious abuses. In 1994, for example, the U.S. General Accounting Office (GAO) conducted a thorough study of the nation's stockbrokers. Their finding: Almost 10,000 currently active brokers had been caught swindling clients.[12] It's reasonably safe to assume that if they swindle, they also misuse information.

The industry's response was that these 10,000 brokers are "just a small minority." However, the GAO study covered only brokers who were caught in the act and whose offenses were so serious they had to go through formal proceedings and be disciplined. The GAO's study did *not* include brokers who were disciplined informally, let alone brokers who were cheating their customers and getting away with it.

As a rule, it is likely that fewer than 1 in 10 crimes committed by brokers is ever detected, reported, or prosecuted. Therefore, it's reasonable to estimate that at least 100,000 brokers (i.e., over one-fifth of all the brokers working in the United States today) could potentially be guilty of a variety of offenses.

Many of these brokers have been found guilty of stealing hundreds of thousands, or even millions, of dollars from their clients.

- A Chattanooga-based broker was disciplined by the National Association of Securities Dealers (NASD) for making unauthorized transactions, churning a customer's account with unsuitable recommendations and/or trades, and overstating the value of the account by $146,000.

- A Florida-based broker was fined $3.65 million for collecting over $1 million in purchase payments from customers and failing to invest them as directed. He also gave forged account statements to at least one customer; he told others that their funds were invested in mutual funds and so forth, when, in reality, he was using these funds for his own business activities.

- A Mississippi-based broker was censured, fined $757,500, and ordered to pay $101,525 in restitution. He sold stock out of one customer's account without authorization, forged the customer's signature on a check for the proceeds of almost $30,000, and then changed the customer's address in his firm's records so that they wouldn't get their statement. To top it all off, he then prepared a fictitious statement that didn't disclose the sale and sent it to the customer directly. He also withdrew $96,552 from other customers' accounts, converted the funds to his own use, changed their addresses in the firm's records, and told the customers they would only get statements once every six weeks.

For many, many more examples, check the records at www.sec.gov and www.nasdr.com. When you review the list, always bear in mind two things: (1) These represent the minority who got caught. There are many more who got away with it. (2) And just because they got caught doesn't mean investors got their money back. Since 1995, the SEC has recovered only $1.69 of every $10.00 owed to investors by swindlers and schemers.[13]

Even more troubling, however, are the many cases in which the entire firm is involved. Take IPOs, for example, often an irresistible target for manipulators. First, the brokerage firms let their preferred clients (i.e., large investors, politicians, or special VIPs to whom they owe a favor) buy in at the offering price, which most investors can rarely get. Within a day or two, the price of the new issue goes sky-high. Then the brokers and the preferred clients *flip* the stock. They get out with a windfall profit, and the little investor gets stuck with an inflated price. In short, while you are buying, they are selling. Sooner or later, the truth comes out. An analyst says, "Hey, this stock isn't worth half of what they say it's worth," or the company just starts losing big-time dollars. That's when the stock crashes and small investors take it on the chin, over and over again.

Robomatics, which was originally issued at $7⅞, promptly plunged to 50 cents! Crescent Airways, which came out at $5 a share, also wound up at 50 cents. North American Advance, issued at $9, fell to $1.50. Perhaps the most shocking IPO disaster was VA Linux, a software company that went public on December 9, 1999, at $30 a share and closed *that day* at $239.25 a share. Just over 15 months later, on March 23, 2001, it closed at $3.44. Thousands of investors lost up to 99 percent of their money, while the underwriting firms lined their pockets.

An even more common crime perpetrated by entire firms is penny stock manipulations. In a typical scheme, stock promoters assume control of a small, struggling company and all of its stock. Then they launch a huge public relations campaign, including promotional videos, press releases, and planted news stories, while greasing the hands of brokers, independent financial advisers, and newsletter editors. Next,

> [s]tarting at . . . pennies per share, it only takes a modicum of trading to push up the stock price of one of these small companies. Sometimes the same 1,000-share block of stock moves in a circle among a number of buyers who are in on the scheme, trading slightly higher each time it changes hands, to give the impression that the share price is rising. When the price rises to a suitable level, the promoters and other insiders dump their shares and leave the company's legitimate investors holding virtually worthless stock.[14]

With all this going on, you'd think someone would have warned you. Unfortunately . . . .

WARNINGS FALL ON DEAF EARS, OR NEVER SEE THE LIGHT OF DAY

The *Washington Post* conducted a survey of the industry and reported that stockbrokers regularly lie as a "pervasive and routine part of doing business." But the response from readers was muted. *Money* Magazine, CNN, *Smart Money,* and others ran special stories about broker dishonesty. Still not much response. I wrote a special report detailing the abuses, with the headlines "Wall Street Is Ripping You Off" and "Major Wall Street Firms Deliberately Deceive Investors with False Reports."[15] Some listened. For most, however, my message fell on deaf ears.

Even the National Endowment for Financial Education (NEFE) published a stinging 16-page attack on stockbrokers. The report described sales abuses that would make your hair curl! It told of brokerage firms that took away the sales staff's shoes every morning until they met their sales quotas with high-pressure sales campaigns to investors. It talked about rampant lying and abuse throughout the industry. And it named names. Major Wall Street firms were enraged. They threatened to sue. And the NEFE immediately pulled its report out of circulation.

Regulators also tried to warn investors in an effort to combat the cheating, lying, and outright stealing. They set up a series of complex rules by which brokers must abide. They added a host of programs for educating and reeducating brokers. And they ran massive sting operations to break up the largest stock scams. It's abundantly clear, though, that all of this was sorely inadequate. No matter what they did, the regulators ran up against the reality that *the system itself undermines the relationship between the broker and the individual investor.*

The brokerage firm is represented as a source of objective research. Unfortunately, as I told you earlier, it is primarily a source of marketing hype.

The individual brokers are represented as investment counselors. Unfortunately, they are often forced to be little more than salespeople, that is, pushing stocks that the company wants to sell.

In short, the firm and the company want you to *buy* precisely the same investments that they want to *sell* . . . and be rid of.

Therein lie the powerful and fundamental conflicts of interest that are continually tugging at the broker to act against the client's best interests. There are, naturally, many brokers who want to do right by their customers. However, to continually achieve that goal, they must ultimately sacrifice their own financial interests. For the broker, the whole truth and nothing but the truth could mean lower sales results, fewer bonuses, and even reduced chances for promotions.

That's why, despite the GAO's landmark study, despite massive efforts by the regulators to reign in the offenders, despite the broad publicity given to broker scams by the media, there was little movement toward change.

REGULATORS AND LEGISLATORS FINALLY BEGIN TO WAKE UP, BUT THE HORSE HAS LEFT THE BARN

In the wake of the tech stock disaster of 2000 and 2001, a U.S. House committee held special hearings on the threats to the independence of Wall Street analysts. The SEC issued a stern warning to all investors using Wall Street advice. The NASD immediately followed with strict guidelines to brokers to disclose conflicts of interest.[16]

Each of these efforts deserves every bit of encouragement and applause. Unfortunately, the horse is already out of the barn–$5 trillion already lost. Moreover, all the investigations, warnings, and guidelines to date have largely failed to address the underlying cause of the abuses: that Wall Street's interests are in conflict with the interests of the investors.

It remains to be seen if substantive changes will be made. In any event, you can't wait for the market to recover, the regulators to act, or Wall Street to reform. You must take concrete steps now to protect yourself from further damage, start recouping from any recent losses, and grow your wealth in years to come.

If you were a victim of the Great Stock Market Scam, you can either crawl into a corner and hide, or you can bounce back fighting. You can either accept your fate meekly, or you can turn the tables on Wall Street and use this calamity to your great advantage. The latter course is your better choice. Read on for specific instructions.

CHAPTER

2

FIVE LESSONS FROM THE GREAT STOCK MARKET SCAM

Many people over 50 who were burned in the stock market are looking for a quick fix—high-risk investments that will help them get all their money back in a hurry. Don't make that mistake—it's not wise to compensate for yesterday's losses by piling on still more risks tomorrow.

But shying away from investing altogether is also unwise: In the months and years ahead, if you withdraw to the sidelines, you may be missing the chance to buy sound investments precisely when they are the cheapest, and when most of the downside risk has been wrung out of them.

Let's begin by taking some valuable lessons out of the early twenty-first-century disasters.

LESSON 1: STOCKS HAVE HIDDEN RISKS THAT NO ONE TOLD YOU ABOUT

Most investors knew that there was a chance their stocks could go down, at least for a short while, but they never dreamed they could go down so far and so quickly. They had no inkling of the multiple, hidden risks that can drive their stock portfolios into the gutter:

- *The risk of earnings lies.*   A stock is selling for $40. Its earnings are $2 per share. So it's valued at 20 times earnings, and this is considered fair. Suddenly, it's discovered that the earnings are a bald-faced lie: The true earnings of the company are only one-half of what was stated (i.e., $1 per share). "Oh, no!" exclaim the investors. "At 20 times earnings, it's really only worth $20 per share." The stock promptly plunges to $20–an instant 50 percent loss to shareholders.

- *The risk of Wall Street hype.*   Distorted ratings and reports by Wall Street firms drive thousands of investors into the stock, including sophisticated pros. This extra buying pushes the stock up to four times what it's really worth. The truth about the company is finally revealed, and the stock promptly reverses all its gains–an 80 percent loss to investors.

- *The risk of fraud.*   A group of brokers manipulate the stock's price. Their favored clients get the best prices, whereas small investors pay more on the way in and get less on the way out. What would normally have been a 20 percent loss becomes a 40 percent loss instead.

- *Failure risk.*   The company goes out of business–a 100 percent loss. Unusual? Not quite. Since January 2000 alone, 555 Internet companies have gone under. Since 1990, bankruptcy has claimed 390 insurance companies, 932 banks and thrifts, and tens of thousands of business corporations.[1]

- *Recession risk.*   Here's just one scenario among many: Due to the bust in tech stocks, the economy begins to fall, driving corporate profits into a tailspin. Nearly all stocks, whether tech or not, plunge further. The potential loss is anywhere from 30 to 80 percent, depending on the depth and duration of the economic decline.

- *System risk.*   Wall Street firms have staked their reputation (and their own money) on stocks and high-risk investments. When their investments plunge in value, the weakest brokerage firms run out of capital and largely withdraw from trading. The mechanism for buying and selling stocks begins to falter. Many investors find that they are effectively locked into their shares and cannot sell at any price. The potential risk? Unquantifiable!

Whether *all* of these risks will be realized is a matter of opinion. So far, we've seen firm evidence of earnings lies and Wall Street hype. In addition, a recession began in March 2001, and we've seen a growing number of failures. System risk has been the concern of the U.S. General Accounting Office (GAO) but, at this point, is merely a scenario—not a forecast.[2]

However, even if you combine only a *few* of these risks, it's clear that the total potential for loss is far greater than most people realized.

So, rule number 1 of investing: *Never underestimate the risk.*

As of this writing, the brunt of the damage has been in the technology sector: the $5 trillion lost in the stocks, a near wipeout in tech company profits, and massive layoffs of tech staff. However, there is no convincing evidence whatsoever that the risk is limited strictly to the tech sector. What happened to Intel and Microsoft can happen to Ford and GM. In addition, the plunge that we've seen in the Nasdaq can be repeated in the Dow Jones Industrial Average or the S&P 500 Index.

LESSON 2: "FREE ADVICE" CAN COST YOU A FORTUNE

You can get "free advice" from many sources—not only from your stockbroker, but also from your insurance agent, your financial planner, and other professionals. This isn't really advice, and it certainly is not free.

You saw how free advice, embedded in the hyped-up ratings and research reports issued by major Wall Street firms, cost investors a fortune, luring them into Nasdaq stocks that brought losses averaging over $60 for every $100 invested near the peak. In subsequent chapters, I'll show you how free advice in other areas (from bonds to insurance) can also be quite expensive.

With free advice, you can actually get hurt in three different ways:

1. You pay significant commissions that, despite any assurances to the contrary, inevitably wind up coming out of *your* pocket.

2. You buy investments that are more likely than usual to be underperformers or outright losers.

3. You wind up getting stuck with plans or programs that lock you in with various kinds of exit penalties. Then, when a better, alternative opportunity comes your way, you have to either pass it up or pay through the nose to switch.

In short, taking free advice can be like walking into the ring with a professional wrestler. First, he socks it to you with commissions. Then, he dumps you into bad investments. And last, he pins you down on the mat and won't let you go. Therefore, rule number 2 of investing is: *Never act on so-called free advice.*

How can you tell? It's actually quite simple. Everyone you deal with in the financial industry is either a *salesperson* or an *advisor*. It is impossible for anyone to be both at the same time.

Salespeople will tell you that they are not charging you for the advice. They will tell you it "comes with the service" or it's covered by the transaction fees or commissions. That's a dead giveaway.

Advisors tell you, up front, what fee they are going to charge you, charge the fee, and then tell you what they charged you. It couldn't be clearer.

The fee may be roughly $100 per year for a subscription to an investment newsletter or $100 per hour for a personal consultation. Unless you have a very large, complex estate, I believe you shouldn't have to pay more than $200 to $300 per year for all the advice you need. That's cheap insurance that can save you, or even make you, a fortune.

Still not sure how to distinguish between a salesperson and a true advisor? Here's what I suggest. No matter whom you encounter in the financial industry, be it a stockbroker, insurance agent, financial planner, or banker, ask these three questions:

1. *Do you (or your company) make more money the more I buy?*   If the answer is yes, you've got a serious problem right off the bat. Often, the best investment decision is *not* to buy. Sometimes, an even better decision is to *sell,* stashing the proceeds in cash. If buying nothing or selling is going to be a negative for your advisor's earnings, you don't have an advisor. You've got a salesperson posing as an advisor.

2. *Who pays your commissions or fees?*   If he or she says it's someone other than you, this person is lying. Shake hands, say good-bye, and walk out the door. To my knowledge, no financial institution really pays sales commissions out of its own pocket. If a salesperson is making commissions, it always comes out of *your* pocket, directly or indirectly.

3. *Where are you getting the information or report that you're giving me?*   If the answer is a source that will benefit from your purchase, you can throw the info into the trashcan. Almost invariably, the story is carefully and skillfully tilted to just one side (i.e., the side *they* want you to see). Even much of the factual data it contains may be cherry-picked to lead to only one possible conclusion: *Buy.*

We saw that repeatedly in the Great Stock Market Scam. And you *will* see it again in virtually every financial industry. With these three questions, though, you can discard the salespeople and find the true advisors. True advisors are those who:

■ *Are always compensated by you.*   Not by the companies whose financial products you buy.

■ *Are always compensated for their time or their information.*   Not for a sale.

■ *Are always* your *advocates and defenders.*   Whether it's just a normal, friendly transaction or it's a heated legal dispute, it's always crystal clear which side your advisor is on: yours and only yours.

It bears repeating: Free advice is neither free nor advice. Sooner or later, it will cost you a fortune in terms of mediocre performance, or worse, outright losses.

Is this being overly harsh on ethical brokers, sales agents, and financial planners? Perhaps—but only in the sense that it's not really their fault. It's the system that's rigged against you.

You see, even the most well-meaning salespeople still have to make a living. They can't do that very well if they tell their clients to stay out of a risky stock market, avoid mutual funds that charge a big fee, or stick with insurance policies that pay the lowest commissions. Nor can they afford to recommend investments that involve zero fees, zero commissions, and zero transaction costs, *which happen to be some of the best investments in the world today.*

If they consistently give you this kind of advice, they can't put food on the table for their families, let alone send their kids to a good college. And they'll never, ever be eligible for the big bonuses and rich rewards that inevitably flow to the top-performing salespeople.

Many salespeople do try to be as ethical as they can be, within the limitations of the system. They're friendly and helpful. They bend over backward to do right for their clients. However, they're still salespeople. Work with them to buy the products you want, but get your information and advice elsewhere.

LESSON 3: WALL STREET'S OLD "RULES OF THUMB" ARE PURE BS

The bias that was uncovered in the Great Stock Market Scam goes beyond just recommending bad investments. It also is the source of many investing rules promulgated by Wall Street pros and blindly accepted by most investors. Following are some examples of common myths.

Myth 1: "Always Invest in Stocks for the Long Term"

You've probably heard this in its many permutations: "Historically, stocks have always moved higher," it is said. "Bull markets are longer than bear markets," goes the argument. Maybe. But most of the stats they cite assume that you bought stocks *after* a major decline, when they were dirt cheap. The reality is that few people ever buy at those levels. Indeed, most people tend to buy most of their stocks *after* a major rise, when the stocks are extremely pricey. For example:

- If you bought the average Dow Jones Industrial stock before the Crash of 1929, you would have lost 89 cents for every dollar. Even if you had both the cash and the courage to hold on (few did!), you'd still have to wait 24 years (a full generation) before you could recoup your original investment . . . and *another 20 years* before you could catch up with an investor who just earned a steady 5 percent yield during that period.

- If you bought the average Dow stock at its peak in 1973, you would have lost 45.1 percent in the following two years. The Dow touched an all-time high of 1051 on January 11, and then dropped for two years, hitting 577 in December 1974. It did not cross above 1000 again until eight years later.

- Losses in so-called conservative stocks were just as bad. If you bought the average utility shares, considered safer than most stocks, your losses would have been 88.2 percent in 1929 through 1932 and 52 percent in 1973 and 1974.

The typical retort from Wall Street: "*Another major stock market crash like 1929 or 1973 is unlikely to ever occur again.*" Oh no? It just did. If you bought the average Nasdaq stock at its peak, you'd be down 68.4 percent at the trough. Any rallies since then have barely made a dent in the losses.

As of this date, even the most optimistic Wall Street experts are estimating that it could take at least eight years before tech stocks recoup to their peak levels. Moreover, if you invested in any one of hundreds of tech companies that failed in 2000 and 2001, you will *never* recoup that money.

Rule number 2 of investing: *Don't hold on to stocks or mutual funds for the long term.* As soon as an investment loses more than 10 percent of your money, get rid of it. If it isn't working for you after three months, move on to greener pastures.

Myth 2: "Don't Sell in Panic—It's Probably the Bottom"

Why is it that when big Wall Street firms sell, it's supposedly based on reason, but when you or I sell, they say it's based on emotion?

The classic example they like to remind you of is the Crash of 1987, which took the Dow down 36 percent in a big hurry, and then was over almost as quickly as it began. "People who sold at the bottom of the Crash of 1987 missed out on the biggest bull market in history," they say.

There are two problems with that argument: First of all, even if you sold at the very worst time in 1987, there were many, many opportunities to buy back into the market in subsequent months.

Second, their recommendation not to sell didn't work too well in 2000 and 2001. The pundits unanimously declared a bottom in April of 2000 when the Nasdaq was off 37.1 percent. Then, they declared another bottom in December 2000, when it was down 55.4 percent. If you followed their advice, instead of getting hurt just once, you got killed again and again.

Then, ironically, when the Nasdaq did hit a bottom of sorts, in April of 2001, that's when the majority of so-called experts on Wall Street themselves began to panic.

Reflecting the nearly unanimous pessimism of Wall Street experts, *Business Week* advised its readers to dump their shares even if they had already plunged 80 or 90 percent. *Time's* front cover featured a mean bear and warned of more big trouble ahead. Nearly all the great bulls on Wall Street temporarily abandoned their optimistic bent and warned you about events that had *already* happened.

Rule number 3 of investing: *Sell BEFORE the panic stage.* In practice, that means selling just as soon as your stocks fall below a predetermined loss level with which you're comfortable.

Myth 3: "Mutual Funds Have Smart Managers—They Will Give You Diversification, and They Will Protect You"

The reality is that mutual funds are neither manna from heaven nor the holy grail of investing. In the great stock market years between 1997 and 1999, only 24 percent outperformed the S&P 500.

In 2000 and 2001, the smart, sophisticated, mutual fund managers running tech funds got scammed just like everyone else. In fact, every single one of 200 tech stock funds lost money, with 72.5 percent of the funds losing *more* than the Nasdaq Composite Index. So much for expertise and diversification![3]

Rule number 4 of investing: *Diversify over a broad spectrum of totally different kinds of investments, including cash and bonds.* However, don't count on diversification alone to protect you from adversity.

Rule number 5 of investing: *Always invest in the funds that are the best performers NOW and dump the rest.* For more instructions on this, see Chapter 5.

Myth 4: "Buy More and You Will Lower Your Average Cost"

Their rationale is: "If your 100 shares of stock were a good buy at, for instance, $50 a share, then they've got to be truly a *great* buy at $10 per share." Therefore, all you have to do is buy another 100 shares and you can lower your average cost to $30 per share.

The reality, however, may be that the stock is in a fundamental, confirmed downtrend, and the natural tendency is for that trend to continue. If it does, you'll be losing money twice as fast. Instead of losing $100 every time the stock drops one point, now you'll be losing $200.

Stop for a moment and look behind each of these "words of wisdom" from Wall Street. When you do, you'll uncover one simple agenda: They want you to *buy*. After you buy, they want you to *buy more*. When the day comes that you want to sell, they'll want you to *hold*. That's the only way they know how to keep you as a customer.

It's the same pattern you saw with Wall Street's stock ratings, and the same pattern you will continue to see from almost any salesperson or organization. Don't fall into their trap.

Rule number 6 of investing: *Add to winning investments—not to losers.*

LESSON 4: BIG-NAME, WELL-RESPECTED FIRMS ARE EQUALLY DANGEROUS

From past experience, most of us know better than to entrust our money to small, unknown, fly-by-night operations. The recent experience on Wall Street, though, is a stark reminder that big names are no guarantee of safety either.

Quite to the contrary, in the Great Stock Market Scam, it was actually the bigger, well-respected brokerage firms that had the biggest stakes in the investment banking business and, therefore, the most conflicts of interest.

The interim chairman of the Securities and Exchange Commission (SEC) even singled them out in her testimony before Congress, telling the world, for the record, that almost *all* of the *major* Wall Street firms were *guilty* of *serious* conflicts of interest.[4]

The firms most involved in investment banking are not fly-by-nights. They are huge, "well-respected" firms like Goldman Sachs, Morgan Stanley, Crédit Suisse First Boston, Citigroup-SSB, and Merrill Lynch.[5]

The recent history of failures and frauds in other financial industries confirms that the largest are often among the most guilty or risky. Prudential Life Assurance of America, the largest of all American insurance companies, was caught with its hands in the cookie jar to the tune of $2 billion. Executive Life went down the tubes with $10 billion of investor funds. Bank of New England lost $14 billion.

Rule number 7 of investing: *Don't assume* big *necessarily equals* safe *or* trustworthy.

LESSON 5: DON'T EXPECT THE AUTHORITIES TO PROTECT YOU

Most investors assume that *someone* in government will protect us from all of this. Not true. In the Great Stock Market Scam, the authorities didn't start making noises until *after* the damage had been done. Nor was there any assurance that these noises would result in substantive changes.

Until the bust, the authorities were usually content to let Wall Street firms have their way. The U.S. Treasury Department was actually quite delighted to let Wall Street continue on its merry path, just so long as its Internal Revenue Service continued to rake in its share of the tech boom profits.

Although the rampant, pervasive, unconscionable conflicts of interest were *well known* by anyone on Wall Street or in Washington who was paying attention, no one lifted a finger to stop them. Indeed, it is in the *very nature* of these booms that the authorities have neither the will nor the power to stop them.

How is the individual investor protected from Wall Street's scams? One mechanism in place is a system of *arbitration*. The system is supposedly designed to protect you, but it is also designed to protect the brokerage industry from lawsuits. Unfortunately, right now, it's achieving neither.

The large brokerage firms that are guilty of serious conflicts of interest are vulnerable to a wave of arbitration filings from the millions of investors who lost money in the tech wreck, based on their skewed advice.

Many investors, however, are getting only a fraction of the money that's due them in arbitration settlements, mostly because brokerage firms are going out of business before paying up. According to a recent GAO study, although the number of arbitration claims has risen dramatically, 80 percent of the money is not being paid up, due primarily to brokers going broke.[6] So much for the notion that the government will protect you!

Rule number 8, the final rule, of investing: *Arm yourself with the knowledge you need for protection.*

BOTTOM LINE: YOU'RE ON YOUR OWN

That may sound a bit discouraging at first, but you should actually welcome it with great optimism and hope. No matter what your age, you have the power to successfully guide your own financial future.

You don't need the free advice from your broker, banker, insurance agent, or any other financial professional.

You don't need to rely on anyone else to tell you what to buy, what to sell, or what to do with your money. You can do it entirely on your own if you want to. And you can do it a lot more effectively than you probably realize.

If you still need some advice and guidance, that's okay, too. Just be sure it's *real advice,* not disguised promotions.

CHAPTER

3

BROKEN BY YOUR BROKER? HERE'S HOW TO GET MONEY BACK

In late February 2001, a doctor in Brooklyn filed an arbitration case against Merrill Lynch that was unique in the history of such actions against brokers. According to his securities lawyer, it was one of the very first arbitrations that not only named the brokerage firm, but also named a research analyst.[1]

The analyst was none other than the Internet stock superstar Henry Blodgett, who had continually recommended InfoSpace, even as it plunged from $160 to just $10 a share. Merrill settled for $400,000, a landmark event that opened the door to a new wave of similar claims.

Why was this so significant? In the past, it was taken for granted that you could not blame Wall Street analysts for being wrong because they expressed their opinions based on their research.

Now, however, there is a new twist in the way this situation is interpreted: If the research analyst was unduly biased by serious conflicts of interest, you may have stronger grounds for filing a claim against the analyst, the individual broker that passed that advice on to you, and the firm they represented.

The Securities and Exchange Commission's (SEC's) testimony before Congress (directly implying that almost all major firms are guilty of serious conflicts of interest) is your open invitation to proceed.

If you feel that you have been a victim of the Great Stock Market Scam, and have suffered serious losses that you can tie to the recommendations of an analyst at a major Wall Street brokerage firm, you can file an arbitration claim against your broker and get money back.

If that's your decision, the sooner you file, the better your chances for success. Otherwise, the case and the evidence can go stale. Or worse, hundreds—perhaps thousands—of other investors could file their claims before you do, possibly driving the firm out of business.

Meanwhile, it will be almost impossible for you to sue your broker in court. When you opened your account with your brokerage firm, you signed a customer agreement, waiving your rights to sue, and agreeing to submit to binding arbitration instead. It will also be difficult to challenge the fine print of the customer agreement because the U.S. Supreme Court has held that the arbitration provisions you signed are binding and enforceable.[2]

The arbitration system gives you a fighting chance of getting some money back, but don't count on getting *all* of your money back. Following are the actual stats, based on a June 2000 study by the U.S. General Accounting Office (GAO):[3]

Fact 1. The good news is that your chances of getting a judgment in your favor are better than 50-50. Considering all of the frivolous cases that are filed, I don't think that's bad at all.

Fact 2. Now for the bad news—investors receive an average of only 22 percent of the amount claimed in compensatory damages.

Fact 3. A surprisingly large percentage, 49 percent, of the arbitration awards were *not* paid at all. In addition, 12 percent were only partially paid.

Fact 4. It gets worse. The GAO estimates that the amount of unpaid awards was about $129 million, or a whopping 80 percent of the $161 million awarded to investors during 1998.[4]

Fact 5.   Here's the killer—the main reason awards were not paid is because the broker-dealers went out of business, according to the GAO.

Put all of these stats together and it becomes evident that the brokerage industry is paying out only a small fraction of the amounts claimed, far less than they'd have to pay in court. This is the dirty little secret about arbitration. It's also the reason the industry has been pushing so hard and so long for mandatory arbitration agreements.

Unfortunately, steps have been limited primarily to educational programs to better inform investors. These programs are positive, but they do little to correct the two fundamental reasons brokers are defaulting on arbitration award payments: (1) weak finances and (2) too many claims.

The GAO puts it this way:

Ultimately, recovering losses caused by undercapitalized, financially irresponsible, or unscrupulous broker-dealers is difficult, if not impossible, for investors.[5]

Something obviously needs to be done about this. However, don't hold your breath waiting. Instead, be sure to get your claim in *quickly*. Critical steps in the process include:

Step 1.   Decide whether you will be using a lawyer. It's not a requirement, but you can be sure that the other side will have legal representation, probably from in-house staff.

If you feel your losses are under $10,000, you won't need an attorney, not only because the potential rewards don't justify the costs, but also because there's a simplified arbitration procedure for claims under $10,000. If you believe that you've lost more than $100,000, you should probably hire a good attorney to help you, at least at each major step in the process.

What should you do if your losses are between $10,000 and $100,000? An initial consultation with an attorney is still recommended to put you on the right track. Any further involvement will depend on what you and your attorney decide from there.

If your existing attorney does not have securities experience, get his or her recommendation for a securities lawyer in your area. To find an attorney with experience in arbitration claims, call the Public Investors Arbitration Bar Association at (888) 621-7484, or go to their Web site at www.piaba.org, go to the top of the left column, click on "Find an Attorney." Then, click on the red words at the top of the page, "Find an Attorney Now." You can search either by your zip code or state.

Step 2. If you can afford it, a straight fee-for-time arrangement with an approximate estimate of the full costs discussed ahead of time is recommended. If that is not within your budget, you may find an attorney who will be willing to represent you on a contingency fee (i.e., a percentage of the proceeds). However, these attorneys tend to use a cookie-cutter, one-size-fits-all approach, which could ultimately be weaker.

Step 3. Don't try to base the claim exclusively on a bad rating or on bad advice alone. If applicable, seek to strengthen your claim by showing that a high-risk investment was unsuitable to your investment guidelines, or that there was evidence of churning, misrepresentation, or a fraudulent omission. Furthermore, don't exaggerate the losses. Stick with the facts.

Step 4. Get *all* your facts together up front. This may sound like a trivial statement, but it isn't. In a court of law, you have multiple opportunities to gather facts after you file the original complaint. In arbitration, you don't. It's very difficult—if not impossible—to overturn an arbitration ruling.

Another reason to have all of your facts in hand before starting is that the exchange of exhibits requires customers to identify documents and witnesses ahead of time, whereas rebuttals and witness lists are not required in advance from the brokerage firm. It is not fair, but it's the reality of arbitration.

When the authorities set up this system, the basic idea was to help cut through the red tape that bogs down the courts. In the process, however, the authorities also put a heavier burden on you to produce the facts up front. The following list details what you'll need:

- All agreements with your brokerage firm.
- All documents you provided to the broker or the brokerage firm, showing your investment objectives, investment history, and net worth.
- All monthly account statements with all brokerage firms.
- All confirmation slips, whether to buy or sell securities.
- Any year-end transaction and portfolio summaries; tax returns for all applicable years.
- Any letters between yourself and the broker or brokerage firm, including all correspondence reflecting complaints or any wrongdoing.
- All other mail or letters sent to you or sent by you to the brokerage firm.
- Plus, if you're going to target the research analysts, get as complete a record as possible of their ratings for your stocks. Even though you may be able to get a more complete record of these directly from the brokerage firm later, I recommend you start with information you can gather independently. Use Web sources, such as www.alert-ipo .com, which will give you a complete initial public offering (IPO) history on stocks. Then use either www.edgar-online .com or www.bigcharts.com and look under "Analysts" to see how analysts changed their minds on stock recommendations.
- Also, find out if your firm was one of the underwriters for those same companies. If so, that helps to pin down the conflicts of interest. You can find out by using www.alert-ipo.com to see the original IPO data and the name of the underwriting firm. Check to see if the analysts at that company recommended buying the stock.

Step 5.   Go to your broker to get any additional information that you can. Get as much as you can *before* you even mention your desire to file a claim because brokers are widely known to routinely ignore deadlines on the production of documents, and often make it virtually impossible for you to thoroughly check information.

Step 6.   To start the process, you will have to submit a statement of claim and demand for arbitration. You can simply type a letter with the words *Statement of Claim* at the top. Then, mail it to the brokerage firm itself, via certified mail, with a return receipt requested.

Set out the relevant facts, the basis of the claim, and the damages sought. Then attach relevant documents in support of your claim. This is where the initial consultation with an attorney will be very helpful to make sure you're on strong footing from the very beginning.

At the same time, you will have to include a submission agreement, in which you agree to submit to the arbitration and to be bound by the outcome.

There's also a filing fee and an initial hearing deposit, which varies on the forum and the size of your claim. With claims from $50,000 to $100,000 before the NASD, figure about $500 to $750. In any event, request that the arbitrators take these fees into consideration when they decide on an award.

Step 7.   The primary advantage of arbitration is that it's quicker than most court proceedings, but it's often still too slow. Fortunately, the New York Stock Exchange (NYSE) and NASD give your broker only 20 days to respond with their answer to the statement of claim. This is the document that's going to have all of their defenses and counterclaims.

Step 8.   Now, both sides have their one chance to ask for relevant documents that they want from each other. Although you can expect them to object to some of your requests, you can do likewise, especially if the production of documents places an unreasonable cost and time burden on you.

Step 9.   Next, arbitrators are appointed and the case is set to be heard. If your claim is for less than $30,000, it will be just one arbitrator. If it's for more than $30,000, you will get three. If you have reason to believe that one or more of the arbitrators may be less than impartial, you should object. A strong ground for objecting would be if the arbitrator has been in a previous hearing involving either you or the brokerage firm in the past.

Step 10.   Here's where the big delay sets in. You will probably have to wait from 6 to 12 months before your case is heard. If the backlog of cases begins to pile up in the wake of the tech wreck, it could be longer. Nevertheless, it's still much faster than the courts, where cases can be bogged down for years.

Your hearing will take place in a large conference room, which will look and feel like a formal courtroom setting. This is where you get your chance to present your case and put forward your evidence. However, be ready for cross-examination by the attorneys who are representing the brokerage firm. As in any court, on the one hand you lose points when you show anger with outbursts. On the other hand, you get sympathy when you demonstrate, calmly and methodically, how you've been hurt financially or in any other way.

As with court proceedings, you can also call on expert witnesses to analyze the events and estimate the damages. Also, you will have your chance to make closing arguments to the panel. Unlike a courtroom, however, there is less pressure on you to have the legal knowledge you'd need before a judge and jury. In fact, at least one of the arbitrators will *not* be an attorney. So you are in good company.

Still, as you can plainly see, presenting a case logically, cross-examining witnesses, and making closing arguments are not exactly the types of things that we can do in our sleep. As untrained lay people, we sure could use an attorney's help.

Your arbitration hearing *should* last no more than a day, but, unfortunately, that has not been the case. Two-day hearings have become more common.

Step 11.   You can expect a decision within about 30 days. Don't expect a detailed explanation. It is what it is. Then, it

will take another 30 days for the panel to review it and final-
ize, and still *another* 30 days for your award to be paid.[6]

Step 12.   Suppose the firm doesn't pay on time? A recent
NASD rule states that brokers who fail to pay within the 30
days could lose their license. Mark your calendar, and if you
don't get your money within the time frame, take action
immediately. In your file, you should have the name of the
case administrator at the NASD who handled your case.
Send him or her a letter saying that you haven't been paid,
requesting that the NASD revoke the broker's license. Then
you could also send a copy of this letter to your broker, via
certified mail with a return receipt requested. That should
put the fire under your broker to send your check right away.

In spite of the many steps and waiting periods, this process isn't
as hard as it may seem. Just remember—more than one-half of the
claims are decided in favor of investors, and with what you know
already, your chances are likely to be even better.

One last point is *settlement*. At almost every stage of the process,
there will be an opportunity for you to settle with your broker. You
can get your attorney's help in weighing the pros and cons, but
there is no 100 percent "right" course. The final decision on settlement is yours and no one else's.

This gives you a chance to get money back. Your primary focus,
though, should be on the future—safety, yield, and profits—not on
lawyers and courts.

CHAPTER

4

SAFETY AND YIELD ARE YOUR BEST ESCAPE

Do you still have most of your keep-safe money in the stock market? If so, the first lesson for folks over 50 (i.e., that stocks are much riskier than anyone ever told you) applies directly to you right now. The stock market may be a good place for some of your money, but it is simply not the right place for *most* of your money. If that's where you have it, you are taking more chances with your future than you might have thought when you first invested.

This is true whether you believe the market is going up or down. It's true whether your stock portfolio is mostly tech or non-tech, growth stocks or blue chips, considered high-risk or relatively safe. It's true whether you own stocks directly or through a mutual fund, in a 401(k) or a regular brokerage account. You could have bought them many years ago or just recently. You could have profits or losses. It doesn't matter. *The stock market is simply too risky for most of your savings.*

How much of your money should be in the stock market? Take the Risk Self-Test in Appendix A, and then read the instructions that follow. You will probably find that, at the very most, you should have no more than 40 percent of your money invested in stocks or stock mutual funds at any time.

If the *average* Nasdaq stock can lose more than 60 percent of its value in just 13 months, what about the 30 blue-chip stocks in the Dow Jones Industrials? What about all the giant companies in the S&P 500 Index? What about General Electric? Pfizer? Exxon? Mobil? Johnson & Johnson?

No one knows what the future will bring. But remember the first lesson learned from the Great Stock Market Scam: *The stock market is a lot riskier than most people realized.* If you still have most of your investment money in the stock market, you must ask yourself: "Can I really afford this risk? By holding on to these stocks, am I jeopardizing my retirement? My kids' education? My long-term health care?"

If you're 50+ and you take a big loss, *you may not have a second chance to recoup before you retire.* My advice is very simple: Take the Risk Self-Test right now. Find out the maximum amount you should have in stocks or stock mutual funds. Then sell any excess amounts *as soon as possible.*

"But I can't sell now," say many of today's investors. "I can't afford to take the loss." You *already have* taken that loss. It's a reality. In the real world, there's no substantive difference between a paper loss and a realized loss. They're both reflecting the fact that your stock has gone down. Whether you hold the stock or sell it, you cannot change that. That's why regulators require companies to mark their portfolios down to the *current* market value. When you're looking at your portfolio, you should always do the same.

"I can't sell now," say the rest of today's investors. "I can't afford to take the profit and pay the taxes." The fact is that Uncle Sam is your silent, but permanent, partner, whether you sell now or later. Always evaluate your stock portfolio after subtracting the amount you will have to pay in capital gains taxes.

In the final analysis, there is only one question that you need to ask: Is the stock market too risky for me? If you think it is, then it's not time to hold—let alone to buy more. It's time to sell.

If the market has been strong recently, that's great. This gives you the chance to get out at a good price. If the market has been plunging recently, sell half of the excess amount now, and the balance on any rally. Your goal, however, is the same: to reduce your risk to a level that is appropriate for you.

The next question: "Where do I put the proceeds?" I don't think it should be in a bank. Instead, I wish to show you an investment that is . . .

SAFER THAN MONEY IN A BANK

If the Great Stock Market Scam was like suddenly ripping adhesive tape off a sore wound, the Great Banking Scam is like pulling the tape off, one painful hair at a time. At any one moment in time, it may feel like mostly nickels and dimes. Over the years, though, the banks' persistent below-market interest rates on savings—plus their oft exorbitant, unjustifiable fees—have actually taken nearly as much out of our pockets as the great bust in tech stocks.

Between 1990 and 2000, banks have paid out a grand total of $783.5 billion in interest on savings and checking accounts. At the very minimum, I estimate that they *should* have paid $1.5 trillion—the amount that the U.S. Treasury Department paid on the same exact balances. That alone is an extra $800 billion or so that American savers justly deserved, but were denied.

Meanwhile, between January 1990 and March 2001, banks deducted nearly $200 million in fees for regular checking transactions, wire transfers, bounced checks, and other special services. I conservatively estimate that the banks' incremental costs in providing those services were no more than $38 million. Even allowing a decent profit margin, figure another $150 million in money that should be in our accounts, not theirs.

The dimensions of the banking rip-off grow geometrically if you also consider the below-normal interest payments that banks have paid on certificates of deposit (CDs). Throughout most of the 1990s, banks were allowed to borrow money at very low rates and then make as much as one or two full percentage points in pure profit just by parking the money in U.S. Treasury notes or bonds. You could have done that yourself directly, and kept *all* of the yield. I figure that's another $2 or so trillion that belonged to American savers, but instead went into the coffers of America's banking institutions.

The grand total was more than $3.6 trillion, plus interest. That's roughly how much has been siphoned right out of the pockets of

38 million Americans who are trying to make ends meet with a fixed income and Social Security, or drained from millions of other families trying to save for Christmas shopping, emergencies, college tuition, future retirement, or long-term health care.

While banks underpay for deposits, they also grossly overcharge on credit cards—to the tune of more than $10 billion in the year 2000 alone.

"Why didn't the federal authorities do something to stop this outrage?" you ask. Stop it? Are you kidding? The federal authorities are the ones that helped to orchestrate the whole thing in the first place! Sound unbelievable? Let's take a small detour back to the late twentieth century, and you'll see how it happened.

The time is 1991. The place is Providence, Rhode Island. Governor Bruce Sundlun has just shut down all of the state-chartered banks, declaring a statewide moratorium on all withdrawals. Thousands of angry savers are marching down Smith Street to the state capitol, demanding their money back.

Nationwide, over 700 banks have failed in the last 36 months, more than any time since the 1930s. Experts are saying that the savings and loan (S&L) industry is history. Banks everywhere, especially some of the largest in the nation, are drowning in bad real estate loans, bad foreign loans, plus a raft of losses from high-risk trading. The Federal Deposit Insurance Corporation (FDIC) has run out of money to save depositors.

In Washington, D.C., banking regulators and legislators are desperate to save the bankers' necks. They decide to give the bankers almost every advantage they can to help prevent an all-out collapse of the American banking system.

That was the situation in the early 1990s. That's when the Fed acted. It dropped the interest rates that banks have to pay. It let the banks make a huge profit just by buying Treasuries and it gave them the green light to rip off millions of savers with exorbitant fees. The trouble is that even *after* America's banks got back on their feet, they were allowed to *continue* ripping us off to their heart's content.[1]

What's worse, many bankers haven't learned their lessons from the big blunders they made in the 1980s.

First, many banks have jumped back into the business of making high-risk loans, including loans to real estate speculators, to consumers who are already up to their ears in debt, to falling dot-coms, and to high-risk foreign countries that are on the verge of default.

That's why, even before a downturn in the U.S. economy, the bad loans (in arrears by 90 days or more) on the books of America's commercial banks surged 27 percent in 2000, and then surged again by another 7 percent in the first quarter of 2001. This is also why Superior Bank went under in Illinois in August 2001, the largest banking failure since 1999, with nearly $1 billion in assets.

Second, many banks have placed big bets on stocks, bonds, and foreign currencies–often high-risk plays called *derivatives*. In October 1998, when markets were crashing around the world and Russia defaulted on its debt, these derivatives cost Union Bank of Switzerland $240 million. Chase Manhattan lost $160 million. Deutsche Bank lost $770 million. And Crédit Lyonnais lost a whopping $2 billion. And that was *without* a worldwide economic recession.

One would think that governments would have stepped in and forced banks to limit their exposure to these highly leveraged derivatives. They haven't. In 1998, U.S. banks held about $27 trillion in derivatives contracts. Today, the U.S. General Accounting Office (GAO) tells us that U.S. banks are involved with more than $40.5 *trillion* in derivatives![2] That's more than four times America's entire gross domestic product, more than 450 times the banking industry's *total profits* in 2000, and it's nearly $142,000 for every man, woman, and child in the country.

Granted, these numbers overstate the risk in that they represent the total face value of the derivatives, which is bloated. However, even if you look strictly at the actual risks that banks are taking, the numbers are alarming: The GAO's figures show that for every $1.00 of capital (after the Fed's adjustments for other risk factors), Bank of America has $1.20 at risk in derivatives, and Citibank has $2.05. At J. P. Morgan Chase, the risk is three times greater at $6.16 in risk per dollar of capital.

Maybe these banks should have taken the same Risk Self-Test that you have been advised to take. They are responsible for the savings of millions of Americans. They obviously should be taking even less risk than the average 50+ American.

At Morgan Chase, however, if just 16.7 percent (a mere one in six) of its bets on derivatives goes bad, it's broke–bankrupt.

Table 4.1   Strongest Large Banks in America

Bank Name	State	Weiss Safety Rating	Total Assets (in millions of $)
Apple Bk for Svgs	NY	A–	6,117
Bancorpsouth Bk	MS	B+	9,390
Bank of Tokyo Mitsubishi TC	NY	A–	4,128
Capitol Federal Savings Bank	KS	A	8,423
Central Carolina B&TC	NC	B+	9,489
Citibank-Delaware	DE	B+	6,160
Columbus B&TC	GA	A–	3,353
Comerica Bk-Texas	TX	B+	3,803
Commerce Bk NA	MO	B+	9,867
Emigrant Svg Bk	NY	A	8,535
First Charter NB	NC	B+	3,061
First Commonwealth Bk	PA	B+	3,430
First Source Bk	IN	A–	3,148
Hudson City Svgs Bk	NJ	A+	9,618
Israel Discount Bk of NY	NY	B+	5,695
Mercantile Safe Deposit & TC	MD	A	3,489
North Fork Bk	NY	B+	14,685
Sanwa Bk California	CA	B+	9,013
Trustmark NB	MS	A–	6,822
Union Bk of CA NA	CA	B+	35,467
United States TC of NY	NY	B+	3,988
Valley NB	NJ	B+	7,957

(continued)

Table 4.1 *(Continued)*

Bank Name	State	Weiss Safety Rating	Total Assets (in millions of $)
Washington FS&LA	WA	A+	6,990
Whitney NB of New Orleans	LA	B+	6,630

There are many disadvantages to keeping your savings in a bank: relatively low yields on most accounts, high costs for transactions, and FDIC limits on its guarantees. However, if you want to do business with a bank, or want to establish a line of credit, you can confidently include these strong banks among those you consider. Because financial risk is minimal, you can make your decision based upon a comparison of the specific costs and benefits of the account. This table contains those banks and thrifts on the Weiss Recommended List (i.e., receiving a rating of B+ or higher) as of August 21, 2001, with total assets exceeding $3 billion. For a complete listing, refer to the *Weiss Ratings' Guide to Banks and Thrifts,* available at many public libraries. Weiss Safety Ratings scale: A = excellent; B = good; C = fair; D = weak; E = very weak; + = high end of grade range; − = low end of grade range.

Source: Weiss Ratings, Inc., Palm Beach Gardens, FL, based on first-quarter 2001 data filed by institutions with the Federal Deposit Insurance Corporation and the Office of Thrift Supervision.

Don't misconstrue what is being said. There are still many strong banks in America today, taking few risks and maintaining plenty of capital. Tables 4.1 and 4.2 show the largest banks with the highest and lowest Weiss Safety Ratings.)

Even when times are good, surging bad loans and big derivatives risk are not healthy; when times are bad, they're downright fright-

Table 4.2 Weakest Large Banks in America

Bank Name	State	Weiss Safety Rating	Total Assets (in millions of $)
Discover Bk	DE	D	21,877
Providian NB	NH	D	16,556
Capital One Bk	VA	D	14,099
Chevy Chase Bank, FSB	MD	D	10,995
Bay View Bk NA	CA	E−	4,847

Table 4.2 *(Continued)*

Bank Name	State	Weiss Safety Rating	Total Assets (in millions of $)
Banco Bilbao Vizcaya PR	PR	D	4,748
IBJ Whitehall B&TC	NY	D	2,755
Union FB of Indianapolis	IN	D	2,566
Beal Bk, SSB	TX	D	2,351
Fidelity Federal Bank, FSB	CA	E	2,195
Superior Bank, FSB	IL	F	1,941
Hamilton Bk NA	FL	E+	1,727
Metropolitan Bank & Trust Co	OH	D	1,702
Matrix Capital Bank	NM	D–	1,607
Liberty Savings Bank, FSB	OH	D	1,558
Ocwen Federal Bank, FSB	NJ	D	1,555
ING Bank, FSB	DE	D	1,481
Guardian Savings Bank	TX	E+	1,323
Sterling Bank and Trust, FSB	MI	D–	1,047

We give these banks a low rating because we believe they are weak or very weak, based on their capital, earnings, and hundreds of other factors. A low rating is not a forecast that they *will* fail. However, weak-rated banks have had a higher-than-average failure rate in the past. Will the FDIC cover your deposits up to $100,000? Yes. But there are other problems and inconveniences that are often associated with weak banks: loss of credit lines, declining service, and a potential disruption in your financial affairs in the event of a failure. If you are shopping for a new bank, we believe you should look for a safer company, especially if you anticipate your account balance might exceed the FDIC's insurance limit. If you already have an account with one of these banks, you should consider leaving once you can do so penalty-free. This table contains all U.S. banks and thrifts that we considered weak (receiving a Weiss rating of D+ or lower) as of August 21, 2001, with total assets exceeding $1 billion. For an updated list, see www.weissratings.com.

Source: Weiss Ratings, Inc., Palm Beach Gardens, FL, based on first-quarter 2001 data filed by institutions with the Federal Deposit Insurance Corporation and the Office of Thrift Supervision.

ening. It is true that the FDIC protects you for up to $100,000 if your bank fails, but it will not protect you from the disruptions to your life and the great potential inconvenience in your financial affairs.

For maximum safety and complete protection from any banking problems in the future, put your keep-safe money in short-term U.S. Treasury securities (i.e., Treasury bills). You can buy these directly from the U.S. Treasury Department by opening an account with your Social Security number (call 800-722-2678 or go to www.publicdebt.treas.gov). You can also buy them through your broker.

However, the simplest and most convenient solution is to put all of your cash into one of the money market funds that specializes in U.S. Treasury securities (see Table 4.3), and to get the maximum yield and safety, consider the program I call "Treasury-Only Savings and Checking."

TREASURY-ONLY SAVINGS AND CHECKING

According to the *Bank Rate Monitor,* in July 2001, America's banks paid you an average of only *1.17 percent* on personal checking. That's *far* below the fair market rate for short-term money today. Without taking any additional risk, you should be getting more than double that much. Meanwhile, on business checking accounts, *banks pay you no interest whatsoever.* By the time you add up all of the service fees that banks charge you (i.e., for regular checking, low balances, too many checks, ATM withdrawals, deposits, and bounced checks), it turns out that *you may actually be paying your bank for the use of your own money.*

You do get better interest with CDs. But there, your *liquidity* (i.e., the access to your funds) is severely restricted by early-withdrawal penalties.

In contrast, with Treasury-only checking you get the very best combination of safety, yield, liquidity, and convenience available in the world today.

Table 4.3 Treasury-Only Money Market Funds

Fund Name	Toll-Free No.	Web Address
59 Wall Street US Treasury MMF	(800) 625-5759	www.bbh.com
ABN AMRO Treas MMF/Common Cl	(800) 443-4725	www.abnamrofundsusa.com
Alliance Treasury Reserves	(800) 247-4154	www.alliancecapital.com
American Century Capital Presv Fund I	(800) 345-2021	www.americancentury.com
American Performance US Treas	(800) 762-7085	www.apfunds.com
BB&T US Treas MMF/Trust Shrs	(800) 882-1872	www.bbtfunds.com
BNY Hamilton Treas MF/Hamltn Classic	(800) 426-9363	www.bny.com
CitiFunds Premium US Treas Resvs	(800) 331-1792	www.citibank.com
CitiFunds US Treasury Reserves	(800) 331-1792	www.citibank.com
DBAB Cash Reserve Treasury	(800) 730-1313	www.alexbrown.db.com
Deutsche Treas Money/Inv	(800) 730-1313	www.deam-us.com
Dreyfus 100% US Treasury MMF	(800) 242-8671	www.dreyfus.com
Dreyfus MM Instr/Govt Secs	(800) 242-8671	www.dreyfus.com
Dreyfus US Treas Reserves/Cl R	(800) 242-8671	www.dreyfus.com
Eureka US Treas Obligs MMF/Retail	(888) 890-8121	www.eurekafunds.com
Evergreen Treasury MMF/Cl A	(800) 343-2898	www.evergreen-funds.com
Evergreen Treasury MMF/Cl S	(800) 343-2898	www.evergreen-funds.com
Evergreen Treasury MMF/Cl Y	(800) 343-2898	www.evergreen-funds.com
Fidelity Spartan US Treasury MMF	(800) 343-3548	www.fidelity.com
Fifth Third US Treas MMF	(800) 257-5872	www.53.com
First Amer Treas Oblig/Cl D—Corpt	(800) 814-3406	www.firstamericanfunds.com
Firstar US Treasury MMF/Cl A	(800) 677-3863	www.firstar.com

(continued)

Table 4.3 (Continued)

Fund Name	Toll-Free No.	Web Address
Franklin Federal Money Fund	(800) 342-5236	www.franklintempleton.com
Gabelli US Treasury MMF	(800) 937-8909	www.gabelli.com
Hibernia US Treasury MMF	(800) 999-0124	www.hibernia.com
HighMark 100% US Treasury MMF/Cl S	(800) 433-6884	www.highmarkfunds.com
HighMark 100% US Treasury MMF/Fid	(800) 433-6884	www.highmarkfunds.com
HighMark 100% US Treasurvy MMF/Retail	(800) 433-6884	www.highmarkfunds.com
Huntington US Treas MMF/Trust	(800) 253-0412	www.huntingtonfunds.com
Independence One US Treas MMF	(800) 334-2292	www.iobsonline.com
JP Morgan 100$ Treasury MM/Vista	(800) 766-7722	www.jpmorgan.com
JP Morgan Treas Plus MM/Vista	(800) 766-7722	www.jpmorgan.com
Merrill Lynch CMA Govt Secs	(800) 637-3863	www.ml.com
Merrill Lynch USA Govt Res	(800) 637-3863	www.ml.com
Nations Treasury Fund/Investor A	(800) 321-7854	www.bankofamerica.com
Nations Treasury Fund/Investor B	(800) 321-7854	www.bankofamerica.com
Nations Treasury Fund/Primary A	(800) 321-7854	www.bankofamerica.com
One Group US Treas Secs MMF/Cl A	(800) 480-4111	www.onegroup.com
One Group US Treas Secs MMF/Cl I	(800) 480-4111	www.onegroup.com
PaineWebber RMA MF/US Govt	(800) 647-1568	www.painewebber.com
Pillar Funds US Treas Secs/Cl A	(800) 932-7782	www.pillarfunds.com
Prudential Govt Sec Tr/US Treas/Cl A	(800) 225-1852	www.prudential.com
Regions Treasury MMF/Cl A/Trust	(800) 433-2829	www.regions.com
Regions Treasury MMF/Cl B/Inv	(800) 433-2829	www.regions.com
Reserve Fund/Government Fund	(800) 637-1700	www.reservefunds.com

Reserve Fund/US Treas Fund	(800) 637-1700	www.reservefunds.com
Riggs US Treasury MMF	(800) 934-3883	www.riggsbank.com
Schwab US Treasury Money Fund	(800) 266-5623	www.schwab.com
Scudder US Treas MF/Cl S	(800) 728-3337	www.scudder.com
SEI Liq Asset Tr/Treas Secs/Cl A	(800) 342-5734	www.seic.com
Sentinel US Treasury MMF	(800) 282-3863	www.sentinel.com
Short Term Income Us Govt/Cl A	(800) 873-8637	www.usfunds.com
Short Term Income Us Govt/Cl B	(800) 873-8637	www.usfunds.com
SouthTrust US Treasury MMF	(800) 843-8618	www.southtrust.com
T. Rowe Price US Treasury MF	(800) 638-5660	www.troweprice.com
US Treasury MF of America	(800) 421-4120	www.americanfunds.com
US Treasury Securities Cash Fund	(800) 873-8637	www.usfunds.com
USAA Treasury MM Trust	(800) 382-8722	www.usaa.com
Vanguard Admiral Treasury MMF	(800) 662-7447	www.vanguard.com
Vanguard Treasury MMF	(800) 662-7447	www.vanguard.com
Victory US Govt Oblig Fund/Inv A	(800) 423-0897	www.victoryfunds.com
Victory US Govt Oblig Fund/Select	(800) 423-0898	www.victoryfunds.com
Vision Treasury MMF/Cl A	(800) 836-2211	www.mandtbank.com
Wachovia US Treas MMF/Instit	(800) 994-4414	www.wachovia.com
Wachovia US Treas MMF/Invmt	(800) 994-4414	www.wachovia.com
Wells Fargo 100% Treas MMF/Cl A	(800) 222-8222	www.wellsfargo.com
Wells Fargo 100% Treas MMF/Svc	(800) 222-8222	www.wellsfargo.com
Wells Fargo Treas Plus MMF/Class A	(800) 222-8222	www.wellsfargo.com

If you want maximum safety from nearly every risk imaginable (e.g., price risk, default risk, fraud risk, and so forth), this is the place to be. The yield is better than most equivalent checking and savings accounts at a bank, the costs are significantly lower, and you'll never lose a dime from a stock market decline. For the largest funds, with some of the best features, see Table 4.4.

THE ADVANTAGES OF TREASURY-ONLY SAVINGS AND CHECKING

The basic vehicle for Treasury-only savings and checking is very simple: Instead of using banks, you primarily use a special kind of mutual fund, a Treasury-only money fund.

A Treasury-only money fund invests all of your money in short-term U.S. Treasury securities (plus other securities that are backed 100 percent by U.S. Treasuries). It uses a bank, but strictly as a custodian for the securities, and those accounts are completely segregated from the bank's deposits or assets.

The Treasury-only money fund also provides you with check-writing privileges so that you can use the money fund as your personal or business checking account. The advantages are many:

Advantage 1: Higher Yields

In recent years, Treasury-only money funds have yielded at least double the yield that is offered on the average personal checking account in the United States. If you assume an average balance of $5,000, and you can boost your average yield from 1.5 to 3.5 percent, your interest income, when compounded, can actually be 2.6 times greater. Assuming that there is no change in these rates, over a 10-year period you would boost your interest income from $809 to $2,092.

In your business checking account, if you assume an average balance of $50,000, your interest income with a Treasury-only account over 10 years will be $20,917. That's *a total 10-year return of nearly 42 percent on your money* that you might not have earned otherwise.

Furthermore, in a business of fairly average activity, I estimate that you will also be able to take better advantage of the *float* (i.e., the funds remaining in your account while checks written against them have not yet cleared). With this float, your average daily balances can increase by 50 percent or more. Assuming an average daily bank balance of $75,000, your total yield on your $50,000 book balance jumps to $31,376 over 10 years. Obviously, this is not petty change; rather, this is a very significant, untapped source of revenues. But this is just the beginning.

Advantage 2: Low Fees

When a bank quotes you yields, on any kind of account, it always quotes you the yields *before* deducting all of the service fees mentioned earlier. With bank charges and fees currently at their highest level in modern history, it's almost impossible for most bank customers to collect anything near the advertised yield.

In contrast, when a money fund quotes you its yield, it is *after* deducting all of its expenses and most fees. Of course, the past or current yield is no guarantee of future results. However, at least the yield quoted is the *net* yield that investors in the fund are *actually* earning.

How much of a difference can this make? In most cases, a very large one. Indeed, after deducting the myriad bank fees, most Americans today are getting a net yield of *close to zero* on their accounts, and many wind up losing money. In other words, instead of the bank paying *you* for the use of your deposits, you're actually paying *them* for the so-called privilege. Examples include:

- Banks rarely spend more than $2 to process a bounced check; however, they charge you close to $30.
- Banks spend nothing to receive a wire transfer from another bank; however, they charge you $10 or more.
- Banks charge you for having too many transactions, and they charge you if you have too few.
- Banks charge you on your way in to make deposits, and they charge you on your way out when you make withdrawals.
- Banks charge a hefty fee if you use the automated teller machines. With some accounts, many banks charge you a fee if you use live tellers.

In contrast, as you can see in Table 4.4, most Treasury-only money funds charge you nothing or very little for each of these situations.

Advantage 3: One Account for Both Checking and Savings

At banks, most customers divide their money between a checking account (where they give up most of their yield) and a savings account or CD (where they give up immediate access and liquidity). No matter what, it's almost impossible to get *both* optimal liquidity *and* high yield in the same bank account.

In contrast, money funds let you keep nearly all of your cash assets, whether for savings or for checking, in one single account. This means that whether you're investing $1,000 or $1 million:

- You have complete access to *all* of your funds at all times.
- You can withdraw the *entire* amount, with no penalty whatsoever. Just write a check or request a wire transfer, and it's done.
- Your money consistently earns competitive, current market yields.
- You never have to worry about leaving too much in your checking account at low rates. The full amount is available for checking at all times, earning full interest.
- You continue earning interest on your money up until the moment your check clears. The longer it takes for your payees to cash their checks, the more interest you make on this float.
- If you want to use your account as your most active checking account to pay most of your bills, that's even better. The more you use it, the more you take advantage of the float.
- In short, you are always getting maximum liquidity and maximum yield on your *entire* balance.

You'll have no more shuttling back and forth between checking, passbook savings, money market accounts, CDs, and other complex combinations. Instead, you'll be able to have one large account that meets nearly all of your needs—checking, savings, and investment. (You may still need one more small account, which will be discussed later.)

Advantage 4: No Limit to Your Account Size

When you use banks for your saving or your checking, you have to go through a series of contortions to keep your money safe from failure, including:

- *Spreading your CDs among various accounts.* This means that you would have to keep track of several accounts at the same time.

- *Making sure that your initial investment in each CD is actually under the $100,000 limit.* Otherwise, the accumulation of accrued interest could put your balance over the limit, and that portion would not be covered by the FDIC.

- *Calling your bank almost daily to make sure (in the case of large checking accounts) that the account is not over the $100,000 FDIC limit.* If there are several large checks outstanding, your bank balance could be over the limit. If the bank were to fail at that time, any excess amount could be a total loss!

Here is the crux of the dilemma with any bank checking account. To make sure that your funds are covered by the FDIC, you need to keep your balance under $100,000; however, to maximize your interest on the float, you'd want your balances to be as *high* as possible, with no limit at $100,000. The two goals are obviously in conflict. If you want the full insurance coverage, you'll probably have to forget about the float.

With Treasury-only money funds, I believe that insurance is a moot point. It's not even an issue because your funds are invested strictly in securities that are guaranteed directly by the full faith and credit of the U.S. Treasury Department. There is no limit on the Treasury's guarantee of its obligations, whether you're a beginning saver with just a few thousand dollars or Bill Gates with many billion.

Unlike bank accounts, there is no limit to your account size with a Treasury-only money fund. This is another reason for keeping nearly all of your cash in one single, easy-to-manage account.[3]

All of the assets in Treasury-only money funds are invested in short-term U.S. Treasury securities (plus some securities that are fully backed by the U.S. Treasury). These are widely considered to be the safest securities in the world.

Nor does the U.S. Treasury Department distinguish between where or how the Treasury bills are held. Whether you own them directly or through a Treasury-only money fund, they are still Treasuries, and they are still guaranteed.

Indeed, everyone in the financial industry (except perhaps for some bankers) would agree that the direct guarantee of the U.S. Treasury Department is actually stronger than the guarantee of the FDIC. That's why U.S. Treasury securities merit a higher credit rating than bank CDs.

There have been more than 3,000 bank and S&L failures in the last 20 years, causing savers and businesses serious inconveniences and even outright losses. In contrast, there has never been a default on U.S. Treasury securities, even when the government was temporarily shut down due to a budget dispute, even when the entire country was torn by the Civil War.

Advantage 5: Exempt from Local and State Taxes

The income that you earn on both Treasury-only money funds and bank accounts is subject to *federal* income taxes. There is no difference between banks and this program in that regard.

However, when it comes to local and state income taxes, there is a big difference: *The dividends that you earn on Treasury-only money funds are exempt. The income that is earned on bank accounts and CDs is not exempt.* Be aware that I did not account for the added benefit of this tax exemption when I compared the yields on bank deposits with those on Treasury-only money funds. Therefore, depending on your city's or state's tax laws, the after-tax yield advantage with a Treasury-only money fund could be even greater.

Also, don't forget about this key advantage when comparing Treasury-only money funds with other money funds that invest in prime commercial paper or bank CDs. The dividends on Treasury-only funds are usually exempt; those of most other money funds are *not* exempt. Therefore, the apparent yield advantage that some of them provide could be deceptive.

Advantage 6: Truly Free Checking

Nearly all banks charge you—one way or another—for your checking privileges. They may charge you a fee for each check you issue. They may charge you a flat monthly service fee. Or they may charge you a combination of both.

Sometimes, banks *say* they're giving you free checking, but require large minimum balances, paying little or no interest. No matter what, you're paying for checking—and probably too much.

The specific rules on how to maintain your average balances to qualify for free checking can be complex and hard to follow. Furthermore, they vary from bank to bank, and can change whenever your bank is bought out by another institution. Keeping track can be almost like a full-time job.

Most Treasury-only money funds do *not* charge you any extra fee for check-writing privileges. You can write as many checks as you want, as often as you want. With most Treasury-only money funds, when they say "free checking privileges," they really mean it. They guarantee that:

- You will never have to pay an extra monthly fee for checking.
- You won't have to worry about how much it costs you to write each check. They're all free.

This is not true for *all* Treasury-only money funds. Many do levy certain charges for special services, but they're almost always lower than the charges at banks. Moreover, if you shop carefully for the right fund, you can reduce even these charges down to virtually zero.

Advantage 7: Immediate Liquidity

As with any financial institution, there will be a holding period for the out-of-town checks that you deposit to your account. However, your money goes to work for you right away, generating interest income immediately. If you deposit your money via wire transfer, you can avoid the holding period–your funds will be available immediately. *In short, except for the holding period, all of the funds received by your Treasury-only money fund are available to you all of the time.*

There are three ways you can withdraw your money from your Treasury-only money fund:

1. You can write a check against the balance in your account to yourself or to another payee.
2. You can call or send a fax to your money fund's shareholder service department, giving them instructions to issue a wire transfer. (Before the fund can accept your wire instructions, however, you will have to file a signed authorization ahead of time. This can be done when you open your account.)
3. You can request that a check be sent to you directly from the fund. You can also authorize telephone instructions for redemption by check when you open your account.

No other kind of account (e.g., with banks, S&Ls, credit unions, brokers, or insurers) can give you this level of immediate access.

THE DISADVANTAGES OF TREASURY-ONLY SAVINGS AND CHECKING

As you can see, there are tremendous benefits in using this plan: Treasury-only money funds offer you the opportunity to earn more. They can save you a great amount of money and time. They give you far more access to your money, opening up new investment opportunities, and potentially transforming the way you do business. However, there are also some disadvantages.

Disadvantage 1

Many money funds impose a minimum amount for each check, usually $100. Therefore, you may need a small checking account for checks less than $100.

Disadvantage 2

The money fund selects the bank that acts as its custodian, and it will probably be an out-of-town institution. For most payees to whom you write checks, this is not a problem. They're glad to be paid on time and will accept any form of payment. However, in your business, employees may want to cash their checks locally, which may not be possible with an out-of-town bank.

HOW TO SET UP YOUR TREASURY-ONLY SAVINGS AND CHECKING ACCOUNT

Whether you are an active investor or not, whether you have a lot of money set aside or just small amounts, you should follow these steps to open your account.

Step 1

Decide what type of account you want to open. For your personal checking account, it could be established as an individual, joint, custodian, or trust. (In addition, you can also use your Treasury-only money fund to open a separate account for your IRA or other retirement accounts.)

Step 2

Select any one of the Treasury-only funds in Table 4.3 or 4.4. If it's not listed in the tables, make certain that it invests exclusively in short-term U.S. Treasury securities or equivalents. These equivalents can include *repurchase agreements,* which are fully backed by U.S. Treasury securities or other Treasury-only money funds. All of these qualify for state and local income tax exemption in most states.

Be careful, though. If a money fund invests in non-Treasury instruments (i.e., certain U.S. government agency securities, commercial paper, bankers' acceptances, or bank CDs), it does *not* qualify for full local and state tax exemption. In short, make sure you are dealing with a Treasury-only money fund.

Step 3

While you're on the phone, ask a few questions about the costs associated with check-writing privileges.

"How many checks will you provide for me at no charge?" For personal accounts, at least the first 20 to 25 checks should be free. If you want additional checks, it's reasonable to expect a printing charge, but it should not be more than $15 per 200 checks.

"Will you charge me a per-check transaction fee?" If the answer is yes, and you anticipate a relatively active account, don't do business with this fund.

"What is the minimum dollar amount for which I can make out each of my checks?" It should be no more than $100. If it's over $100, this fund may not be suitable for your Treasury-only savings and checking plan.

"What is the minimum balance that I must maintain in my account, and will you penalize me if my balance falls below the minimum?" If the minimum is too high for you or if there is a penalty, look elsewhere.

"Do you accept deposits of second-party checks?" If the answer is no, this isn't the right fund for this plan.

Step 4

Ask the fund: "What is your seven-day simple yield?" Make sure you use this exact terminology: *seven-day simple yield.* This is the past seven days of income on a fund, expressed as a percentage of the fund's net asset value and calculated on an annual basis.

Because the yields are calculated daily, they are bound to vary. Don't pay much attention to yield differences of up to ¼ of a percentage point (0.25 percent). However, if the seven-day simple yield is ½ percent (0.50 percent) or more below that of other Treasury-only money funds, you may want to consider another fund.

Step 5

Ask the fund to mail you a fund prospectus, along with the appropriate account application. Read it carefully before investing. You may also download the prospectus and application from the fund's Web sites listed in Table 4.4.

Step 6

If you are not sure about what forms and documents you will need to submit to open an account, now is the time to ask. Some typical types of accounts, along with the documentation needed, include:

Type 1: Individual or joint account, minor custodian account. You'll need the application and the signature card (indicate the number of signatures that will be required to cash a check).

Table 4.4   Largest Treasury-Only

Fund Name	Toll-Free No.	Web Address	Minimum Balance to Open Account	Cost to Print Checks
Alliance Treasury Reserves	(800) 247-4154	www.alliancecapital.com	$1,000	No charge
American Century Capital Presv Fund	(800) 345-2021	www.americancentury.com	$2,500	No charge
American Performance US Treas	(800) 762-7085	www.apfunds.com	$5,000	No charge
Dreyfus 100% US Treasury MMF	(800) 242-8671	www.dreyfus.com	$500	No charge
Evergreen Treasury MMF/CI A	(800) 343-2898	www.evergreen-funds.com	$1,000	No charge
Gabelli US Treasury MMF	(800) 937-8909	www.gabelli.com	$3,000	No charge
HighMark 100% US Treasury MMF/Retail	(800) 433-6884	www.highmarkfunds.com	$1,000	No charge
Huntington US Treas MMF/Trust	(800) 253-0412	www.huntingtonfunds.com	$1,000	No charge
One Group US Treas Secs MMF/CI A	(800) 480-4111	www.onegroup.com	$1,000	No charge
Regions Treasury MMF/CI A/Trust	(800) 433-2829	www.regions.com	$1,000	No charge
Reserve Fund/ Government Fund	(800) 637-1700	www.reservefunds.com	$1,000	First 185 checks free
Scudder US Treas MF/CI S	(800) 728-3337	www.myscudder.com	$2,500	No charge
T. Rowe Price US Treasury MF	(800) 638-5660	www.troweprice.com	$2,500	No charge
U.S. Treasury Securities Cash Fund	(800) 873-8637	www.usfunds.com	$1,000	First 15 checks free
Vanguard Treasury MMF	(800) 662-7447	www.vanguard.com	$3,000	First 20 checks free

These are some of the largest Treasury-only money funds. All provide equivalent safety. But if you want to use the fund for the Treasury-only savings and checking described in this chapter, you should focus on those that offer checking with no minimum dollar amount per check, or a relatively low minimum per check. Funds

Maximum Number of Checks without Extra Charge	Maximum Number of Deposits without Extra Charge	Charge for Each Transaction over Maximum #	Charge for Each Bounced Check	Wire Transfers out of Your Account	Wire Transfers into Your Account
Unlimited	Unlimited	No charge	No charge	No charge	No charge
Unlimited	Unlimited	No charge	No charge	No charge	No charge
Unlimited	Unlimited	No charge	No charge	No charge	No charge
Unlimited	Unlimited	No charge	No charge	No charge	No charge
Unlimited	Unlimited	No charge	No charge	No charge	No charge
Unlimited	Unlimited	No charge	$15.00	No charge	No charge
5	Unlimited	Not allowed	No charge	No charge	No charge
Unlimited	Unlimited	No charge	No charge	$11.00	No charge
Unlimited	Unlimited	No charge	No charge	No charge	No charge
Unlimited	Unlimited	No charge	No charge	No charge	No charge
Unlimited	Unlimited	No charge	No charge	$10 if amount is under $10,000	No charge
Unlimited	Unlimited	No charge	No charge	No charge	No charge
Unlimited	Unlimited	No charge	No charge	$25 if under $5000	No charge
Unlimited	Unlimited	No charge	No charge	$10.00	No charge
Unlimited	Unlimited	No charge	No charge	$5 if amount is under $5000	No charge

with a $500 minimum amount per check or more are fine for savings, but are not practical for an active checking account. Take a look also at all the special transactions that you can get for no charge. When was the last time your bank did NOT charge you for a bounced check, for example?

For joint accounts, unless you specify otherwise, they will probably be opened as *joint tenants with rights of survivorship* (JTWROS), meaning that the entire account balance will pass to the survivor in the event of death of one of the joint owners.

If you want the account to be registered as *joint tenants in common* (JTIC), be sure to specify that in writing when you open the account. JTIC means that each person owns a set percentage of the account; if one person dies, his or her percentage does not automatically go to the survivor, but goes into the deceased's estate to be distributed.

If you wish a *custodian account for a minor child* (UGMA), don't forget to use the child's Social Security number for correct IRS reporting.

Type 2: Trust or guardianship. You will need the application and the signature card (indicate the number of signatures needed to cash a check). Plus, you will need certified copies of the appropriate trust documents or court papers appointing a guardian and any power-of-attorney forms, if applicable. [*Hint:* Put the trustee name(s) first on the account registration to reduce the paperwork that would be needed whenever an account transaction is requested (e.g., Jane S. Doe, TTEE Doe Family Trust).]

Type 3: IRA, Roth IRA, or other retirement account or rollover. Ask for the IRA or retirement plan application and agreement. This information should include a new account application, a transfer authorization, and a rollover certification form.

- If you're opening a *new retirement account,* fill out the new account application only.
- If you're *transferring a retirement account directly between custodians,* fill out both the application and the transfer authorization. Also be sure to include a copy of the most recent statement from your current custodian.
- If you have an *IRA rollover* and there is a distribution from a retirement account that you are going to transfer to the Treasury-only money fund, fill out both the new account application and the rollover certification form. (*Impor-*

tant: Due to IRS regulations, check writing is not possible on IRA accounts.)

Step 7

With the aforementioned documents, also provide the basic wiring instructions to the fund. If there is no space on the application, put the following information in a separate, signed letter:

- Your bank's name, city, and state
- Your bank's American Bankers Association (ABA) number
- Your bank's wire transfer account number
- Your account number at the bank
- All registered names on the account

Note: The account title on your bank account should be the same as the title on your Treasury-only money fund account.

Step 8

Don't forget to sign the application. Then make your check payable to the Treasury-only money fund and mail it with your new account materials. You should receive written confirmation of your deposit in the mail within a few days, and a checkbook within about two weeks. Look over these materials carefully to verify that all is correct. Be sure to call the fund immediately if there is any discrepancy, and don't use your checks if they are printed incorrectly.

HOW TO MAXIMIZE YOUR YIELD WITH TREASURY-ONLY SAVINGS AND CHECKING

Once you have completed the preceding eight steps to establish your Treasury-only account, proceed with the following steps.

Step 9

Keep only a minimal amount in your local bank. Most people maintain balances of between $500 and $2,000 for petty cash and small, occasional checks.

Step 10

Use a major credit card for as many of your purchases as possible. Then, to avoid any interest charges, *pay off your credit card in full each month* with one check written off your Treasury-only money fund.

Step 11

To maximize your total yield and liquidity, transfer the bulk of your cash funds to the Treasury-only money fund account. These can include any investment funds you wish to keep liquid and available for upcoming opportunities, most of your regular spending money, and most of your keep-safe savings.

Step 12

Write all of your checks that are above the fund's per-check minimum from this account. These should include checks for paying your mortgage, rent, monthly credit card bills, utility bills, and any large purchases at establishments that give you a better price for non–credit card purchases.

Step 13

If you need a large amount of cash or want to buy traveler's checks, just call your Treasury-only money fund and give them instructions to transfer the money to your local bank. In most cases, if you call before 3:00 P.M., you should have the funds in your account the very next business day.

Step 14

At most funds, you may deposit your salary and any checks payable to you directly into your account. Just endorse the checks with your signature on the reverse side and include the words *for deposit to,* followed by your account number at the fund. Then simply mail your deposit to the fund. (You may use the deposit slip and envelope that most funds provide you with your monthly statement.)

As always, *do not send cash in the mail.* If you have cash deposits, make them at your local bank and then send the funds to your Treasury-only money fund via either a check or wire transfer.

If you want to know if your check has cleared your fund, and you don't want to wait for the written confirmation in the mail, just call the fund's shareholder services at its toll-free number.

You will receive monthly statements from the fund showing all of your checking transactions plus any other activity, including deposits, dividend income credits, and so forth. Canceled checks are not usually returned to you automatically, unless you specifically ask for them.

That's it! With these steps, you will now have superior safety overall, significantly greater effective yields, greatly reduced bank charges, and maximum liquidity.

This is what I recommend for most of your money. The higher your score in the Risk Self-Test, the larger the percentage of your funds that should be kept in Treasury-only savings and checking.

Alas, no plan is perfect. There is always a price to pay. In this plan, the price is that interest rates on short-term, immediately available funds are currently low. They're a lot better than what you can get in a bank nowadays, but still low in comparison with what most of us would like to be earning on our money. However, once you've put most of your money away in a safe place, you will be ready to venture further, aiming for far higher returns.

CHAPTER 5

PROFITS ARE YOUR BEST REVENGE

Wall Street firms financed a great boom in technology that generated a king's ransom in valuable assets. Then, they presided over an equally great *bust* in the stock market, giving you the opportunity to buy all that wealth at flea-market prices. Therefore, instead of dwelling on the past, we should look optimistically toward better profit opportunities.

In this chapter, I'm going to lead you through four alternative investing approaches, from a basic, complete, safe, no-risk-no-worry method, to an aggressive, active-trader approach. Before we get there, however, I'd like to introduce you to the key investment vehicle you should be using, regardless of which approach you choose: mutual funds. As you'll see, mutual funds allow you to capitalize on just about any strategy while also providing a number of advantages that go above and beyond most other investments. Their advantages include:

Advantage 1: The mutual fund industry gives you more and better information than any other investment industry. You can find out virtually everything you need to know about the people who are making the investment decisions on your behalf, what they're doing with your money, what the bottom-line performance is, and how much they're charging you for the effort. You can make apples-to-apples comparisons of their performance, the risk, and the costs versus those of any other mutual fund. You can get the information promptly for free. You can slice and dice the information almost any way you want, sorting funds by category, yield, safety, performance, and a host of other criteria. Also, you can do this without relying on anyone, whether salesperson or advisor, all from the comfort of your living room.

Moreover, the data are almost always unbiased and accurate, strictly conforming to legal guidelines and standards regarding exactly how they are calculated and when they are disclosed. The kind of fudging of information found in other investments is almost impossible. Mutual funds provide a greater level of disclosure than almost any other investment product.

Advantage 2: Mutual funds offer the best protection from failure or fraud. When you put your money into a brokerage account, you can be adversely affected if the brokerage firm fails. If you put your money into a cash-value life insurance policy, you can get hurt if the insurance company fails. Even in a bank, any money beyond $100,000 could be in jeopardy. When you invest in a mutual fund, however, your money is segregated from the assets of the management company.

No matter what, the securities and funds of the mutual fund are held in escrow at a separate financial institution. This is a Securities and Exchange Commission (SEC) requirement. No mutual fund can do otherwise. This is also true for mutual funds that are managed by a brokerage firm or bank. Even if the broker or bank fails, your money in the mutual fund will remain separate.

Needless to say, none of these protections guarantees investment success. If the mutual fund managers buy investments that tank, your investment goes down the tubes as well. However, there are also thousands of mutual funds that never put a penny of your money in the stock market, and are rarely, if ever, subject to losses.

The key question is: Which mutual funds should you select, when, and how much? Let's look at four different approaches, starting from the safest to the most aggressive. Choose the *one* approach that best fits your abilities and goals.

Approach 1: No Risk, No Worry

If you have no room for even *one dime* of losses, and no patience for even a few minutes of research, you leave yourself only one alternative: Park all of your money in the safest possible place, earn whatever short-term yields are available, and sleep at night.

In Chapter 4, I have given you a list of the Treasury-only money funds, all of which are among your safest choices. I have also shown you how to maximize your yield and liquidity.

Unfortunately, however, your 401(k) probably does *not* offer a Treasury-only money fund as one of its options. If you require the no-risk-no-worry approach, you will have to use the next best alternative: First, check to see if your 401(k) includes a government-only money market fund. These funds invest in other kinds of government securities beyond just U.S. Treasuries, but they offer most of the same advantages.

Second, if there is no government-only money market fund, check for *any* money market fund. These loan your money out to private companies, such as banks and large corporations, for a very short term and rarely to high-risk companies. They are still among the safest kinds of mutual funds.

Third, if there is no money market fund at all (which would be unusual), find a bond fund.

Whatever your choices may be, go for the safest one of all. If, at some time in the future, you feel that you want to be more aggressive again, allocate a modest portion of the total (e.g., from 20 to 40 percent, depending on your risk tolerance) to a balanced or value fund, which can take advantage of future opportunities in the stock market.

Approach 2: Evaluate Your Risk Tolerance, Then Invest Accordingly

An obvious problem that contributed to the losses in the Great Stock Market Scam was the mismatch of what investors could afford to risk and how much risk they were actually taking. Your primary goal in this approach is to properly evaluate your tolerance for losses and then invest according to the following five steps.

Step 1: Take the Risk Self-Test, found in Appendix A of this book. This will tell you if you should prioritize safety or performance when choosing mutual funds and other investments. It will also tell you how much of your assets to allocate to the programs recommended in this book.

Step 2: Thousands of public libraries in America carry our Weiss Ratings guides. Consult the *Weiss Ratings' Guide to Stock Mutual Funds* and the *Weiss Ratings' Guide to Bond and Money Market Mutual Funds.* Or for more information, you can call 1-800-289-9222 or log on at www.weissratings.com.

Step 3: In the guide, follow the instructions that are appropriate for your risk tolerance level. If you have a high risk tolerance, focus on our listings of mutual funds with the best Weiss Performance Ratings. If you have a low tolerance for risk, focus on our lists of funds with the best Weiss Risk Ratings.

Step 4: Avoid load funds with a 10-foot pole. Load funds are those that charge up-front or back-end commissions—to enter or exit. Proponents of the load funds (including stockbrokers who routinely get a share of the fees) use all kinds of pat arguments to overcome your natural resistance to the fees. If they give you that song and dance, hang up or walk out.

For example, they will tell you that the fees on load funds are no more expensive than those on no-load funds. The only difference, they say, is that the load funds take the fees in one chunk, while the no-loads spread them out over time. That argument only holds if you're willing to commit to a single fund or fund family for at least six to eight years—a pretty weak strategy in any environment.

Suppose you're like the average investor who switches funds every two years or so. Suppose you *really* want to use mutual funds efficiently and switch as often as every month or two. Either way, the loads are a real killer.

Another sales tactic you'll often hear for load funds goes something like this: "You get what you pay for. If you want better performance and management, you have to pay a fee to get in." This is also not true! Weiss Ratings has analyzed the average performance of 1,436 no-load funds versus 2,072 load funds. The result was precisely the opposite of what the load funds argued: The no-load funds produced a better overall performance. So scratch load funds off your list.[1]

Step 5: Broaden your horizons.   Don't restrict your investing to traditional stock market mutual funds. Instead, *truly* diversify your investments by allocating funds to a wide variety of mutual fund types. These should include the standard categories, such as value funds, growth funds, balanced funds, and most important, mutual funds that can help you avoid completely the risk of a declining stock market. These are mutual funds that *never* put one dime of your money in stocks of any kind—foreign or domestic. In the United States alone, there are 3,834 bond mutual funds that specialize in bonds of all varieties (e.g., Treasury bonds, corporate bonds, tax-exempt municipal bonds, and so on). You can earn yields that are equivalent to most long-term bond yields. Plus, if the market price of the bonds in the portfolio rises, you benefit from the appreciation as well. There is a risk of loss, but on average it's far less than the risk in stock mutual funds.

Approach 3: Eliminate the Volatile Funds in Your 401(k), Then Rotate among the Others

The money in your retirement plan is important, so you should devote some time every week to make it grow for you. That, plus access to the Internet, is all you'll need to follow this far more flexible, and potentially very profitable, approach. This approach is especially appropriate for your 401(k), where any higher returns can compound without the burden of current taxes.

Federal law mandates that your employer give you a variety of choices. These should include a balanced fund, a growth fund, a small-cap fund, a bond fund, plus perhaps an international fund and an index fund, as well as a money market fund. Your goal should be to avoid the funds that move up and down too much and then, using strictly the nonvolatile funds, invest always in the best performers. Follow these six steps:

Step 1.   Get from your HR or benefits manager the names and ticker symbols of all the mutual funds that are available to you in your 401(k).

Step 2.   Eliminate the mutual funds that are too volatile (i.e., the funds that jump up and down too suddenly). Go to www.morningstar.com, and then:

   A. Find the box called "Enter Ticker." Type in the five-letter ticker symbol of your fund and press "Go."
   B. Click in the left-hand menu on Modern Portfolio Theory (MPT) stats.

WARNING: WEB SITES *WILL* CHANGE THEIR LAYOUT!

This and subsequent chapters provide very specific directions on using today's publicly available Web sites. However, they often change their structure and layout. If so, you'll need to adjust your steps accordingly!

C. Find at the top of the screen a number for the fund's *beta* (i.e., the measure of volatility in relation to the overall market). If the beta of the fund is greater than 1.5, forget it. Leave it to the riverboat gamblers and speculators. If it is 1.5 or less, put it on your list of buy candidates.

D. Repeat this step for all of the funds in your 401(k). However, you will not have to look up any money market funds, because their beta is always very low.

E. You will now have a short list of funds in which you can invest.

Note: Steps 1 and 2 only have to be done once a year. Typically, your 401(k) will not change funds more than once a year, and the beta for each fund doesn't change that much either.

Step 3. Find out which of your funds are in an uptrend by going to www.bigcharts.com and doing the following:

A. Find the box "Enter Symbol." Enter the five-letter ticker of your fund.

B. Click on the red box at the top of the screen that says "Interactive Charting."

C. Click on the left-hand side, on the box that says "Indicators." A new menu will appear.

D. Go to the left side, and find the box "Moving Averages."

E. Pull down the menu for "Moving Averages," and select "Simple Moving Average" (SMA).

F. To the immediate right of SMA, find another white box with the number 9 in it. Replace the number 9 with the number 50.

G. Click on the red box "Draw Chart." You will now see a graph that shows two lines. The black line is the value of your fund; the beige line is a 50-day SMA of the fund's ups and downs.

H. Ask this simple question: "Is my fund (the black line) now trading above the SMA (beige line)?" If it's not, set it aside. If it is, keep it on your list of buy candidates.

Step 4. Pick out the fund with the best performance over the last month. Go to www.morningstar.com, and do the following:

    A. Find the box "Enter Symbol." Enter the five-letter ticker of your fund.

    B. Click on "Trailing Returns" (in the left-hand menu). You'll see a series of time periods from "1 day" all the way up to "10 years." Make a note of the 1-month trailing return.

    C. Do the same for all of the other funds in your 401(k) that are still on your buy list.

Step 5. Rank your funds, from the highest return to the lowest, investing 100 percent of your money in the fund with the highest return.

Step 6. Next weekend, repeat steps 3 through 5.

- As long as that fund stays in the number 1 or number 2 position, *hold.*
- As soon as that fund falls to number 3 or lower, *sell.*
- If you have a loss of more than 5 percent in the fund from the time you bought to the most recent Friday close, *sell.*
- Then, take the proceeds from that sale, check to see which fund is the new number 1, and *buy* it.

That's it! It's really very easy. In this program, sometimes you will hold a fund for many months, sometimes for only a few weeks. But, on average, expect to be switching no more than every two or three months. When the stock market is doing poorly, this program should automatically put you in a money market fund or bond fund. Otherwise, you should be in one of the better- or best-performing stock funds available in your 401(k). There are no guarantees of success, but this plan should keep you out of trouble while still giving you the opportunity to make very good, steady returns.

Approach 4: For Your Taxable Money, Invest in the Best and Dump the Rest

Some funds that were hot last month will be dogs tomorrow; they will be replaced by a new set of hot funds. Imagine the amazing performance you'd have if you could always be in the cream of the crop!

Bill Donoghue, one of the nation's foremost experts on mutual funds, pioneered an approach with precisely that goal. His motto is: "Invest in the best, and dump the rest." That's also the basic principle behind the approach that is recommended to you here.

This program, developed by Tony Sagami, will take no more than 15 minutes of your time each week. It will free you from every single scam and piece of bad advice that Wall Street could possibly conjure up. In addition, it will give you the potential to personally outperform nearly every mutual fund manager in America!

It may take a few hours for you to set it up, and it will require a modest investment in software and data. However, if you are investing $30,000 or more, I think it could pay for that cost many times over. Here's what you should do:

Step 1.   For this program, select a discount brokerage firm that:
- Is a "mutual fund supermarket," handling hundreds of different mutual funds
- Charges low, discount commissions
- Does *not* discourage frequent switching from fund to fund

Which mutual fund supermarkets qualify? Well, both Charles Schwab and Fidelity are among the firms that discourage trading. So for this program, cross them off your list. That leaves firms like Ameritrade, Waterhouse, E-Trade, and Quick & Reilly.

"I don't want to use a broker for my mutual funds," you say. "I'm happy just calling my mutual fund company up directly." That may sound easier to you, but it would make it impossible for you to take advantage of this strategy. First, restricting yourself to just one mutual fund family (even large ones like Fidelity or Vanguard) would limit your choice of funds too severely. Moreover, if you start switching from fund to fund too often, you'll soon get a nasty-gram from the fund telling you to stop. If you pursue it, they may even suspend your switching privileges.

At the brokerage firm, you avoid this problem entirely. Because your mutual fund supermarket will carry many different fund families, any switches you make will rarely involve the same fund family more than once or twice. Therefore, you're very unlikely to violate the mutual funds' rules.

Step 2. When you open and fund your account, make sure that you specify that you want all of your cash balances placed into a money market fund of your choice–not a "cash" account, which earns interest for the broker only. If there is a government-only money market fund available, that would be my first choice. But with the bulk of your funds safely tucked away in the Treasury-only money fund that you chose for "Treasury-Only Savings and Checking" (Chapter 4), a standard money market is fine for the purpose of this program.

Step 3. Get a list of all of the mutual funds that are available at your brokerage firm. You can probably find one on their Web site, or they will give you a brochure with a complete listing. At most of the major mutual fund supermarkets, they will have anywhere from 800 to 3,500 funds available.

Step 4. Select the mutual funds that you will use in this program. Start with all of their funds and make the following eliminations:

- Eliminate any fund that charges an up-front or back-end sales load. There are a few that charge a very minimal 0.25 percent redemption fee, which I don't think will hurt you too much. Check your discount broker's brochure or Web site. It should make it very clear what the fees are.
- Eliminate any fund that requires a minimum holding period. You want total flexibility. Sometimes you'll be in for several months, but sometimes for only several days.

- Eliminate any fund that requires a minimum investment of more than $10,000.
- Eliminate bond funds and money funds, except the one you chose when you opened your account.

That will leave you with between 100 and 500 funds, depending on your broker.

Step 5. Which funds to invest in now? In the accompanying box, I show you how to rank them by their 1-month alpha, easily the most reliable measure of risk-adjusted performance. You will do the ranking once a week, preferably on a Saturday or Sunday.

Step 6. On Monday morning, before the market opens, enter your order to buy the number 1–ranked fund with 50 percent of your money. Then put the other 50 percent of your money in the number 2–ranked fund.

Step 7. As long as these two funds stay *within* the top 10 percent of the funds in your universe, *hold*. For example, if you're using a total of 300 funds, it has to be ranked number 30 or better.

Step 8. As soon as that fund falls *below* the top 10 percent of the funds in your universe, *sell*. (In a universe of 300 funds, that would be number 31 or lower.)

Step 9. If you have a loss of more than 5 percent in the fund from the time you bought to the most recent Friday close, *sell*.

Step 10. Then, take the proceeds from that sale, check to see which fund is the new number 1, and *buy*. If you already own fund number 1, place the proceeds into fund number 2 instead.

I believe this is the *ideal* way to invest in the best and dump the rest. It should give you a wide diversity of funds to work with, including:

- Good representation in *all* of the nine fund styles that are tracked by Morningstar: large blend, large growth, and large value; medium blend, medium growth, and medium value; small blend, small growth, and small value.

- A good cross section of funds with top Weiss Performance Ratings and a good selection of funds with top Weiss Risk Ratings.[2]

- Some sector funds (i.e., specialized in individual stock market sectors).

- Some index funds (i.e., designed to track in lockstep with the performance of major stock market indexes).

- Some international funds. These will help you profit from rising markets overseas, a good feature especially when U.S. markets are not doing as well.

- One or two *reverse index funds*. These are funds that are designed to actually make you money when the market is going down!

As with the 401(k) program, expect to be switching no more than every two or three months. When the entire stock market is doing poorly, this program should automatically put you into a money market fund, or even a reverse index fund, to profit from the decline. Otherwise, you should be in one of the better- or best-performing stock funds in the country. The mutual fund game is *survival of the fittest*. And your goal is to always ride with the funds that are leading the pack.

The results can be amazing. Indeed, if you had used this program faithfully over the past seven years, you would have gotten a better result than with any single mutual fund in America. For example, an investor using this type of program could have started with $10,000 on January 1, 1993, and grown it into $125,993 by August 21, 2000. Needless to say, duplicating this performance in a down market would be very difficult. But it gives you a good idea of its potential power.

HOW TO RANK YOUR MUTUAL FUNDS WITH ALPHA

The key measure is the fund's *alpha*. It's based on Nobel Prize–winning economics, and it helps you to find the funds that are moving up the most, with the least danger of decline.[3] In simple terms, it measures the excess return over and above the expected return. In other words, it helps you pick out funds that perform better than the average.

Many investment services or Web sites calculate alpha in the wrong way: They use only monthly data, and then they go back three years. However, even in normal times, what was hot a few months ago could be a dog today. In turbulent times, data that are more than one month old are practically useless. So don't use the ordinary alpha that you can find on the Web. Instead, follow these eight steps:

Step 1. Buy software to track your funds with daily data. There are many good packages available, and almost all of them will calculate the alpha for you automatically. Among the best:

- *MetaStock (800-508-9180 or www.metastock.com).* Software cost: $449. Estimated data costs: $35 per month.
- *Monocle (877-606-6243 or 512-263-1191; www.monocle-systems.com).* Software cost: $450. Estimated data costs: $25 per month.

  If you're a whiz-bang computer expert, and you want to have the largest number of technical indicators, then you'll be happier with MetaStock. If you are at a beginner or intermediate level, Monocle would be your better choice.

Step 2. Each software program will let you set up your own personal trading family, or portfolio, of funds. Just make sure that you include *all* of the funds that are currently available for your "Invest in the Best" program (approach 4 of this chapter).

Step 3. Follow the computer program's instructions for downloading at least two months of daily price data.

Step 4. Eliminate one more group of funds. Cut out any fund that is too volatile. In the program, look for the section in your software called "Indicators" or "Stats." Select the indicator "Beta." Then remove from your portfolio any fund that has a beta of 1.5 or greater. Once you have done this once, you need not do it again.

Step 5. Again, under "Stats" or "Indicators," select "Alpha."

Step 6. The program will ask you to fill in the number of days you wish to use. Enter 30.

Step 7. Rank your funds by alpha, with the highest-alpha funds at the top and lowest at the bottom. In Monocle, for example, click on the descending arrow.

Step 8. Next weekend, download the latest week of data and repeat steps 5 through 8. Do it faithfully. Never miss a week. If you're going to be gone for a while, park your money in a money market fund until you get back.

MUTUAL FUND SUPERMARKETS

The premise behind the mutual fund supermarket is convenience. You open an account at one of the discount brokerage firms listed in Table 5.1. They, in turn, give you access to hundreds of mutual funds, from scores of fund families, all in one central location.

You get the added bonus of having all of your account information (including fees) for all of the funds that you own on one consolidated statement. It will also include any stocks and bonds that you purchase through that brokerage firm, which is especially helpful at tax time.

(continued)

Supermarkets bring ease to making selections among the multitude of funds with different investment styles, objectives, and costs. In addition, when sold through supermarkets, some top funds have much smaller minimum investments, perhaps $2,500 rather than $25,000.

There are three fees that you should be concerned about:

1. *Front-end sales loads.* Avoid these like a plague.

2. *Back-end sales charges greater than 0.25 percent.* Avoid these as well.

3. *A transaction fee (a commission).* These fees are inconsequential and to be expected. For example, Price Waterhouse charges a flat $24 for a round-trip trade (a purchase and a sale). Others are similar. You don't want to ignore a great fund because of a $24 fee. Fortunately, with almost all of the funds, you will be charged no transaction fee at all. Either way, it should not be a deal breaker.

Table 5.1   Mutual Fund Supermarkets

Brokerage Firm Name	Toll-Free No.	Web Address
Ameritrade, Inc.	800-454-9272	www.ameritrade.com
CSFB Direct Fund Center (formerly DLJDirect)	800-825-5723	www.csfbdirect.com
Fidelity Funds Network	800-522-7297	www.fidelity.com
National Discount Brokers (NDB) Mutual Fund Center	800-888-3999	www.ndb.com
Schwab Mutual Fund Marketplace	800-266-5623	www.schwab.com
Siebert Fund Exchange	800-872-0444	www.msiebert.com

Table 5.1   *(Continued)*

Brokerage Firm Name	Toll-Free No.	Web Address
TD Waterhouse Mutual Fund Network	800-934-4448	www.tdwaterhouse.com
Vanguard Fund Access	800-662-7447	www.vanguard.com

These brokerage firms provide the standard services of most discount brokers. Plus, they offer one more critical feature: the ability to trade a large number of mutual funds with no, or low, transaction costs. This is essential in today's volatile and uncertain world. You need the flexibility to run quickly from funds that are underperforming or falling, and jump into funds that are swinging with the times. You can't do that if you're being charged an arm and a leg at each fork in the road. *Warning:* Some firms, like Fidelity and Schwab, discourage active switching. So, if you're going to follow my approach 4 prescribed in this chapter, avoid those firms.

CHAPTER 6

INVESTING IN INDIVIDUAL STOCKS?

Even if you're over 50 and cannot afford to take large risks, at the right time you may want to allocate a modest portion of your portfolio to more aggressive investing. In fact, I believe you may be able to buy some of Wall Street's former favorites for as little as 10 cents on the dollar. You can pick up discarded dot-coms for as little as one penny on the dollar. You may even be able to pick up bargains in big-name blue chips as well. You just need to know when to wait for even better bargains, and when to jump in with both feet. That will require a healthy combination of discipline and skepticism.

Step 1: Get the Real Scoop on Corporate Earnings

In Chapter 1, I demonstrated how easy it is for corporations to manipulate their earnings reports. How do you get to the real story? *Follow the cash.* A company can artificially bloat up its sales by virtually giving away money to buy its products. Or it can book the sales even before its products come off the assembly line. However, none of these generate cash.

To cut through most (but not all) of the fluff, I recommend that you pay close attention to each company's *cash flow*. No matter how much the company may pad its performance figures–no matter how many bogus, intangible assets it creates on its books–it cannot create cash that's not there.

Follow that cash, and you'll almost always be a lot closer to the truth. Don't let the steps I outline in the accompanying box scare you. They are actually very easy for anyone with a knowledge of simple arithmetic. I give you instructions on how to get the information from the Web. But your broker or financial advisor can also get the information for you.

HOW TO TELL IF A COMPANY MAY BE MANIPULATING ITS EARNINGS

If you're relying on faulty earnings information to pick stocks, you owe it to yourself to take these 10 steps. All it will take is a few minutes to calculate:

1. On the Internet, go to www.yahoo.com and in the first paragraph at the top, click on "Finance."
2. In the upper left side of the screen, find the box "Get Quotes" and enter the ticker symbol of your company.
3. Immediately to the right of that box, you will find a pull-down menu. Select the item "Fundamentals" and press "Get Quotes."
4. In the box that appears, look in the column on the right labeled "More Info," and click on "Research."
5. Click on "Financials."
6. Next, click on the words "Cashflow Statement."
7. On the Cashflow Statement, find the "Cash flow from operating activities" or "Cash flow from operations," and write that down. Let's imagine that it's a negative $20 million. Right there, you know that this company is not bringing in real money from its core business.

(Continued)

8. At the top of the page, click on "Income Statement," and find the net income for the current period. Let's assume that it's $10 million. This is obviously not in sync with the cash flow. The company says it's making money, but the actual *cash* is going out the other way. That gives you a second warning sign.

9. You could stop right here. But there are still a couple more issues that a good researcher should check into: Is this a significant discrepancy? Is it better or worse than some of the other stocks you're interested in? To answer these questions, click on "Balance Sheet" (also at the top of the page). About halfway down, find the most recent number for the company's "Total Assets," and write that down. Let's assume it's $100 million.

10. Subtract the net income from the cash flow. In this case it would be a negative $20 million minus $10 million, equaling a negative $30 million. Then divide that result by the total assets. In this case, it would be negative $30 million divided by $100 million, or negative 30 percent. That's not good. Indeed, I believe that any company with a figure greater than 10 percent (whether negative or positive) is an indication of possible earnings manipulations. Don't trust this company's earnings.

Is this approach infallible? No. But no matter how quickly a company's earnings are going up, if cash flow isn't going up at the same pace, something's fishy. If cash flow is consistently going down while reported earnings are going up, you can be relatively sure something's wrong.

Step 2: Use Only Independent Stock Ratings

Quite a few independent research organizations, having no ties to the companies being rated, rate stocks. Independence doesn't guarantee success, but it does remove one of the greatest causes to failure. Some examples include:

- *Morningstar* (800-735-0700 or www.morningstar.com). Covers approximately 7,000 stocks.

- *Standard & Poor's* (800-546-0300 or www.standardandpoors .com). Covers 1,700 stocks

- *Stock Scouter* (www.moneycentral.msn.com). Covers over 6,000 stocks

- *Value Line* (800-634-3583, www.valueline.com). Covers 1,700 stocks

- *Weiss Ratings* (800-289-9222, www.weissratings.com). Covers 9,431 stocks

Most ratings focus primarily on performance with, at best, a nod to risk. Our Weiss Ratings are the only ones of which I am aware that are completely balanced between these two critical considerations. We measure risk by studying the stock's volatility and valuation, plus the risks the company itself may be taking in its operations and its balance sheet. We believe it is just as important to *protect* your money as it is to grow your money, and we personally insist that each and every rating we issue respects this fundamental principle.

Please bear in mind that all of these are *stock* ratings, designed to help you decide whether to buy, sell, or hold the stocks. They are entirely separate from credit or financial safety ratings that are issued on many of the same companies.

Step 3: Monitor Your Stock's Performance Regularly

No matter how good your stock picking, you've still got to expect underperformers and outright losers. After you've selected particular stocks for your portfolio, don't forget to track their performance weekly. If they're doing well, hold. If they're doing poorly, get out and don't look back.

Remember, contrary to the old Wall Street lore, "buying for the long term" was a total failure for most investors in the first two years

HOW TO MONITOR YOUR STOCK'S PERFORMANCE

1. Go to www.bigcharts.com.

2. Click on the red button that says "Interactive Charting."

3. Enter the ticker symbol of your stock in the box titled "Enter symbol or keyword" (it also works for funds).

4. On the left-hand side, click on the button that says "Compare to" and select S&P 500.

5. On the left-hand side, choose six months as the "Time."

6. Click on the red "Draw chart" button. You should get a graph comparing your stock to the S&P.

7. Then, ask two simple questions: First, is my stock making me money? Second, is my stock doing at least as well as the S&P 500? If the answer to either of these questions is no, dump it, and don't look back. If the stock happens to turn back up just after you've sold it, don't let that bother you. Forget about it. Based on the information you had, you made the right decision.

of the new millennium, and could continue to be a misguided approach for many years to come.

Instead, in this new era of rapidly shifting tides, you have to stay flexible and be ready to move on. No matter how great a company may appear, the proof is in the pudding. If the stock doesn't perform, get out. How do you evaluate your stock's performance? The simplest way is to follow the seven steps in the preceding box, entitled "How to Monitor Your Stock's Performance."

Step 4: Find a Safe Broker

The main message of this book is: Don't use a broker for advice on what to buy or sell, or even when to buy or sell. But a good broker can give you helpful instructions on *how* to buy or sell. In addition, he or she can be a good source of basic information about the market and the investments.

If your priority is trading mutual funds, use the same discount broker that you selected in the previous chapter. Otherwise, follow the steps in Appendix B for selecting a good broker. Favor those who work at one of the brokerage firms with a Weiss Safety Rating of B+ or better. However, other factors (e.g., low commissions and the flexibility of their mutual fund supermarket) may also need to be weighed in your final choice.

In Table 6.1 are lists of the large retail brokerage firms that are the strongest financially. But the lists are not exhaustive. There are

Table 6.1   Strongest Brokerage Firms in America

	State	Weiss Safety Rating
Full-service brokerage firms		
Choice Investments Inc.	Texas	A+
Foresters Equity Services Inc.	California	A+
Vectormex Incorporated	New York	A+
Jefferson Pilot Securities Corp.	New Hampshire	A
Middlegate Securities Ltd.	New York	A
Northern Trust Securities Inc.	Illinois	A
Peoples Securities Inc.	Connecticut	A
A. G. Edwards Inc.	Missouri	A−
Dime Securities Inc.	New York	A−
Vanguard Capital	California	A−
Discount brokerage firms		
Muriel Siebert & Co. Inc.	New York	A+
Downstate Securities Group Inc.	Florida	A
Centura Securities Inc.	North Carolina	A
Scudder Financial Services Inc.	Massachusetts	A

(Continued)

Table 6.1 *(Continued)*

	State	Weiss Safety Rating
Discount brokerage firms (continued)		
Westminster Securities Corporation	New York	A
DJF Discount Brokers Inc.	New York	A
D. L. Baker & Co. Incorporated	Ohio	A–
Summit Financial Services Group LP	Pennsylvania	A–
Suntrust Securities Inc.	Georgia	A–
Fifth Third Securities Inc.	Ohio	A–
On-line brokerage firms		
Investex Securities Group Inc.	New York	A
Onlinetradinginc.Com Corp.	Florida	A
Recom Securities Inc.	Minnesota	A
National Discount Brokers Corp	New Jersey	A–
Interactive Brokers LLC	Connecticut	A–
U.S. Rica Financial Inc.	California	A–
Sunlogic Securities Inc.	California	A–
Wallstreet Electronica Inc.	Florida	A–
Vision Securities Inc.	New York	A–
Wall Street Access	New York	A–

This is a sampling of the highest-rated full-service, discount, and on-line brokerage firms rated by Weiss Ratings, Inc. An A–, A, or A+ rating indicates that the company offers excellent financial security and has the resources necessary to withstand even the most adverse economic and market conditions. But safety can't be your *only* criterion for picking a broker. You should also consider commission rates, available services, and the degree to which the firm can help you meet your long-term planning needs. Since we can't list every safe broker, if yours is *not* on this list, don't assume it's unsafe. For a complete listing, see the Weiss Ratings' *Guide to Stock Brokerage Firms,* available at many public libraries.

Weiss Safety Rating scale: A = excellent; B = good, C = weak; D = weak; E = very weak; +: upper end of grade range; –: lower end of grade range.

Source: Weiss Ratings, Inc., Palm Beach Gardens, FL, based on the latest available data filed with the Securities and Exchange Commission (SEC) as of June 2001.

many other safe firms that, due to space limitations, are not included here. For a complete list, see the Weiss Ratings' *Guide to Brokerage Firms,* available at many public libraries.

A high rating doesn't guarantee honesty. However, well-capitalized firms are less prone to engage in illegal or unethical behaviors and less likely to hire unethical brokers. Moreover, a high rating greatly reduces your risk of getting caught in a failure.

Step 5: Save a Fortune in Commissions

Consider this scenario: You're not a buy-and-hold investor. But you're not an active trader, either. Starting with $100,000 in your brokerage account, you buy about 20 different securities, with an average initial value of $5,000 each. Then, you buy and sell each one only twice a year, with an average profit of 5 percent per trade before commissions. With consistent profits like those, you'll retire rich, right?

Not necessarily, according to our regular surveys of the commissions charged by the 500 brokers we rate.

If you're paying top-dollar commissions (actually charged by 27 percent of the firms rated by Weiss Ratings), your entire $100,000 will be totally *wiped out* by commissions by the end of year nine. Why? Because although your trading is consistently profitable before commissions, *after* commissions you will actually *lose* money every year, until every single last penny in your account is gone—all into your broker's pocket.

You can avoid this disaster simply by using a broker who charges you the *average* commission rate among the brokers surveyed by Weiss Ratings. That's what most investors like you are doing today. But, assuming the exact same scenario with the exact same profits, the results are *still* very disappointing. All you'd make is a meager $21,675 in profits. And that's after 10 long years, with every single trade profitable and with reinvestment of profits at the beginning of every new year.

The *only* way to make good money in the market is to find a safe broker with commissions on the low end of the scale. Instead of just $21,675, you'd walk away with $108,374 in pure profits to you, *after* commissions. In other words, just by switching from average commissions to low commissions, you'd multiply your profits by nearly *five* times.

As you can see, you don't have to be an active trader for this to make a huge difference. And you cannot be content with just "discount commissions." With truly low commissions, your profits compound and multiply quickly. With average commissions or higher, it's like paying a huge tax on every single transaction. You not only pay the commissions . . . you also miss out on all the yield and profits you *could* have been making on the money that was sucked out of your account.

Where can you find the broker with the lowest commissions? Shop around, asking each broker to tell you what he or she would charge you for the following three scenarios:

1. 100 shares at $10 per share

2. 100 shares at $100 per share

3. 1,000 shares at $20 per share

That way, you can compare apples with apples at as many different brokers as you wish. If your broker says "it depends," explain that you need a specific response in order to decide whether to open an account. If he or she still refuses to give you clear information, take your business elsewhere.

If you don't want to do this research on your own, refer to the Weiss Ratings' *Guide to Brokerage Firms,* which uses these same three scenarios to provide an updated review of the commissions quoted by nearly 500 different brokerage firms representing 99 percent of the business.

Already using a dirt-cheap on-line broker? Great! But quite a few of the on-line brokers are new firms with little experience and inadequate capital. See Table 6.2.

If you want to trade on-line, make sure that the firm (1) is financially stable and (2) is also available via phone or in person in case of any problems or questions regarding on-line trading.

Table 6.2 Lowest-Rated Brokerage Firms

Name	Grade
Ascend Financial Services Inc.	C–
Brookehill Equities Inc.	E+
Burke Christensen & Lewis Secs Inc.	C–
Cuttone & Company Inc.	D+
D. E. Frey & Company Inc.	C–
Interfirst Capital Corp.	D+
Landmark Securities Corp.	E
Preferred Capital Markets Inc.	D
Seattle-Northwest Securities Corp.	D+

You should try to avoid brokerage firms that are financially insecure (i.e., those with a Weiss Safety Rating of D+ or lower). A C grade is acceptable, especially if most of your money is invested in mutual funds, but should be monitored periodically. Important: The grades of these and other firms could change. For an updated list of the weakest brokers, visit www.weissratings.com. Weiss Safety Rating scale: A = excellent; B = strong; C = fair; D = weak; E = very weak; +: upper end of grade range; –: bottom end of grade range.

Source: Weiss Ratings, Inc., Palm Beach Gardens, FL, based on the latest-available data filed with the Securities and Exchange Commission (SEC) as of June 2001.

Step 6: Reduce the Risk of Dealing with a Dishonest Broker

See Appendix B for specific instructions on how to reduce your risk of dealing with a dishonest broker.

Step 7: Get a True, Honest-to-Goodness Advisor

There are three alternatives that I recommend, and they're not mutually exclusive.

CERTIFIED PUBLIC ACCOUNTANTS

There are 250,000 certified public accountants (CPAs) in this country who have the potential to be as good—or better—advisors than the so-called financial planners. They don't peddle investments; they don't make commissions on sales. Furthermore, it's impossible to put together a comprehensive financial plan without extensive tax knowledge, which is one of their fortés.

Some CPAs lack experience with financial instruments. But to get around that weakness, you can hire a CPA who has specialized training in financial planning, under the designation *personal financial specialist* (PFS). Don't confuse them with certified financial planners. They're different, and, I think, much better. To find them, follow these four steps:

1. Go to www.cpapfs.org.
2. On the right-hand side, you'll see an icon labeled "Find a PFS Near You."
3. Click on "Continue with CPA/FPS search."
4. You should see a map of the United States. Click on your state, and you'll get a list of all of the PFSs in your area.

Or, if you don't have access to the Internet, an equally good way to go is to call the American Institute of Certified Public Accountants (AICPA) at 888-777-7077 and ask for their Publication No. G00616. (Those are zeros, not the letter O.) They will send you a list of the CPAs in your area who are PFSs.

Don't use CPAs as active money managers to trade the market. Even though they may be certified to perform that function as well, it's not their specialty, and the results could disappoint you.

FEE-ONLY FINANCIAL PLANNERS

These are the only financial services professionals whose name tells you how they charge you. These advisors usually do not work on commission, but rather, they charge either an hourly fee or a fee that is a percentage of your assets (usually around 1 percent).

Use advisors who charge you an hourly fee. They have nothing to gain by giving you any particular advice because they get the fee regardless of what happens in your account. Furthermore, 1 percent of your assets can be a big drain, especially on the portion of your money that is allocated to the safest (but lowest-yielding) investments. And, because you are aware of that, it gives your advisor an incentive to invest a larger portion of your funds more aggressively than may be right for you.

To get a list of the *right kind* of financial planner, call the National Association of Personal Financial Advisors (NAPFA) at 800-366-2732 or go to www.napfa.org. You can get the phone numbers of genuine *fee-only* advisors in your area. These fees may seem like an extra expense, but they will actually save you a lot of money and possibly a lot of trouble. Please bear in mind, however, that not all fee-only planners are purely advisors. Some do sell commission-based products.[1]

INVESTMENT ADVISORS

Just like you'd want to know who's the best doctor for whatever ails you, or who's the best lawyer to represent you, it's equally important to find an advisor who can best help you achieve your financial goals. You don't want to pick up the yellow pages and select one that's local because it's convenient, or even one whom your friend or neighbor recommends to you.

Financial newsletters can be excellent sources of investment advice if you know what you're looking for. But advisory letters usually specialize in various investment markets (e.g., stocks, options, mutual funds, tax advice, and so forth). Rarely will you find a newsletter that can give you great investment advice in all areas, so it's best to find one that specializes in the area in which you're interested and that fits your goals.

Why subscribe to a financial newsletter? You'll receive more objective investment advice than you could possibly be getting from a commission-hungry broker. Or, you may want to supplement the advice that you're getting from other sources. For performance ratings of over 160 financial newsletters and their investment portfolios, refer to the *Hulbert Financial Digest* by calling 888-485-2378 or logging on at www.hulbertdigest.com.

CHAPTER 7

PROTECT YOUR WEALTH!

What are your most important financial decisions after you turn 50? In previous chapters, we've reviewed how to escape the dangers of stocks and invest more safely with greater flexibility. Now, think also about the assets that you have worked so hard to accumulate—stocks that have been in the family for many years, real estate that may make up a big chunk of your net worth, collectibles, and other possessions.

Many people are counting on these kinds of assets to help support them in their older years. These assets have gone up in value for decades, so they blindly assume that they will *continue* to go up in the years to come. That could be a big mistake.

In fact, there is abundant evidence in the world today that many of your assets could suffer from *deflation*—an actual decline in their value. Whether that scenario actually unfolds or not, the danger is now real enough to merit serious consideration, and even some protective action on your part. Let's start with the biggest of them all:

YOUR REAL ESTATE: SHOULD YOU HOLD NO MATTER WHAT? SHOULD YOU SELL? WHEN?

One possible consequence of the great tech boom and bust is an equally great boom and bust in real estate. This is especially true in high-tech regions of the country. Indeed, during the tech boom, rents in many of the hottest markets (e.g., New York, Boston, San Francisco, and so on) doubled and tripled. Office rents in downtown San Jose, California, a high-tech hotbed, zoomed 23 percent in 2000 alone. New tech companies, hot off their initial public offerings (IPOs) and flush with cash, were snapping up commercial real estate and bidding up the prices into the ozone.

Then the music stopped, and the party came to an end. Failed dot-coms shut their doors and pulled out of their leases. The struggling survivors downsized and relocated to smaller digs, and landlords were suddenly faced with a rash of vacancies.

In San Francisco's South of Market district, formerly home to many tech start-ups, available sublease space stood at just 800,000 square feet before the tech bust. A few months later, that number skyrocketed 275 percent to 3 million square feet, as companies closed down and moved out. At the same time, rents in some commercial buildings plunged by 40 percent. One study projected that 80 percent of the remaining dot-com companies in the Bay Area would collapse in the months ahead. If so, another 4 million square feet of office space would become vacant.

In New York, more than 20 percent of the office space that was leased by dot-coms was returned to the market soon after the tech stocks collapsed. In Seattle, the vacancy rate more than doubled. And in parts of Silicon Valley, commercial vacancies reached a whopping 12 percent.

But the impact was not limited to offices. High-end home prices in high-tech regions plunged rapidly from their peaks, especially in the San Francisco Bay Area. Middle-end home values also fell, although not as sharply.

For you, the key questions are: Will this new trend be limited to homes in high-tech areas? Or will it spread to the rest of the country? If so, what should you do?

Unfortunately, your real estate broker is *not* the place to get answers. When was the last time you walked into a real estate office, showed an interest in some homes, and heard the agents tell you, "These properties will probably be going down in value"?

If they are going to express that view, they might as well say, instead: "Please don't buy my properties. Go home and come back another day." Like a stockbroker, there is a conflict of interest. The agents' agenda is to sell. They know that declining real estate is a deal killer. They might tell you they're cheap. But they have to be masochists to tell you that they're going to get even cheaper. Quite to the contrary, real estate brokers around the country have been telling you that rising home values are as sure as the sunrise—that buying a home is always a great investment.

They fail to mention that home prices can fall—sometimes dramatically. They tell you little about the terrible real estate recessions of 1974 and 1975, and 1989 through 1991, when home prices fell by between 20 and 25 percent in some areas. They never mention that all it may take is an average real estate decline to wipe out 100 percent of your home equity.

In every bubble in history, from the Tulip Mania in the 1600s to Wall Street in the Roaring 1920s, real estate prices ran up enormously just before they fell. And indeed, in the last five years of the last century, along with the rise in stock prices, housing prices went ballistic in several regions: In just the last year of the tech boom, residential real estate climbed 19 percent in San Diego, 25.5 percent in San Jose, and 33 percent in Boston. And throughout the United States, the number of homes that sold for $1 million or more shot up 51 percent.

The big danger stems from the fact that homeowners have been borrowing against their properties, using the proceeds to load up on more stocks, or to pour more money back into large purchases. Too many families have mortgaged themselves to the hilt. As a result, the home equity of most Americans has gone down, down, down.

The Federal Reserve reports that, in 1982, homeowners had an equity that averaged 70 percent of the home's market value. By 2001, with home prices much higher, you'd think they'd still have at least that much—maybe even more. Not so. The average equity in a home had plunged to 55 percent. And for many Americans, it was much less—30, 20, 10 percent—even zero percent.[1] (See Figure 7.1.)

The same kind of boom and bust you saw in the Great Stock

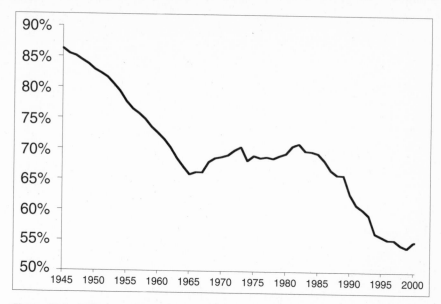

Figure 7.1 Watch out: The equity on America's homes has plunged! If you consider your home to be primarily an investment, or you own other investment real estate, you should consider selling as a real option. One reason is that Americans now have more debt and less equity on their homes than ever before. If they lose their jobs, they could come under intense pressure to sell, forcing prices down. Just 20 years ago, the average American family had 70 percent equity in their home. But by 2001, the average equity had dropped to 55 percent. And that was just the average. Millions of Americans had nearly zero equity.

(*Source: "Flow of Funds for the U.S." Table B.100: "Balance Sheet of Households and Nonprofit Organizations", Section 102,* Federal Reserve Statistical Release, Z.1.)

Market Scam could be replicated in your home. To keep your assets safe and avoid getting hurt by any real estate disaster, follow these four steps.

Step 1: Steer clear of debt. When interest rates are lower, mortgage companies will probably try to lure you into refinancing your home and taking out bigger loans. While this strategy may seem an easy way to get some spending money, especially if your home's value has appreciated, don't fall for their sales pitch. It makes sense to refinance to lower your monthly payments or pay off burdensome credit card balances. But you should not acquire further debt simply to get more spending money.

Step 2: Unload commercial real estate. If prices go down—even just a bit—many brokers will insist "this is the worst time to sell." Or they may even try to persuade you to buy more. Don't believe them. It's no different than Wall Street's stock ratings—they almost always give you buy or hold signals—never sell signals.

If you can get a good price and you're not in love with your holdings, now is the time to sell, especially if you're in debt and could not service your debt if your tenants leave. Remember, too, you may get an opportunity to buy great properties for much less in a few years.

Step 3: Sell second or vacation homes. These are also vulnerable. You'd be much better off taking your cash out and stashing it away in a safe place, even if the interest isn't that great.

Step 4: Consider your home. A home is not just an investment. It's where you live, where you have your memories, where your children stay or visit. Don't sell your home if you don't want to move and are comfortable with the payments. However, if you were thinking about selling anyway, or if you consider your home to be primarily an investment, then you may not want to wait. Sell now and rent for a few years. Then, if you wish, you can always buy back once prices have dropped or once the danger of a decline has blown over.

CRASH PROTECTION FOR YOUR STOCKS

Suppose you are neither willing nor able to sell, no matter what. You have to keep your real estate. You have to hold your stocks. Nevertheless, you want to protect yourself against a decline in values. What do you do?

For real estate, there's no good answer—just be sure to build a good cash nest egg and reduce your debt. For stocks, there is no perfect solution to this dilemma, either—you're never going to be able to continue owning these assets and still be fully protected against a decline. That's why, if you are adverse to risk, my first recommendation is to liquidate your excess stocks now before they decline further.

But if you insist on holding your shares, there *are* specialized investments you can buy today that will act as an indirect hedge. These are investments that are designed to actually go *up* in value while the markets are going down. I recommend that you consider reverse-index funds, such as the following:

- *Rydex Ursa Fund (RYURX).* Designed to go up 10 percent in value for every 10 percent decline in the S&P 500 Index
- *Rydex Tempest (RY/TPX).* Designed to go up 20 percent for every 10 percent decline in the S&P
- *Rydex Arktos Fund (RYAIX).* Designed to go up 10 percent with every 10 percent decline in the Nasdaq 100 Index
- *Profunds.* Similar funds that do essentially the same thing

Consider these investments for your crash protection program. If the stock market goes up, they will produce a loss, but your gains in your stock portfolio should easily cover it. If the stock market goes down, you will at least have one investment working in your favor. The four steps I recommend are the following:

Step 1: Evaluate your stock portfolio. Is it almost entirely tech stocks? Or is it mostly blue-chip and other stocks, with just a sprinkling of techs?

If you have an excessive amount invested in blue-chip and other stocks that you can't sell, I think you should put a modest portion of your money into shares of the Rydex Ursa Fund, or equivalent. That way, if your stock portfolio is falling, your Ursa shares will be rising, helping to offset the loss.

If you have a large portfolio of tech stocks that you can't sell, you should buy shares in the Rydex Arktos Fund. That way, even if your tech stocks fall still further, at least your Arktos shares will be rising, helping to offset the loss.

Step 2: Estimate your risk of loss. No one knows for sure whether the stock market is going up or down–let alone how much or how quickly. But based on past history, you can put together a couple of scenarios to evaluate your current exposure to risk. Consider these historical examples:

- The average Nasdaq stock fell by over 60 percent in the 13 months from March 2000 to April 2001.
- In Japan, the Nikkei Stock Index, which represents both blue-chip and technology companies, fell by 71 percent from 1990 to 2001.
- In the early 1970s, the Dow Jones Industrial Average fell 43 percent from peak to trough.

These are all very severe declines that hopefully will not be duplicated in your stocks. But they do give you some parameters. Without going over the deep end or conjuring up far-out doomsday situations, *it is not unreasonable to assume a 30 to 70 percent decline in your stock portfolio.*

To make it simple, take the current value of your portfolio and cut it in half. If your portfolio is worth about $100,000 at one time, your loss risk, in this scenario, is $50,000. If you have $50,000, your risk is $25,000, and so on.

Step 3: Decide how much of that risk you want to protect yourself against. If you wanted to protect yourself against the *entire* amount, you'd have to invest about dollar for dollar in one of the reverse-index funds.

There's nothing wrong with that. But most people prefer to buy only *partial* protection to cover, for instance, about half or even one-third of their portfolio. If your intent is to cover half, then for every $1 of current value in your stock portfolio, you simply put 50 cents of your money into Rydex Ursa or an equivalent fund. Assuming that your stock portfolio is worth $100,000, you'd be investing about $50,000 in Ursa.

Step 4: Raise the funds for your crash protection program. Where do you get that extra $50,000? You could take it from your cash assets. But if you did, you'd in effect be moving money from a safe investment (such as one of the Treasury-only funds I recommended in Chapter 4) to a much more aggressive investment. That's not very prudent.

My recommendation is to liquidate at least enough from your stock portfolio to finance this program. You don't have to liquidate the full $50,000 worth of shares to raise the money. You'd only have to liquidate $33,333. The reason is that after you liquidate the shares, you will only need to protect the remaining $66,667 in your stock portfolio. The $33,333 is the exact amount you need to cover half of your portfolio risk.

The formula is simple: If you want a program that will protect you against half your risk, and you don't want to take money from another source, you should liquidate one-third of your shares to generate the money. I think it's cheap protection.

"CRASH INSURANCE"

If you feel that you cannot afford to reallocate assets to a reverse-index fund, an even cheaper way to protect yourself from a market decline is to take out some "crash insurance."

I'm not talking about a policy you buy from an insurance company. But the principle is very similar: You pay a "premium" that covers a specific period of time, anywhere from just a couple of months to as much as a few years. If the crash happens during that period, you can get a pay-off that may be double, triple, possibly even up to 5 or 10 times the premium you paid, depending on the timing, speed, and depth of the decline.

If the crash does not happen, you lose the entire premium you paid—no refunds. But you can never lose a dime more. Because the entire premium *can* be lost, this is obviously not a program for all of your money—not even half or a quarter of your money. But it is something to consider for a small portion of your money as a hedge against a potentially vulnerable stock portfolio.

Step 1: Learn about LEAPS put options. LEAPS stands for *long-term equity anticipation securities,* the key word being *long-term. Put options* are options that give you the opportunity, but not the obligation, to sell a security to profit from its decline.

Putting the two concepts together, a LEAPS put option gives you a relatively long period of time (up to a few years) to profit from a market decline. There are no guarantees either way, but if the decline takes place in that time frame, you can cash the LEAPS in for a very substantial profit. If the decline does not take place, you write them off, just like you would with premiums you pay in an insurance policy.

Step 2: Understand the advantages and disadvantages of LEAPS.

- *Advantage 1.* When you *buy* LEAPS or any other options, you can never lose more than you invest. You could lose everything you put into them, but never a penny more. Unlike futures or other speculative investments, no matter what happens, you are 100 percent protected from losses that exceed your initial investment. You can never get a margin call.
- *Advantage 2.* On average, you can get more leverage from LEAPS than you can with the mutual funds mentioned earlier. Even the most aggressive mutual fund is designed to give you a 20 percent return for every 10 percent decline in the market. With LEAPS, you could make 50 percent or even 100 percent from a 10 percent market decline, depending on the market conditions.
- *Advantage 3.* You can invest in options with a lot less money. The mutual funds I told you about typically have minimums of $25,000. Even if you buy through a broker in lesser amounts, you should have at least a few thousand to invest in the reverse-index mutual funds. However, you can find LEAPS options that cost as little as $200.

Be warned. If you are investing a substantial portion of your savings in options, you are probably taking excessive risk. The main rule of all options investing is: *Never invest more than you can afford to lose.*

Now let's look at the disadvantages.

- *Disadvantage 1.* More leverage is a double-edged sword. If your LEAPS put option can make you a 100 percent profit on a 10 percent decline, it means you could also lose 100 percent if the market rises 10 percent.

- *Disadvantage 2.* Unlike mutual fund shares, all options have an *expiration date.* This means the market decline needs to take place *before* they expire.

- *Disadvantage 3.* Just as an insurance policy has a *deductible,* all options have a strike price (i.e., the price level at which the option really begins to work for you). You could buy a LEAPS with a strike price that is right at today's market—like a no-deductible policy—but it would probably be prohibitively expensive.

- *Disadvantage 4.* If they're short term, put options can be very volatile and should be watched daily, even hourly. But long-term options are much more manageable. That's why I recommend that you stick primarily with LEAPS, which are the long-term variety of put options. (This assumes that you are doing this on your own and don't want to worry about tracking them so closely.)

Step 3: Evaluate your stock portfolio. Ask yourself: Does my stock portfolio contain almost entirely tech stocks? Or does it have mostly blue-chip and other stocks, with just a sprinkling of tech stocks?

- If it's mostly tech stocks, the investment you will buy is LEAPS put options on the Nasdaq 100 Shares (symbol: QQQ).

- If it's mostly nontech stocks, the investment you will buy is a LEAPS put option on the S&P 500 LEAPS Index (symbol: SPXL).

- If your portfolio is concentrated in a particular sector, you may be able to find a suitable LEAPS put option that is specialized in that sector as well. A complete list is available from the Chicago Board Options Exchange by calling 888-OPTIONS or logging on at www.cboe.com. At their Web site, click on "Options Products," then "Product Specifications." It will bring you right to the list of LEAPS.

Step 4: Decide how much in portfolio value you want to cover. Allocate a maximum of $500 to LEAPS put options for every $10,000 in portfolio value you would like to cover. Therefore, if you want to cover $20,000, your maximum budget for this crash insurance program would be $1,000; if you want to cover $40,000, the maximum amount would be $2,000; and so on.

Step 5: Select the specific LEAPS put options you will be buying. Unfortunately, it is not possible to give you a specific security recommendation in this book, because the appropriate selection will vary depending on a variety of factors: how much time has already transpired, where the stock market is, how much further it is expected to decline, and so forth. But as a rule, I recommend you buy the following:

■ LEAPS put options that have at least one year remaining before they expire.

■ LEAPS put options that have a strike price that is at least 10 percent below the current market level.

Step 6: Learn more about options—and the full range of possible outcomes when you buy them. This is the subject of the next section of this chapter.

OPTIONS: A GUIDED TOUR

Options are usually used for speculation. They give you the opportunity to make runaway profits, with a risk that's strictly limited to the amount you pay for them.

However, it's not unusual to lose the full amount invested. Therefore, right now, my goal is to introduce options to you strictly as a vehicle to help you *protect* your wealth. Before I tell you more about how they work, I want to stress that unless you are a speculator:

■ Your first goal should be to liquidate any shares you own that are in excess of your current risk limits.

- You should buy options only if you cannot unload those shares and feel you need some protection against any further losses.

- When you buy options, you should focus strictly on *put* options—those that are designed to go up in value when your stocks go down.

- You should invest only in modest amounts, using funds you can afford to lose.

- If you want to go beyond protection and use options for pure speculative opportunities, the brief introduction I give you here will not suffice. You will need to learn more and probably will need more timely trading advice than is possible in a book or even most newsletters.

Since you may be unfamiliar with options, I will walk you through each step slowly, and take you through as many possibilities as I can.

To begin with, forget about learning a whole bunch of complex options strategies. Instead, start with the kind of options you are probably most familiar with.

Example 1

The time is a few years ago. You walk into the office of your local real estate broker. She takes you out to see a beautiful house in a great neighborhood. The price is good, too. But you're not quite ready to buy. You consider renting—just to try it out.

You meet the seller and he says: "OK. I'll rent you my house with an option to buy." You like that and you hash out the terms. The going price for similar homes is roughly $150,000. But everyone thinks that prices in the area are going up. So the seller says he'll give you an option to buy the house at $155,000.

The term is 12 months. If you don't exercise the option within that time frame, that's it. You've lost your chance. You figure: You need a place to live anyhow. The option is the icing on the cake. If you don't use it, you've lost nothing. If you need it, you've got it. So you accept the deal.

Example 2

A few months later, you get a call from a headhunter, offering you a new job to join a competitor. You're flattered, but you have no intentions of leaving your company.

He offers you better pay. Your response is, "No." He offers you all kinds of great benefits. "Still not interested." But then he starts telling you about stock options, and you suddenly find yourself paying closer attention.

"Here's the deal," he says with genuine excitement. "This is one of those up-and-coming, high-tech companies with incredible growth potential. Similar companies with lesser products have recently gone absolutely, totally berserk in the stock market.

"One such company first offered its shares for $2 and zoomed to $98 per share. Another was worth just $10,000 not too long ago and is now worth more than Boeing Aircraft. As a welcome-aboard bonus, this company will *give* you an option to buy 10,000 of its shares at $5 anytime within the next five years. That's a pretty good strike price, $5.

"The stock is selling for $2.75 right now. So you can't do anything with the options at this particular moment. But you just wait. This stock is headed for $10, $20, maybe even $50, just like those other high-tech stocks. When that happens, you can cash in—big time! No matter what the shares are selling at, you still get to buy at $5.

"Let's be conservative," he continues. "Let's say the stock only reaches $10. In effect, you go in there and you buy the 10,000 shares for 5 bucks a pop. That's $50,000. Then, you turn right around and sell them for $100,000. Bingo! You've bagged a hefty $50,000 profit."

The headhunter pauses and then says: "This is how CEOs have become multimillionaires in recent years. This is how thousands of people have transformed themselves from hired hands into owners of some of the nation's richest companies. Now, I'm giving you the opportunity to do the same."

You call your broker for some advice. Provided you want to switch jobs, he thinks it's a good deal for several reasons. First, even if all their promises fall by the wayside, you've lost nothing by accepting the option. When you hold an option, it means *you* decide whether to buy. If it turns out that the company is a total flop, you throw it in the trashcan. You don't lose a penny.

Second, unlike options that you buy from your broker, this option doesn't cost you diddly-squat. The company is offering to *give* it to you—free. If you wanted to buy similar options in the stock market, you'd have to pay for the privilege, especially with any option that gives you so much time. Some options are extremely cheap. But no one in the market ever gives them away.

Still, you want to negotiate a better deal. You call back and say: "I want more time—ten years instead of five. Plus, I want a lower strike price—three dollars instead of five dollars."

The headhunter's answer is immediate: "No way! An option to buy at $3, like you're asking for, would be too valuable to give away. If the stock goes up just 25 cents, to $3, you'd already be *at* the money. If the stock goes up just 50 cents, to $3.25, you'd already be 25 cents *in* the money. Plus, you'd have a full 10 years for this to happen.

"Heck, in 10 years, this stock could be worth 100 bucks! Then you'd buy it for $3, sell it for $100, and take out a $97 profit on each share. Multiply that by 10,000 shares, and you've got close to a million. There's no way this company is going to give away that much."

You hang up and forget about the whole thing. But it wasn't a waste of time because without realizing it, you've learned most of what you will need to know about options: You've learned what the *strike price* is—the price where you can exercise the option and buy the stock. You've learned what the *expiration* is—when the option expires, of course. You've learned concepts like *at the money* (when the market is at the same level as the strike price) and *in the money* (when the market has surpassed the strike price).

More important, you've learned some basic rules:

Rule 1. The closer the current share price is to the option's strike price, the better the chance of reaching the strike price in the allotted time—and the more valuable the option is.

Rule 2. The more time you get, the more an option is worth.

Rule 3. The payoff can be large, but the risk is limited. When you purchase an option, you *can* lose every penny you invest, but never a penny more.

These same principles apply to put options. The main difference is that put options are designed to profit when prices go *down*–ideal for protection in a market decline.

The same principles also apply to LEAPS put options. The main difference is that most put options are for just a few months. LEAPS put options are issued for much longer terms, up to a few years.

And just as call options made people a lot of money when the market was booming, put options can make a lot of money if the market busts.

It's very simple: Instead of giving you the right to *buy* at a predetermined price, the put options give you the right to *sell* the stock at that price.

For example, let's imagine that you expect the shares in ABC Company to drop from $100 to $50. You can buy a put option (i.e., the right to sell the stock) at $90. If the share price drops to $50, you can buy it for $50, and your option lets you sell it for $90– giving you a profit of $40.

As you may have noticed, you don't have to exercise the option to get your money out of it. You can sell it on the open market anytime before expiration. In fact, you should not exercise options at all because your goal is to make a profit by buying and selling the options, not by owning or selling the stocks.

This makes life a lot simpler. All you want to do is buy the LEAPS put options low and sell them high, just like a stock or any other security in which you regularly invest.

For a better idea of how put options work, let's give it a whirl with some play money. Consider this put option contract:

Number of shares:	100
Underlying stock:	ABC Co.
Expiration:	1 year from now
Strike price:	$90

Then consider these four questions:

1. How much would you pay for this particular option?
2. How much could you sell it for?
3. How much could you lose?
4. How much profit could you make?

First, how much do you have to pay for it? That's easy. You can just ask your broker, check the newspaper, or the Internet. Let's say the ABC put option is going for $5 per share. Because all options are for 100 shares, that means it costs 100×5, or $500, per contract.

How much could you sell it for? Let's consider several scenarios:

The "Oops!" Scenario

You just happen to buy at exactly the wrong time. Instead of falling as you expected, ABC shares start going up immediately to $130. Now, the $90 strike price, which seemed to be within easy reach when you bought it, is further away. Meanwhile, the time just keeps ticking by.

A few months later, you ask: How much is the option worth now? With much less time remaining before it expires, and with the strike price now at least 40 full points away, your put option is worth practically zero. In fact, the amount you'd pay for commissions is probably more than the money you can get out of it.

But look at the positive side. If you had put $10,000 into one of the reverse-index funds, and the market went up, you'd have $5,000 in losses. Worse, the more the market goes up, the more you'd lose.

Not so with LEAPS put options! Even in this worst-case scenario, all you've lost is the $500 you invested, plus a small commission. No matter how far ABC rises, that's the *most* you could ever lose.

The "Nowhere" Scenario

ABC goes down a small fraction one day, up a bit the next day. But despite some excitement here and there, it always seems to wind up pretty much in the same spot. With every day that passes, your option goes down in value. It reminds you of an hourglass dropping grains of sand with each passing moment.

Suddenly, in the last few days before your option expires, ABC finally falls a few points. But it's too late. The stock doesn't fall below $90 until three weeks after your put option expires.

The irony is that you were right about ABC: It did go *down,* just like you thought it would. But that's not good enough. You also had to be right about the timing. You bought the put option too soon. By the time the shares really started to fall, your time ran out. The end result is that the option expires worthless (same as the "Oops!" scenario).

The "Break-Even" Scenario

ABC falls apart right out of the starting gate. Your timing is perfect. And it continues to tumble nearly every day. The stock falls below $90, you're *in the money,* and you're delighted.

But *in the money* does not necessarily mean *in the profits.* Remember, you paid $5 per share, or $500, for the contract. So by expiration time, for you to break even, ABC not only has to fall below the strike price of $90, it has to fall beyond it by $5—to $85.

And that's exactly what happens. If you exercised the option at that point, you'd sell 100 shares of ABC for $90 per share. And you'd be able to buy them for $85 per share, netting you $5 per share.

For 100 shares, that's $500—exactly what you invested in this deal in the first place. You make nothing and lose nothing, except some commissions, of course. But look at the positive side: You bought protection from the possibility of a more serious decline. And you still recouped the cost of your premium.

The "Double-Your-Money" Scenario

As in the previous scenario, ABC falls sharply right out of the box. Within a few weeks, it reaches the strike price of $90. Within a few months, it falls through the $85 level, which would be the break-even point at expiration. But we're still months away from expiration, and ABC continues to fall.

At expiration, ABC is trading at $80. If you exercised your option, you'd be able to buy the 100 shares of ABC at $80 and sell them for $90. That's a nice $10 difference, or $1,000. But you don't exercise the option. Instead, you just sell it to someone else for the $1,000. You never have to exercise, you can always sell your option to close your position.

Not bad. You go in with $500 and walk away with $1,000—double your money, or a 100 percent profit. For investors used to stocks and bonds, this may sound like a fantastic result. But, with the purchase of options, a small move in the stock can often double your money.

The "Home Run" Scenario

ABC just keeps plunging, practically nonstop. It falls below the $90 level in the first week. So almost immediately, your option is in the money. This is a very good sign. Then in the second week, ABC falls below $85—your break-even point. And it just keeps crashing. Now, it's selling at $65, and there is still a lot of time remaining. You have two choices:

1. You can wait until the very last month or week, in the expectation that ABC will go still lower and you'll make even more.

2. You can sell your put option now, take your profits, and run. In your head, you calculate how much you think it's worth: $90 minus $65. That's $25 in the money. So you figure it should be worth $25 times 100 shares. That's a nice round $2,500.

You figure if you sell it now, you can walk away with five times your original $500 investment. Not bad at all! You call your broker and ask his or her advice. To your pleasant surprise, you discover that the put option is actually worth about $1,000 more than you estimated, close to $3,500. Why? Because the $2,500 you figured is strictly the put option's *intrinsic* value (i.e., the amount that someone would profit from the sale of the stock if they exercised the option today).

Now, in addition to the intrinsic value, this option still has *time value*. There is quite a bit of time left before it expires, and that time is worth something. In fact, investors feel the time remaining is actually worth a lot: an additional $1,000 on top of the $2,500 intrinsic value.

Why is that time worth so much? Because ABC is moving down sharply and steadily every day. Like you, other investors are also assuming this trend will continue, and they're willing to pay the $1,000 for the chance of making those extra bucks.

"That's fine," you say. "Let them have that chance!" You cash out and walk away with $3,500 minus commissions. Subtract the $500 you originally invested, and you have a profit of $3,000–a gain of 6 to 1.

The "Grand-Slam Home Run" Scenario

When you first buy the ABC put option, the stock is pretty quiet. In fact, the market is so quiet, you can practically hear a pin drop at the specialist's desk on the trading floor. With that lack of movement, few people are interested in buying options, and the few who do aren't willing to pay the usual price for them.

Their logic is simple: "Even if ABC is trading at $100, and the strike price is only 10 points away (at $90), what good is it? At this rate, it will take a month of Sundays for ABC to fall to $90. In this dead market, you'd be lucky if ABC reaches $95 in a year," they reason.

People already holding the ABC put options get discouraged. They try to find someone to take these options off their hands, but there are no takers–except you and a few others. Instead of paying

$500 for the option, you pick it up for a song—at only $2 per share, or just $200 for the 100-share contract.

Suddenly, ABC announces that it missed Wall Street's earnings expectations by a mile. At the same time, the entire sector gets clobbered and comes alive with activity. Instead of moving by just a meager 10 cents or less every day, the stock plunges (and surges) in leaps and bounds, with huge gyrations of as much as $5 or even $10 per day.

Within days, ABC is selling for $65. You hurriedly call your broker to find out how much the option is worth. You can hardly believe your ears: It has surged from the $200 you originally paid for it to $4,000.

Why is it worth so much? There are three reasons:

1. *Intrinsic value.* You know how to figure that: It's the $90 − $65 = $25, or $2,500 for the contract of 100 shares.

2. *Time value.* With many months remaining, that's worth a good deal.

3. *Volatility.* Just as the options lost value when the market went dead, they have now *gained* tremendous value as the market has had a sudden burst of activity. ABC stock is not just falling in larger increments. It's also gyrating wildly all over the lot: down 10 points in just a few hours of trading, rising 5 points in minutes, then down again soon thereafter.

These gyrations, even if they're sometimes in the wrong direction, make the options far more valuable, and this increased value accrues to your benefit.

Adding together (1) the intrinsic value, (2) the time value, and (3) the volatility factor, your ABC put is now worth $4,000, or a remarkable 20 times more than you paid for it—an explosive investment return.

Is this possible in the real world? Yes. It actually happens, provided you can be in the right place at the right time.

This gives you the full range of possibilities. Now let's sum up some of the basics:

- Options give you the right, but not the obligation, to buy or sell a specific investment at a specific price, within a certain period of time.

- If there is no profit, you can just let them expire worthless. The profit is potentially very large. But the potential loss is always limited to the amount you invest and never a penny more.

- You have access to two kinds of options: not just options to buy (*call* options), but also options to sell (*put* options) to protect you from a declining market.

- LEAPS put options are a special variety, which are ideal for "crash insurance" because they give you much more time and don't have to be tracked as closely.

- LEAPS put options are available not only on individual stocks, but also on stock indexes, including the Dow Jones Industrial Average, the S&P 500, and the Nasdaq 100. This gives you the opportunity to, in effect, protect most of your portfolio without buying a large number of individual options.

(Please note that LEAPS are typically sold on a special version of these indexes representing one one-hundredth of the full value. On the Dow Jones, for example, instead of a strike price of 8,000, the strike price would be 80.)

Here are the basic terms you should know:

premium.   This is the price you pay for the option. An expensive option has a high premium; a cheap one has a low premium.

strike price.   This is the price at which the option lets you buy or sell the underlying stock or stock index. For example, a call option on ABC stock with a strike price of 90 gives you the right to buy 100 shares of ABC at $90. A call option with a strike of 110 gives you the right to buy the 100 shares at $110, and so on. Similarly, a put option on ABC stock with a strike price of 90 gives you the right to sell 100 shares at $90.

expiration. Remember, the option only gives you the right to buy or sell within a specific period of time. Once that time period is over, the option expires. If the market has not moved enough, or if it has gone in the opposite direction from what you expected, the option could expire worthless. This information is built into the brief description of the option. As an illustration:

- A Microsoft January 120 call is an option to buy 100 shares of Microsoft stock at the price of $120, with this option expiring in January.
- June 800 S&P 500 Cash Index put is an option to sell one contract of the S&P 500 Cash Index at 800, with this option expiring in June.

There are two cautions that you should always remember, however:

1. Options can also be like lottery tickets. You can't lose more than you spend on each ticket. But if you buy tickets every day, month after month, your cost can add up to an unlimited amount over time. That's why your investment in options should be small.

2. Second, whenever you invest in options, you should always bear in mind the primary disadvantage about which I told you: Options are wasting assets. When you buy an option, you are essentially buying time. So if the market remains unchanged, the value of the option will naturally decline as time goes by. And to profit from options, the expected move has to happen–or, at least, get underway–before the option expires.

With these cautions in mind, use them wisely to take out "crash insurance" and help protect your wealth.

Next, consider ways to protect yourself from the other risks that you are bound to encounter in the years ahead, the subject of the following chapters.

CHAPTER 8

THE GREAT
INSURANCE
COVER-UP

The Great Stock Market Scam should have come as no big surprise to anyone who got caught in the Great Insurance Cover-Up a decade earlier—an event that was particularly damaging to folks over 50. The pattern was the same: giant, big-name companies, hyped-up promotions, distorted ratings, unabashed conflicts of interest, plus mass sales forces driven by big commissions and frequent disdain for the customer. The victims were the same: investors like you who longed for a larger nest egg and a comfortable retirement. And the end of the story was also similar: huge losses and shattered hopes for millions of Americans.

Only the actors and scripts were different: life insurers instead of brokerage firms, insurance commissioners instead of securities regulators, high-yielding annuities and life insurance instead of high-flying stocks.

Before you spend one dollar on insurance, follow along while I take you on a virtual tour of the Great Insurance Cover-Up. Some people in the industry will tell you it's history, and it is. But it's also directly relevant to the decisions you will be making in the months and years ahead.

You ask: How was it possible for big, conservative, long-established, insurance companies to get swept up into fly-by-night-type schemes? For an answer, we start in the 1970s, when the whole scheme was incubated.

Back in those days, insurance companies sold you mostly insurance. You paid them a premium. They paid you on your claims. It was simple but some people in the industry began thinking that just selling insurance wasn't enough. Mutual funds were growing like gangbusters. Savings and loans were hot on the tail of American savers. Even conservative banks were spreading their wings. Insurance executives figured they wanted a piece of the action, too.

"Instead of just selling insurance policies, we can sell investment programs with a veneer of insurance," they reasoned. "Instead of just watching money come in one door (as premiums) and go out the other door (as claims payments), we can actually *hold* onto people's money—like a bank or mutual fund," they figured.

They wanted to expand beyond the dull and boring business of selling insurance to the jazzy and exciting business of selling investments. They wanted to be in the *money* business. Trouble is, they had little or no experience. And from day one, they screwed up royally.

Their first big blunder was that they violated a cardinal rule of the investment industry: *Never guarantee results.* Anyone who's ever been in the investment industry for any length of time knows that guaranteeing results on an investment is a no-no. On a bank's certificate of deposits (CDs), maybe. But an investment program, never! Only novices without training or scruples would make such a dumb mistake. Yet, that's what hundreds of America's largest life insurance companies did from their first day in the investment business.

As we'll see in just a moment, it got them—and their customers—into *big* trouble in the early 1990s. And unless the insurers change their ways, it will continue to get them into trouble in the years to come.

You see, investment companies, like today's mutual funds, had learned from previous failures in the past. They'd been through hard times before: the stock market panics of the early twentieth century, the Crash of 1929, and the Great Depression. They learned the hard way that you cannot predict the future. And since you cannot predict the future, you cannot guarantee your customers investment results. When you do, it invariably leads to more blunders, even lying and cheating.

That's why, after the Depression and World War II, the Securities and Exchange Commission (SEC) established some strict rules and guidelines about this. They said, in effect: "If you run an investment company, you cannot—must not—promise your customers a high return on their investments. In your advertising materials, or in your sales pitches, you can't say that a particular result is 'certain,' or 'guaranteed.'" Today, even if you put your clients' money strictly in U.S. government-guaranteed securities, you can't use those terms.[1]

That's why you'll never see a mutual fund with a name like "First Guaranteed Mutual Fund," or even "Safe Mutual Fund." (One guy got away with the word "Strong" for his mutual fund, but that's only because his last name happened to be Strong.)

Most life insurance executives seemed to know very little about these rules, and if they did, they didn't seem to care. Right from the starting gate, they began to offer investment products—like deferred annuities—with *guaranteed high rates of return*. And they had no qualms about hyping the guarantees in their advertising and sales campaigns.

Then, as if that wasn't enough, the insurance companies created *guaranteed investment contracts,* or *guaranteed insurance contracts,* called GICs, and hawked those to large institutional investors.

Not coincidentally, right around that time, interest rates in the United States were unusually high. Even U.S. Treasury bond yields were close to double digits. So the insurance companies figured it would be a piece of cake to deliver on their promises to investors. All they had to do was take the money from investors, put the money into bonds with high fixed rates of return, take out a share for themselves, and then pass the rest on back to investors.

But they forgot about one detail: What to do if interest rates and bond yields went down, which is exactly what happened. Interest rates and bond yields went down.

This presented a serious dilemma. The insurance companies had guaranteed to pay a high yield, for instance, 10 percent, but the best they could earn on safe bonds was maybe 9 percent or 8 percent. They obviously had to do something to fix that problem—and quickly. How do you deliver high guaranteed yields when interest rates are going down? There's only one way: You have to buy the bonds of smaller, or financially weaker, companies.

Consider, for a moment, what bonds are and you'll immediately understand the situation they were in. When you buy a bond, all you're doing, in essence, is making a loan. If you make the loan to a strong, secure borrower, like the U.S. government or a major blue-chip corporation, you're not going to be able to collect a very high rate of interest.

If you want a truly high interest rate, you're going to have to take the risk of lending your money to a smaller, less secure borrower—maybe a start-up company, or maybe a company that's had some ups and downs in recent years. And you can get *great* interest rates from companies that have been having "a bit of trouble" paying their bills lately. (Whether you'll actually be able to collect that interest is another matter entirely.)

What's secure and what's risky? In the corporate bond area, everyone—in or out of Wall Street—long ago agreed to use the standard rating scales established by the two leading bond rating agencies: Moody's and Standard & Poor's. The two agencies use slightly different letters, but their scale is identical: triple-A, double-A, single-A, triple-B, double-B, single-B, and so on.

If a bond is triple-B or better, it's "investment grade." That's considered relatively secure. But if the bond is double-B or lower, it's "speculative grade," or simply "junk." It's not garbage you'd necessarily throw into the trashcan, but in the parlance of Wall Street, it *is* officially known as *junk*.

The point is that there is a clear, specific, universally accepted definition of what is a junk bond and what isn't. A junk bond is any bond with a rating of double-B or lower. Period. And that's what insurance companies started to buy—junk. They bought double-B bonds. They bought single-B bonds. They even bought a lot of bonds that had no rating at all, but which, if rated by Moody's or S&P, would almost certainly be classified as junk.

Promising guaranteed high yields was the first big blunder, which then led to the second big blunder: junk bonds. Like a modern-day Pinocchio, these junk bonds then led to the lies and cheating you'll see in just a moment.

Unbelievably, many insurance companies *still* didn't get it. Despite the obvious risks, they wanted to *continue* growing this very lucrative new business line. They wanted to offer high guaranteed yields to even *more* investors. "This is a fantastic business," they said. "Look at how many customers we're bringing in! Why should we stop now?"

Even more unbelievably, a few insurance companies, such as Executive Life of California, Executive Life of New York, Fidelity Bankers Life, and First Capital Life—took the concept one giant step further. These companies weren't just reluctantly forced to buy junk bonds to fulfill old promises. Their entire business plan was *deliberately based on* junk bonds practically from day one.

They contracted with large Wall Street brokerage firms to sell their plans to investors through their extensive branch networks. They attracted investors by the droves with their promise of high, guaranteed yields. They became giant *junk bond* insurance companies.

Imagine that! Insurance companies, supposedly created to be your fail-safe protectors, speculating heavily in one of the riskiest investments on Wall Street! Naturally, the key to their success was to keep the junk bond aspect hush-hush, while playing on the faith people still had in the inherent safety of insurance. But to make the whole scheme work, they needed two more elements: the blessing of the established ratings agencies and the cooperation of the insurance commissioners.

The blessing of the rating agencies was relatively easy. Indeed, for years, the standard operating procedure of the leading insurance company rating agency, A. M. Best & Co., was to "work closely" with the insurers. If you ran an insurance company and wanted a rating, the deal that Best offered you was very favorable indeed. Best said, in effect: "We give you a rating. If you don't like it, we won't publish it. If you like it, you pay us to print up thousands of rating cards and reports that your salespeople can use to sell insurance. It's a win-win."

Three newer entrants to the business of rating insurance companies (i.e., Moody's, Standard & Poor's, and Duff & Phelps) offered essentially the same deal. But instead of earning their money from reprints of ratings reports, they simply charged a big fat fee for each rating–$25,000 *or more* per rating, per year. Later, Best decided to change its price structure to match the other three, charging the rated companies similar up-front fees.[2]

It seemed then, during the late 1980s and early 1990s, that, not surprisingly, the ratings agencies gave out good grades to almost everyone. At A. M. Best, the grade inflation got so far out of hand that no one in the industry would be caught alive buying insurance from a company rated "good" by Best. Everyone (except the customers) knew that Best's "good" was actually *bad.*

Soon, the grade inflation even began to infect Best's "A" grades. According to the *New York Times,* the decision makers at Best were so intent on "working with the companies," they became reluctant to "hurt the poor companies" with a downgrade, despite obvious problems such as huge junk bond portfolios. So, in many cases, instead of downgrading, Best's executives told their analysts to start using little, lowercase letters next to their "A" grades–cryptic "moderators" that only Best could fully understand, like *w* for *watchlist,* or *c* for *conditional.*[3]

Best said these moderators were very important. But at the same time, Best allowed the insurance companies to continue advertising the "A" ratings to the public *without* the moderators. In effect, Best had two sets of ratings: one for the customers and one as a butt-covering device for the professionals. It was like two sets of accounting books: one for your own internal reference that told the real story, and one for the tax collector to cheat on taxes. Pinocchio would be proud.

How Executive Life Got Everything It Wanted—Almost

Fred Carr, the CEO of Executive Life, was somehow able to persuade Standard & Poor's to give his company a triple-A (AAA) rating, despite a business model that was predicated largely on junk bond investing![4]

Moody's, the least liberal of the established rating agencies, was shell-shocked and pissed. They couldn't believe Carr got an AAA rating from S&P. So they did something they rarely do. They decided to go ahead and rate Executive Life with no request from Carr and no payment, giving them a grade of A1, which wasn't so great. But Carr could care less. By that time, he had gotten everything he needed from the insurance ratings agencies. He knew he could leverage the AAA rating from S&P, combined with his high guaranteed yields, to get filthy rich. And he did just that.

Getting the insurance *regulators* to cooperate was not quite as easy. In fact, the state insurance commissioners around the country had been concerned with the industry's rising investments in junk bonds and unrated bonds for quite some time, and they set up a special office in New York, the Securities Valuation Office, to monitor the junk bond situation.

What is a junk bond? The answer, as I've explained, was very simple: any bond with a rating from S&P and Moody's of double-B or lower. But the insurance companies didn't like that definition. "You can't do that to us," they said, in effect, to the insurance commissioners. "If you use that definition, everybody will see how much junk we have." The commissioners struggled with this, but amazingly, they finally obliged.[5]

It was like rewriting history to suit the new king. Rather than use the widely accepted standards, they actually invented a brand new, cockamamie bond-rating system of their own that conveniently misclassified the bulk of the junk bonds as "secure bonds." The result was the insurance companies kept buying more and more junk, and no one—let alone you and me—had any way of knowing how much. Pinocchio would be green with envy.

These deceptive practices were an outrage, and I felt I could not sit by idly as millions of investors were duped. Therefore, to help warn the public of the dangers, I decided to issue Weiss Ratings on insurance companies.

The deceptions went on for several years. Finally, however, after a few of us screamed and hollered about this sham, the insurance commissioners finally realized they simply could not be a party to the Great Insurance Cover-Up any longer.

They decided to bite the bullet. They adopted a new scale that used the standard double-B definition, and reclassified over $30 billion in "secure" bonds as junk bonds. It was the beginning of the first scene in the final act for the junk bond giants.[6]

The *New York Times* was one of the first to pick up the story; newspapers all over the country soon followed, and the Great Insurance Cover-Up was over. Unfortunately, for millions of investors like you, the fire had barely begun.[7]

The large junk bond insurance companies were falling like dominoes—Executive Life of California with 452,000 policyholders, Executive Life of New York with 102,000 policyholders, Fidelity Bankers Life with 373,000, and First Capital Life with 268,000— each and every one dragged down by large junk bond holdings.[8]

These were the same junk bonds that were bought with people's keep-safe insurance money, hidden away by the secretive insurance companies, and covered up by the state insurance commissioners.

One day everything seemed to be just fine. The next day all hell broke loose. The junk bonds went sour. The institutional investors in those GICs demanded their money back. The insurance companies ran out of cash to meet demands. And their house of cards came crashing down.

At one company after another, the insurance commissioners marched into the headquarters, took over the operations, and declared a moratorium on all cash withdrawals by policyholders. How many policyholders? I checked the records. The failed companies (including Mutual Benefit Life, which was caused primarily by real estate speculation) had exactly 5,950,422 policyholders, including individuals and groups. Among these, 1.9 million involved a cash value.[9]

If you were among these 1.9 million policyholders, your money was *frozen*. They wouldn't let you cancel your policy. The regulators, who had taken over the operations of the companies, wouldn't even let you borrow on your policy. If you had a life-and-death emergency and you needed your money immediately for medicine or surgery, you had to beg and grovel before a state bureaucrat to prove that *your* emergency was more desperate than everyone else's emergency.

Congress was bombarded with calls and letters from angry investors who couldn't get their money back. In response, the U.S. House Subcommittee on Commerce, Consumer Protection, and Competitiveness held hearings to delve into the causes and possible solutions. The U.S. Senate Committee on Banking, Housing, and Urban Affairs followed suit soon thereafter.

What surprised them the most was the fact that most of the large insurers seemed to have failed *even while they still had positive ratings from the major rating agencies,* including A. M. Best, Standard & Poor's, and Moody's. Therefore, as a follow-up, the House Subcommittee requested a special study by the U.S. General Accounting Office (GAO) to compare their ratings to the Weiss Ratings. The GAO later concluded that Weiss was first in warning consumers of future troubles three times more often than A. M. Best, the oldest insurance company rating agency in America. Further, for the six large insurance company failures, the GAO confirmed that all of the rating agencies, except for Weiss, routinely failed to warn consumers until *after* the failures had occurred and it was too late to get out.[10]

The state insurance guarantee associations, which were supposed to make policyholders whole in case of an insurance company failure, choked, and then went limp. They had no money. Unlike the Federal Deposit Insurance Corporation (FDIC), the insurance guarantee association in your state usually didn't have funds in the kitty ahead of time; it raised the money from surviving insurance companies *after* a failure. That worked fine when just a few small companies failed. But when the failures were large, where were they going to get the money? The guarantee system itself failed.[11]

The authorities put their heads together and came up with a "creative" solution. To avoid invoking the guarantee system, they decided to change the definition of when a failed company fails. Instead of declaring the bankrupt companies as failed, they decided to call them "financially impaired," or "in rehabilitation."

Meanwhile, the freeze on all policyholder assets continued— for months. Finally, the authorities created new companies with new, reformed policies yielding far less than the original policies.

Then they offered policyholders two choices: (1) Either you "opt in" to the new company and accept a loss of yield for years to come, or (2) you "opt out," and we give you your share of the cash that we have available for you right now. How much? In most cases, policyholders got back no more than 50 cents on the dollar. It was the greatest disaster in the history of insurance.

BACK TO THE PRESENT

You'd think the insurance companies, and rating agencies, would have learned something from this experience, and indeed they did: how to put a new face on the same old business as usual to get Congressional investigators and the public off their backs.

Best tweaked its rating scale a bit. Its B is now called something closer to "bad" than "good." And all the moderators like *w* for *watchlist* and *c* for *contingent* are gone. Companies with those conditional A ratings were switched to A+. Companies with no conditions attached were bumped up to a new, even higher grade, A++. But Best did it all very quietly. So to this day, most people don't realize that A+ is not Best's highest grade any more—it's actually the second highest grade.

The insurance commissioners, meanwhile, developed a grading system of their own, a single number, to help spot potential failures ahead of time. The industry wanted to keep it secret. The commissioners insisted on making it public. To settle the dispute, they all agreed to a new rule, which says, in effect, that if you're in the insurance business, and you tell a customer what the official grade is—or even just where to go find it—you'll lose your license. By this time, Pinocchio was literally laughing in his grave.

Meanwhile, you'd expect that, *at least,* the insurance companies would have learned the lesson not to ever again get stuck in junk bonds; and indeed, for a few years, junk in the insurance industry mostly disappeared. But starting in the late 1990s, many companies began to drift back to their old junk hunting grounds.

By 2000, there were at least 49 life and health insurers holding more junk bonds on their books than capital.

For every dollar of capital, Fidelity & Guaranty Life (Maryland) had $2.90 in junk; Conseco Direct Life (Illinois) had $2.99; Capitol Life (Colorado) had $3.75; and Illinois Annuity & Insurance (Massachusetts) had $5.27. Can you imagine that? All you'd need is a 20 percent loss in their junk bonds and the company would be wiped out. Broke. Kaput. Overall, just these 49 companies held an astounding $41.4 billion in junk bonds.[13]

Not all insurers holding junk bonds are financially weak. Some companies may have other offsetting strengths. They may have deep pockets (i.e., plenty of capital). In addition, they may be making strong, stable profits.

The moral of the story, however, is clear: Before doing business with any insurance company, make sure that it will be there for you in good times and bad.

Two Fundamental Questions You Should Be Asking Your Insurer

Let me put *you* in the driver's seat of the insurance company—or any financial institution, for that matter. You're the principal, CFO, and the CEO all rolled into one. You own the company, run the finances, and make all of the final decisions. And you want my money.

- My first question to you is: "What risks are you going to take with *my* money?"

- My follow-up question is: "How deep are *your* pockets? In other words, how much of your own net worth (i.e., capital) do you have available to cover for any losses you might take with my money?"

In sum: How much *risk* is involved? And how much *capital* is involved? The more risk you take, the more capital you should have to back it up.

In essence, these are the same questions we asked when we developed our Weiss Ratings of financial institutions. We called it *risk-adjusted capital*. Later, the regulators developed a similar model, calling it *risk-based capital*.

The trouble is that getting the answers from financial institutions isn't easy, especially in the insurance industry. You'd have to drive to your state capital, go to the state insurance department, plead with the commissioner's staff, and then, if you're lucky, you'd get a chance to look over the official financial filings of your insurance company—up to 1,000 pages of schedules and tables that even a CPA would have trouble figuring out. Instead, follow these steps:

Step 1. Get the company's Weiss Safety Rating, which takes into account not only the junk bond holdings but also hundreds of other factors. To get our rating, you can call 800-289-9222 ($15 per company), visit our Web site at www.WeissRatings.com ($7.95 per company), or go to your public library and ask for Weiss Ratings' *Guide to Life and Health Insurers.*

The Weiss rating scale is very similar to a school grading system: A = excellent, B = good, C = fair, D = weak, E = very weak, and F = failed. We also use plus and minus signs to indicate the upper or lower range of each grade. My recommendation would be to try to do business strictly with companies enjoying a grade of B+ or better—and there are many to choose from. The largest among them, based on the most current data, are listed in Table 8.1.

Step 2. If you already have a policy, and your company has a Weiss Safety Rating of B or B−, that's acceptable. However, if its rating is in the C, or fair, range, it's a *yellow flag*. Don't panic. But watch it carefully. If it doesn't cost you anything to switch to a stronger company, do so now. If there's a heavy penalty, which will diminish over time, I suggest you check

Table 8.1 Strongest Large Life and Health Insurers in America

Company	Domicile State	Weiss Safety Ratings*	Total Assets (in millions of $)
Allstate Life Ins. Co.	IL	B+	40,798
American General Life Ins. Co.	TX	B+	10,687
Fidelity Investments Life Ins. Co.	UT	B+	11,742
Great-West Life & Annuity Ins. Co.	CO	B+	25,950
Guardian Life Ins. Co. of America	NY	A	17,983
Hartford Life & Annuity Ins. Co.	CT	B+	43,524
Hartford Life Ins. Co.	CT	B+	81,354
Jefferson Pilot Financial Ins. Co.	NE	B+	12,043
Jefferson-Pilot Life Ins. Co.	NC	A	10,040
John Hancock Life Ins. Co.	MA	A–	61,175
Manufacturers Life Ins. Co. USA	MI	B+	27,843
Massachusetts Mutual Life Ins. Co.	MA	A	66,365
Metropolitan Life Ins. Co.	NY	A–	180,135
Minnesota Life Ins. Co.	MN	A	15,447
Mutual of America Life Ins. Co.	NY	B+	10,415
Nationwide Life Ins. Co.	OH	B+	78,574
New York Life Ins. & Annuity Corp.	DE	A–	31,105
New York Life Ins. Co.	NY	A	74,102
Northwestern Mutual Life Ins. Co.	WI	A+	94,093
Pacific Life Ins. Co.	CA	A	50,886
Principal Life Ins. Co.	IA	A–	73,282

State Farm Life Ins. Co.	IL	A+	28,762
Teachers Ins. & Annuity Asn of Am	NY	A+	120,628
United of Omaha Life Ins. Co.	NE	B+	10,990
Variable Annuity Life Ins. Co.	TX	B+	43,962

*A = excellent, B = good, + = upper end of grade range, – = bottom end of grade range.

This gives you a solid shopping list from which to choose a strong insurer for your life and health insurance or annuities. A high grade doesn't guarantee a good deal. But it does give you a strong assurance that the company will stick around to fulfill its promises. This list contains all life and health insurers on the Weiss Recommended List (receiving a rating of B+ or higher) as of September 5, 2001, with total assets exceeding $10 billion. If you are considering purchasing a new insurance policy or renewing an existing policy, we believe you can safely include these companies among those you consider. Since financial risk is minimal, you can make your decision based upon a comparison of the specific costs and benefits of the policy. For a complete listing, refer to the Weiss Ratings' *Guide to Life and Health Insurers* as well as the Weiss Ratings' *Guide to HMOs and Health Insurers*, available at many public libraries.

Source: Weiss Ratings, Inc., Palm Beach Gardens, FL, based on first-quarter 2001 data filed with state insurance regulators as well as some data provided by the companies directly to Weiss Ratings.

Table 8.2 Weakest Large Life and Health Insurers in America

Company Name	Domicile State	Weiss Safety Rating*	Total Assets (in millions of $)
American Community Mut. Ins. Co.	MI	D	125
American Pioneer Life Ins. Co.	FL	D	106
Aurora National Life Asr Co.	CA	D	4,033
Capitol Life Ins. Co.	CO	D	379
Coventry Health & Life Ins. Co.	DE	D+	116
Golden State Mutual Life Ins. Co.	CA	D	126
Health Insurance Plan of Greater NY	NY	D–	833
Mayflower National Life Ins. Co.	IN	D–	110

(continued)

Table 8.2   (Continued)

Company Name	Domicile State	Weiss Safety Rating*	Total Assets (in millions of $)
Medico Life Ins. Co.	NE	D+	135
Mutual Savings Life Ins. Co.	AL	D	295
National Heritage Ins. Co.	TX	E	919
New Era Life Ins. Co.	TX	D+	143
Old Standard Life Ins. Co.	ID	D	219
Old West Annuity & Life Ins. Co.	AZ	D	105
Penn Treaty Network America Ins. Co.	PA	D–	513
Pennsylvania Life Ins. Co.	PA	D	440
Security Plan Life Ins. Co.	LA	D–	230
Southwestern Life Ins. Co.	TX	D+	1,819
Universal Guaranty Life Ins. Co.	OH	D	216
Wabash Life Ins. Co.	IN	D+	402
Wisconsin Physicians Service Ins.	WI	D	142

*D = weak, E = very weak, + = upper end of grade range, – = bottom end of grade range.

In the early 1990s, six million Americans were caught in failed life insurance companies, with many losing as much as 50 percent of their money. To avoid that possibility, avoid weak life insurers such as these. Their low Weiss Safety Rating does not represent our forecast of failure. But historically, the probability of failure has been high among lower-rated companies. This table contains strictly those life and health insurers considered weak (receiving a Weiss Safety Rating of D+ or lower) as of September 5, 2001, with total assets exceeding $100 million. There also may be other smaller, weak companies that do not appear on this list. If you are shopping for new insurance and you are not a risk taker, try to obtain a policy from a safer company. And, if you already have a policy with one of these companies, consider switching. Try to avoid penalties if you can, and make sure you can find alternative coverage. But in our opinion, the risk of staying usually outweighs the cost of switching. For a complete list of weak companies, refer to the Weiss Ratings' *Guide to Life and Health Insurers*, available at many public libraries. For a brief, updated list of the weakest insurers, go to www.weissratings.com.

Source: Weiss Ratings, Inc., Palm Beach Gardens, FL, based on first-quarter 2001 data filed with state insurance regulators as well as some data provided by the companies directly to Weiss Ratings.

in *at least* yearly. As long as it's still a C, you can wait before making your switch.

If your company's Weiss Safety Rating is a D+ or lower, it's a *red flag*. When the U.S. General Accounting Office (GAO) conducted its study of our rating scale, it said D+ was a warning to consumers of financial vulnerability, and we agree. You still have to weigh the cost and inconvenience of switching (plus whether you can get an equivalent policy with another company), but all in all, I feel the scale is clearly tipping in the direction of *getting out*. Table 8.2 includes a complete list of the life and health insurers in this category.

Step 3. Despite the biases that are inherent in their rating process, it can't hurt to check out the ratings published by our competition as well (i.e., A. M. Best, S&P, and Moody's). Refer to Table 8.3, developed by the U.S. GAO. As you can see, the GAO aligned its scale with Weiss Ratings' A through F. Then, it sought to determine the equivalent scales of the other rating agencies. A few noteworthy points to be aware of:

- You may think Best's top rating is A+. It was, but it's not anymore.

- Companies that do not merit a top rating from Best often advertise their A+ rating from Standard & Poor's. However, the S&P A+ rating is actually fifth from the top of the S&P scale, as it is for Duff & Phelps (now Fitch).

- The B rating from Weiss is still a good rating. Even a C is still in the "secure" range. We don't recommend you buy insurance from C companies. If you're already with one, though, it's not cause for panic.

- Moody's, S&P, Best, and Duff & Phelps all have a full scale of low grades, but they rarely issue those ratings. At some of the agencies, there are no companies receiving the lower grades.[14]

Table 8.3 Confused about What Insurance Ratings *Really* Mean? Refer to This Scale from the U.S. General Accounting Office (GAO)

Ratings	Bands	Weiss*	Best*,†	S&P‡	Moody's	D&P§
Secure	1	A+, A, A–	A++, A+	AAA	Aaa	AAA
	2	B+, B, B–	A, A–	AA+, AA, AA–	Aa1, Aa2, Aa3	AA+, AA, AA–
	3	C+, C, C–	B++, B+ B, B–	A+, A, A– BBB+, BBB, BBB–	A1, A2, A3 Baa1, Baa2, Baa3	A+, A, A– BBB+, BBB, BBB–
Vulnerable	4	D+, D, D–	C++, C+ C, C–	BB+, BB, BB– B+, B, B–	Ba1, Ba2, Ba3 B1, B2, B3	BB+, BB, BB– B+, B, B–
	5	E+, E, E– F	D E, F	CCC, (CC, C) (D), R	Caa, Ca, C	CCC+, CCC, CCC– DDD, DD, D

If you're confused by insurance company ratings, you're not alone. So was Congress! So was the GAO! So they spent many months comparing the Weiss ratings with those of other rating agencies—A. M. Best (Best), Standard & Poor's (S&P), Moody's Investor Service (Moody's), and Duff & Phelps (D&P). They established a rating scale of five bands, which correspond to the five major ratings in the Weiss scale—A, B, C, D, and E (F = failed). Then, they placed the ratings of the other agencies into those bands.

If you are using the Weiss ratings, try your best to initiate new business strictly with companies rated B+ or better. If you are already doing business with an insurer, monitor regularly the safety of companies with a C–, C, or C+ rating; seriously consider leaving the company if it is rated D+ or lower, taking into consideration any penalties plus the availability of alternative coverage.

If you are using the ratings of other rating agencies, bear in mind that conflicts of interest in the rating process compromise the objectivity of the ratings.

*Weiss and Best use additional symbols to designate that they recognize an insurer's existence but do not provide a rating. These symbols are not included in this table.

†Best added the A++, B++, and C++ ratings in 1992. In 1994, Best classified its ratings into "secure" and "vulnerable" categories, changed the definition of its B and B– ratings from "good" to "adequate," and assigned these ratings to the "vulnerable" category. This table contains the GAO's assignment of Best's ratings to bands based on our interpretation of their rating descriptions prior to 1994.

‡S&P discontinued CCC + and – signs, CC, C, and D ratings, and added the R rating in 1992.

§Duff & Phelps has since been purchased by Fitch Investors Services. Duff & Phelps Credit Rating Co. merged with Fitch IBCA in 2000, and minor changes were made to the rating scale at that time. These changes were not reflected in the GAO's 1994 study, but are reflected in the chart.

Source: U.S. General Accounting Office (GAO).

When you are evaluating insurance companies based on a rating, be sure you have this handy scale by your side to give you a clearer picture of what the rating means.

Step 4. As soon as you have a list of the companies you can trust, consider the costs and benefits of the insurance policies they are offering you, the primary subject of the next two chapters.

CHAPTER

WHAT YOU NEED TO KNOW ABOUT LIFE INSURANCE

When you buy a policy to protect yourself against a fire, it's called fire insurance. When it's for an accident, it's accident insurance. So when you want to protect your family from the consequences of your death, it should be called "death insurance," right?

Yes, but long ago, insurance salespeople discovered that no one wanted to talk about their death, let alone buy insurance for it. So taking a chapter out of Orwell's *1984,* they called it "life insurance" instead.

It didn't seem to help much, though. Life insurance was still a very hard sell, and agents who pushed it too hard got a bad reputation for bringing up unpleasant subjects. "Want a row of seats all to yourself on your next flight to Chicago?" went a popular joke. "Then just tell your fellow passengers that you sell life insurance."

Prudential, the Rock-of-Gibraltar largest insurance company in the world, came up with another very "creative" solution. They figured out a way to disguise the life insurance as an annuity, set up a big sales force trained to obfuscate the real nature of the product, and sold it to millions of investors from 1982 through 1995. All annuity policies sold by insurance companies do have a small life insurance component. But that's a far cry from being an actual life insurance policy.

It took many years of litigation before the regulators caught up with them. Prudential execs said they were sorry. The regulators said that wasn't quite enough to make amends. After much heated debate and negotiation, the company belatedly agreed to pay $2.7 billion in restitution to more than 1 million maligned customers, many times more than the largest previous settlement in insurance history. They sold insurance as a "retirement plan," failing to disclose the risks and using policy illustrations, which projected fabulous dividend accumulations as foregone conclusions.

So did agents at New York Life and Allstate. Meanwhile, Equitable Life Assurance Society was fined $2 million for selling more than $100 million of improper life insurance policies.[1] If the larger companies can do it, just imagine what the smaller, fly-by-nights are getting away with![2]

The Prudential, Metropolitan, Allstate, and Equitable messes were finally cleaned up. However, serious problems remain.

Problem 1: The Shroud of Secrecy

Consumers are kept in the dark about everything that counts the most. The junk bond cover-up, the Orwellian "newspeak" of life insurance, and the giant Prudential scheme are just three examples of the secrecy that still surrounds the entire life insurance industry. It's hard to find out how much a product really costs. It's almost impossible to figure out how much you're paying in commissions. It's hard to know what the true yield will be. And unless it's term insurance, it's totally impractical to compare the products of competing insurers side by side.

People in the insurance industry don't pay much attention to it because it's always been that way. But anyone who comes to insurance from the mutual fund industry is appalled. "Can't you tell me what your one-year yield is? Can't you tell me what your expense ratio is? Can't I compare your policy with a hundred other policies?"

The answers, respectively, are No. No. No. You can't do anything even close.

How does the insurance industry get away with this secrecy? By always maintaining that thin veneer of insurance on their investment products. They have to underwrite the policy (i.e., decide whether you're worthy of their insurance coverage). So their message, in essence, boils down to: "You can shop around all you want. But first, *we* have to decide whether *we* will accept you."

If you're shopping for a mutual fund, you will get a prospectus that discloses all the risks. If you're shopping for a cash-value life insurance policy, you get a *policy illustration* that often promises much but discloses little.

What about the actual insurance contract itself (i.e., the actual product you're buying)? You don't get to see that until *after* the underwriting process is complete. You'd have to go through this same process with several companies before you could make a comparison. Shopping around becomes so impractical as to be virtually impossible.

Problem 2: A Patchwork of Regulation

Insurance companies are regulated by 50 state insurance commissions, most of which are too small to deal effectively with the most pervasive problems in the industry. Even the largest state offices, with the biggest funding and staff, pale in comparison to the giants of the industry. If New Jersey, for example, conducted a thorough audit of Prudential, they'd probably be doing nothing else for several years.

Between the shroud of secrecy and the patchwork of regulation, you can see how easy it can be for some of the largest companies to get away with "murder."

The solution that I've proposed to Congress is more disclosure to consumers. Rather than place the entire burden of monitoring, baby-sitting, and punishing the industry on the states, why not give consumers all the information they need to make their own, informed decisions? That way, they could vote with their dollars, punish the bad companies, and reward the good ones.[3]

Indeed, several of the largest insurance company failures in recent U.S. history could have easily been prevented by full disclosure to customers. For example, there would have been nothing wrong with Executive Life or First Capital selling high-yield annuities, provided they made it very clear up front—directly to the buyer at the point of sale—that their annuities were also very high *risk*. Who knows? There may have been a small minority of investors willing to take that risk in order to get the higher yields. These companies could have existed, albeit as small, niche businesses.

Unfortunately, that's not what happened. There was no risk disclosure, and most policyholders had no idea what they were getting into. They thought that they were buying insurance to *protect* themselves against risk—not high-risk investments that invited more losses.

With full disclosure, most people would have shunned Executive Life or First Capital and taken their money to safer companies. In that environment, regulators could mostly concentrate on making sure that the companies give us all the information and *tell the truth*. Sounds very reasonable, doesn't it?

Unfortunately, the large life insurance companies don't think so. Their lobbying arm, the American Council of Life Insurance (ACLI), has consistently fought tooth and nail against any effort at greater disclosure, and no other industry has as much clout—not banking, not all of Detroit.

That's why we have truth-in-lending legislation for banks and why we have lemon laws for automobiles. But there's no such thing as a federal truth-in-insurance law. Individual states do have disclosure requirements, but for most consumers, the information is out of reach, cryptic, or both.

That's also why, when I complained bitterly about this, and began issuing bad ratings on weak companies, the ACLI turned its wrath on me. They sent a personal letter to the editors of all the major media (e.g., *New York Times, Wall Street Journal,* CBS, ABC, NBC, CNN, and others) trying to persuade them to stop quoting me. Even as I testified before Congress, they passed around a packet of information seeking to discredit me, literally behind my back. But their campaign backfired. The more they attacked, the more the major media took an interest in my ratings, and the more praise I got in the press.[4]

Today, nothing has changed. The insurance industry still huddles under its shroud of secrecy. Its lobbyists continue to protect that shroud with a rich budget. Regulators remain relatively powerless. And consumers like you are at the industry's mercy, unless you arm yourself with the information you need to fight back.

Problem 3: Deceptive Practices

The problem of deception in the insurance industry is so rampant, involving so many of the largest and most respected companies, it is virtually impossible for any one person or organization to bring about meaningful change.

The attempts made by Joseph M. Belth, the nation's leading insurance industry critic and watchdog, illustrate how deeply ingrained the deceptions really are. Belth figured that since actuaries are the insurance company specialists who calculate the costs and benefits of insurance policies, they're the ones who would know exactly what the deceptions are and who would be in the best position to nip those deceptions in the bud. So Belth wrote the chairman of the professional conduct committee of the Society of Actuaries, asking a very simple and pointed question: "Is it the professional responsibility of the actuary to take positive action to eradicate deceptive practices, or is it the professional responsibility of the actuary merely to refrain from endorsing deceptive practices?"

The actuaries were perplexed. They debated for a full day on how to respond. But at the end of the day, they concluded that the only possible answer they could give Belth was, ironically, that they were unable to answer his question. The reason, according to one of the actuaries who participated in the debate, shows you just how serious the problems really are in the insurance industry:

> If the committee concluded it is the professional responsibility of the actuary merely to refrain from endorsing deceptive practices, the Society would become the laughingstock of professional organizations. On the other hand, if the committee concluded it is the professional responsibility of the actuary to take positive action to eradicate deceptive practices, the Soci-

ety would condemn many members to being fired by their companies.

Belth was shocked. But he didn't stop there. He wrote stinging letters to the CEOs who presided over deceptions and to the state regulators who were supposed to do something about it. He testified before the Senate Subcommittee on Antitrust and Monopoly, telling them, "the deceptive sales practices found in the insurance industry constitute a national scandal."

That was nearly three decades ago; today, Belth is still protesting, still writing, and still testifying. But virtually nothing has changed. Until this very day, "consumers are trapped. They are victimized by a variety of deceptive methods for portraying the price of the protection component and the rate of return on the savings component in life insurance."[5] Here are just a few of the most common examples:

Account churning. If you've built up a lot of cash in your policy, unethical agents may try to sell you more insurance or switch you to a policy offering a higher yield. Your agent calls you and says that he or she has found something wrong with your current policy. "But if you just switch to the one I've just found for you, you'll be just fine," he or she says. Further, the agent may sweeten the enticement to switch by telling you that your premium will be lower and your death benefit will be higher. What this agent doesn't tell you is that he or she gets another fat commission, which is going to be paid out of your cash values, depleting your investment funds even more than the bad policy.

But it's not just the agent who's responsible: Some of the largest insurance companies, such as American General Life, John Hancock Mutual Life, Metropolitan Life, and Prudential Insurance Company of America have been hit with class-action lawsuits that ultimately settled for millions, sometimes billions, of dollars, because of insurance agent churning.[6]

The mystery of the vanishing premium. The pitch went something like this: "There's this new policy where the rate of return from the investments is projected to be so fabulous that you will probably be able to stop paying for future premiums after a couple of years–a decade, at most." Unfortunately, the sky-high projections weren't accurate (or guaranteed), and sooner rather than later you'd get a bill in the mail for your premium. It hadn't vanished after all.

The "old-losses shuffle."   When you buy into a new policy, you are effectively buying into the company's existing pool of investments. If those investments have unrealized losses, it is possible that you will get stuck with those losses, even though they were incurred before you came on board. Only thorough analysis of a company's holdings will reveal such a problem.

Selling off your policy.   Your insurance company can sell off your policy to another company without your consent. For example, let's say your insurance policy is with company X. One day, you get a notice in the mail that your policy has been sold to company Y. But you do not want to do business with Company Y because it's low-rated. The industry's response: Sorry, you have no choice.

Viatical settlements.   These are contracts that allow you to buy out the life insurance benefits from a terminally ill policyholder, such as an AIDS patient. The patient gets immediate cash to cover his or her living and health expenses (tax-free), and you get the payoff when he or she dies. The difference between the purchase price and the proceeds is the profit to the investor. Approach these with extreme caution. First, despite claims to the contrary, viatical investments are not guaranteed. If the insurance company underwriting the investment goes bust, so could your investment. Second, one would hope that the terminally ill patient can extend his or her life expectancy as much as possible. To the degree that he or she is successful, your yield will plunge. For example, let's imagine that you invest in a three-year viatical offering a total return of 42 percent. If the terminally ill patient lives six years instead of only three, your total return is halved to 21 percent. You're in for six years–and your annualized return ends up only 3.5 percent per year!

Viaticals are a very private market. Contracts and funds are often held in trusts, lawyers' escrow accounts, and the like. Cracks can develop in any one of the links between the investor and the insurance company actually offering the viatical settlement, further increasing the potential risk. Stay away.

Policy illustrations. The biggest deception does not stem from special situations such as these. It's the one that shows up every day in the normal process of selling insurance. To understand this process, consider first the process of buying a regular mutual fund.

Let's suppose that you've got $10,000 to invest. You decide what your goals are. You research some mutual funds on the Internet and compare their one-year, six-month, and 30-day performance. You send for the prospectuses in the mail, or download them from the Web. You check out their fees. You make a decision. You can buy the fund directly or you can go through a broker. Then, any time you want to see how your investment is doing, you can check in the daily newspaper or search on the Web.

Now, let's suppose that you want to buy a cash-value life insurance policy. First and foremost, you *have* to go to an agent. With very few exceptions, *unless* you go through an agent, you will get nowhere.

But before you can ask about the product, the agent will make sure the shoe is on the other foot from the very beginning. He or she will start asking *you* questions about your medical history, your career, and even your personal lifestyle. He will make it abundantly clear that the burden is on you to prove that you are worthy of the privilege.

Instead of giving you a prospectus, your agent runs one of those policy illustrations I told you about a moment ago. Unlike a prospectus, the illustration is long on big-picture projections and short on specific information. Typically, it tells you little about the allocation of your funds or the breakdown of fees. It discloses nothing about the risk or the financial stability of the insurer. It tells you nothing about the commissions your broker will make.

Rather, its primary purpose is to give you scenarios of future performance based on assumptions about inflation and interest rates. Some companies use conservative assumptions. Some companies try to tweak the results to make the policies look better. Some go off the deep end, making assumptions that make their policies really shine.

In the January 2000 report of the Consumer Federation of America, the nation's largest consumer group, author James Hunt wrote:[7]

> For several years, the National Association of Insurance Commissioners (NAIC) has struggled to draft model rules for life insurance policy illustrations and related sales material . . . Regrettably, the rules, which were essentially written by life insurers themselves, offer little help to consumers and may add to their confusion.

You are wary of this. So you ask to see the insurance contract. You figure it's your right to know what you're buying. But your agent says you can't do that yet. You first have to wait until the underwriting process is complete, and you have been accepted by the insurance company. *Then* they'll let you see the contract.

You've already put a lot of time and effort into this project. You don't want to back out now. So you sign and pay the up-front fee.

You ask the agent what his commission is. The response: "Don't worry about that, the company writes my commission check." The agent doesn't tell you that no matter who writes the physical check, the money comes out of *your* pocket.

A few months go by, and you want to see how well your investment is doing. You open the newspaper but can't find it. You search the Web and still nothing. Except for cryptic statements from the insurer, you have no way of tracking your performance.

WHAT TO DO

What a murky mess! Hopefully, a lot of these problems will be resolved in the years ahead. But don't hold your breath. Right now, you have to use your own common sense and smarts to cope with this industry.

Step 1: Decide whether you *really* need life insurance. If your agent tells you that *everybody* needs some life insurance, tell him or her to go take a hike. Some people need it. Some don't.

The purpose of life insurance is to replace a deceased spouse's income, to cover a mortgage, to pay for a child's education, or to pay for living expenses during the early years following a death. Or it could be to provide an inheritance to a needy child or other relative that you were supporting. If you're not supporting anyone other than yourself, you don't need insurance to replace that support.

Let's suppose that you're a widow or widower with no children. You are in good health and have a comfortable lifestyle. What do you need life insurance for? You probably don't.

Or suppose you do have heirs. Do you need life insurance to help offset the costs they will have to pay in estate taxes? Maybe. But if your estate is under $675,000, it's not subject to estate taxes. And if Mr. Bush has his way, all estate taxes could be eliminated. The most your children may need is some money to cover for funeral and burial.

Moreover, all that money you might have wasted on life insurance premiums may be much better spent on your own health, so you can live a longer and more enjoyable life. Besides, why not spend some of it on your children's or grandchildren's education so they can be even more self-sufficient when you're gone?

The bottom line is that if you are not financially responsible for someone and you are not going to have a large federal estate tax bill, the agent who gives you a big pitch for life insurance is wasting your time.

However, if you *are* responsible for your heirs' well-being, or if they *do* need you for their education, their mortgage, or for any other large expenses, then some life insurance may make sense—provided you can afford the premium.

Step 2: Make sure it's affordable. Your desire to provide for your children and grandchildren with some extra money is a kind and generous gesture. But remember: It may not be cheap. And it's certainly not free. Your premium money has to come from somewhere. If you have to sacrifice your own health care or adjust your lifestyle just to pay your premium, it's not affordable and not for you.

"But suppose," you ask, "even though I don't really need insurance, I *can* afford it. And suppose I really *want* to do something special for my children or grandchildren. Then what do I do?" Then consider giving them the money while you're still alive and able to enjoy their gratitude. Or contribute directly to their IRAs or other retirement accounts.

For example, you could invest in one of the new Section 529 education plans. You can open an account in any state, which can be used for tuition at any age, in any state, and in any educational institution—not just college. Further, an individual can have more than one Section 529 account. So if you want to set one up for a grandchild, you can do it separately from any investment or savings plans that the child's parents might have.

Step 3: Ready to buy life insurance? Okay. Then you'd better get started learning all the jargon. Do you know what a *paid-up addition* is? How about a *mortality charge? Waive-of-premium rider?* If you don't, you're in good company. Most consumers who try to learn about life insurance are overwhelmed by the jargon. As a result, many simply bow to agents' high-pressure tactics without knowing what they are buying or how much it costs.

Typically, once agents have their foot in the door, they begin speaking in a language that may as well be Sanskrit. And because most people are embarrassed by their ignorance, they do not ask questions.

Actually, though, the fundamentals of life insurance are not that complicated. You are the *insured.* You buy the policy by paying *premiums* that entitle you to a specific *death benefit.*

The part of your premium that goes to the life insurance protection is known as the *mortality charge.* The rest may go into savings. When you die, the *proceeds* of the policy (the death benefit) go to whomever you have chosen as the *beneficiary.* Those proceeds can often be paid out as a lump sum or an annuity (an annual stream of income) and they are tax-free to the beneficiary.

Step 4: Decide whether you want to just buy insurance, or buy insurance and an investment at the same time. If you've read this far, you can probably guess which one I recommend: With rare exceptions, you should stick with buying insurance from insurance companies and investments from investment companies.

To buy pure insurance, stick with *term* life insurance, and avoid *permanent* or *cash-value* life insurance. In addition, some term policies are guaranteed renewable, and give you some of the advantages of permanent insurance without the investment aspect.

As you've seen, insurance companies are usually not that good at handling your money. And even if they were, they just don't disclose the facts you need to be a prudent, informed investor. Another plus is that term insurance is less expensive than permanent insurance.

Term insurance can give you all the death benefits you need. And if you want to save more money, you can simply take the difference between its premium and the premium of a permanent policy, and invest it elsewhere (following my guidelines in earlier chapters). Even if you have exhausted your tax-deferred retirement account options, you can always purchase a variable annuity (see Chapter 10).

Step 5: Figure out how much life insurance you need. Remember, the whole purpose is to help your heirs cover critical expenses after you're gone. So if you—or they—already have resources available to partially fund those needs, you need coverage strictly to fill any gaps, and perhaps give them a bit of an extra cushion.

Ask yourself what expenses you are trying to cover. Is it to pay off a mortgage? If so, it's fairly easy to estimate how much you'll need.

If it's to provide your spouse with enough money to maintain his or her current lifestyle, that's a bit more involved. Take a look at your current ages and life expectancies. Then consider your health, and make any adjustments that feel right for you. It's going to be a rough estimate. But that's the best you can do.

If you need some help, check www.humanlifevalue.com. It helps you calculate the amount you contribute to your family in the form of net earnings, health insurance, and some intangibles, such as certain things you do in the home.

Step 6: Decide which type of term insurance you want. Here are your options:

- *Annual renewable term life insurance.* You buy it one year at a time, and your annual premium is recalculated each year based on your current age and life expectancy. Naturally, as you grow older, the premium will go up each year.
- *Level premium term life.* The idea is that you lock in your premium rate for a longer time period: 5, 10, 20, or even 30 years. That rate is established just once at the beginning of the policy, based on the average annual cost for the death benefit over that time. And it's the same during the entire term, regardless of your health. Or so they say.

  The reality is that some companies do not guarantee the premium for a 20- or 30-year term. The guarantee is often for only five years but you may not find out about that detail unless you read the fine print. Ask questions, read the entire contract, make sure you understand everything, protect yourself.

Step 7: Already in a permanent life policy? Then learn about what they're doing for you—or to you. There are two main types of permanent insurance: (1) *whole-life* and (2) *universal-life,* plus several variations of both. The one thing they all have in common is that they all have a death benefit and some kind of investment vehicle that provides for tax-deferred growth of your money.

The difference between term and permanent insurance is that permanent insurance has the added component of *cash value* (also known as *surrender value*). A percentage of each of your payments goes into the savings account that you own, and it gradually grows until it equals the death benefit at age 100. This is known as the *maturity* of the contract (or *endowment* of the policy).

If you would like to tap into your policy before it matures, you can take out a *policy loan.* It sounds great. But it's your money, and they still charge you interest for it. If you would like to terminate the policy before maturity, you will get the cash value (which is *not* the same as the death benefit). But you may also get socked with a big *surrender charge.*

Be warned on surrenders: Remember I told you that most agents will not reveal how much they're making in commissions. One reason is that, on many life insurance policies, it is equivalent to 100 percent (or more!) of the first-year premium. Therefore, if you surrender your policy just after the first year, your cash value could be *zero* because all of your first premium payment went to commission or an up-front revenue for the company. Some companies may pay the commission out over the first couple of years, and you can accumulate a bit more cash value. But most don't.

Some different kinds of permanent life insurance:

- *Whole-life.* Whole-life insurance is issued to provide coverage for your entire life, with part of the annual premium you pay going into a reserve in which you own an interest. This is the "cash value" of your policy, invested by the company along with all of its other investments. I cannot say it often enough: With rare exceptions, the purchase of whole-life insurance is not recommended for anyone. The fact is that you have no control over the investments within the policy. They are not subject to the regulations of the SEC and the NASD. Furthermore, if the insurance company becomes insolvent, your investments can go down with it.

■ *Universal-life.* Universal-life insurance provides you with flexibility to decide how much your premium payments will be and how frequently you will make them. And you can even increase or decrease your death benefit. In other words, as your financial situation and your insurance needs change, your policy can change to accommodate. Here's how it works: Your premium is split out into a mortality charge (i.e., the cost for the life insurance protection), expenses (including commissions and administrative fees), and a savings element (i.e., the portion that goes toward your accumulating cash value).

As you pay your premium and accumulate your cash value, interest is credited to that cash value. As long as there is enough in your cash account to pay for your monthly expenses, you don't have to put any more money into it.

Now, let's step back for a moment to a place where many people make a bad decision. Interest is credited to your cash value after your mortality charge and expenses are deducted. That interest rate could be one of two types: (1) *current interest,* which is a rate that is declared by the company and dependent on the company's performance with the current market conditions, or (2) a *guaranteed minimum* specified in your contract.

This is important because many people will purchase a policy based on those policy illustrations that make assumptions about how much their cash value will increase under the most ideal market conditions. That last detail can often be omitted when an insurance agent is trying to sell a policy. Therefore, many people make their purchase decision based on erroneous assumptions that may be unlikely to pan out. They buy a policy because they are told that it will probably increase to a certain dollar amount, when in reality that kind of increase may simply be unlikely to happen.

■ *Variable universal-life.* This is a variation on universal-life with one addition: It lets you decide not only how much money you're going to invest, but where your money is going to be invested. As with a variable annuity, your money is kept in separate accounts, segregated from the insurance company's assets. That's a plus. And, as with a variable annuity, you assume the investment risk. If you choose great investments, you win. If you make bad choices, you lose. One problem, however, is that the commission and other expenses for these policies can be a big drag on your portfolio.

Step 8: Take full advantage of your "free-look period." This is a 30-day window during which you can review the policy and send it back for a refund. And you *are* insured during this period.

Step 9: Review your policy periodically. Unfortunately, many people buy a policy, put it in a drawer, and never look at it again. It's as if buying it was enough, and now they're covered no matter what. But any policy of a couple of years or more should be periodically monitored for its current relevance and value. Indeed, there are several events that should automatically trigger you to review your policy and perhaps make a change:

- If your health has changed significantly.
- If your spouse or other beneficiary has passed away or changed status in some other way.
- If the insurance company's financial situation has changed enough to warrant a policy change.
- If you have taken any loans from your policy. You could be in danger of your coverage lapsing and owing tax on your loan if you don't replace the money.

Step 10: Get unbiased, conflict-of-interest-free advice. One of the most underhanded aspects of the life insurance industry is that, in the third millennium, you are not likely to encounter any individuals who introduce themselves as life insurance salespeople. Instead, you will encounter "pension consultants," "financial advisors," and "financial planners." Even stockbrokers and bank tellers are selling life insurance when they can. At one investment seminar, the speaker at a workshop passed out literature that declared, in bold letters,

"I won't sell you insurance." However, several customers who got his "free consultation" reported that he tried to sell them some very expensive life policies.

Everywhere, salespeople have been actively creating new titles for themselves, finding new ways to get in front of prospective buyers. Regardless of their shifting titles, however, the substance of what they do has not changed: The life insurance agent, by any name, is someone who *works on behalf of the insurance company.* He or she solicits the business of unsuspecting consumers like you, using a variety of tactics to get a foot in your door.

Now, you might think that a possible strategy is to just ask the person who has approached you if he or she is a life insurance agent, and if the answer is "yes," you will simply say "no, thank you." But it's not that easy. In fact, he or she might even say something like, "I'm no agent, I'm a *broker;* I work for *you*." The truth is that brokers—and all other people who sell life insurance products for commission—are working for *themselves*.

Insurance brokers may indeed research most of your possible options and gather the material that you will need to make your decision. But how do you know that they haven't limited the search to the companies that pay them the highest commission?

Then there's the "financial planner" who wants to analyze your financial situation, and who creates a personalized, comprehensive financial plan (or estate plan) for you. However, when you meet, you discover—if you are really paying attention—that beneath all the talk of saving on taxes and growing your money, your new financial plan really revolves around an insurance policy that you may not need.

Always ask: "Who do you work for?" "In what capacity?" "What are your credentials?" You might even ask, "Who owns the company you work for?" And although you might get some kind of explanation that hints about compensation, always ask: "Will you earn a commission from the sale of this product?"[8]

Amid all of the specialists trained to sell you insurance

products, I promise you that there are ethical people who are waiting to serve you right now. You just have to find them. In this environment, the ethical agents have a hard time making a better-than-average living, while the sharks have a field day. Your best weapon is your own education about what you are up against plus a healthy level of skepticism about the sales process.

There are agents who know exactly what they are doing when they sell you a policy that is inappropriate or unnecessarily expensive and gives them the highest commission. There are also agents who know exactly what the policies say and mean, and they are on a mission to find you the best deal and even educate you.

But somewhere in the middle (and I'm afraid this accounts for the vast majority of agents), there are also well-meaning people who were sold a bill of goods while they were being trained in insurance products. They have been conditioned by the industry, they think they know what they are talking about, they tell you what you want to know (*according to what they have been told*), and they are most likely not out to cheat you! But you get cheated anyway because your well-meaning agent is in the same position you are in: He or she believed what the experts said.

What are you supposed to do? Is there a foolproof way to differentiate between the sharks and the ethical agents? Unfortunately, no. But you do have several good alternatives:

1. Use a fee-only insurance advisor. Many certified financial planners (CFPs) work strictly on a fee basis. The money they charge for their advice will be small in comparison to the amount they can save you. Make sure you look for a *certified* financial planner, as anyone can call himself or herself a financial planner. And CFP or not, be sure to always ask if the person will get any commission from the sale of insurance products.

2. Enlist the services of a fee-only advisor, such as Glenn S. Daily. He can be reached by phone at 212-249-9882, by e-mail at gdaily@glenndaily.com, and at his Web site at www.glenndaily.com.

3. Enlist the services of companies like Katt & Company, a national fee-only life insurance advising firm based in Michigan. Peter Katt, CFP, the founder of the firm and the author of *The Life Insurance Fiasco: How to Avoid It,* can be reached at pkatt@peterkatt.com. The general firm number is 616-372-3497, and their Web site is at www.peterkatt.com.

Because the fees of some fee-only advisors can be pretty steep (some are well over $250 an hour), if you are thinking about life insurance because you are looking for a way to cover your estate taxes, then it's worth it to pay an expert to do your work.

If not, look to an on-line quote service for help (e.g., www.quotesmith.com or 800-556-9393, www.quickquote.com, www.insure.com, or www.term4sale.com). Other companies may say they'll give you free quotes, but that is often a loss-leader to get you to buy from the companies they represent. Beware of general agents giving free quotes.

4. If you have already visited an agent and you have some policy illustrations or you already purchased a policy, you can enlist James Hunt of the Consumer Federation of America (www.consumerfed.com). Mr. Hunt will analyze your existing policy at $45 for the first illustration ($75 for second-to-die policies), and at $35 for additional policies sent at the same time. In addition, the Consumer Federation's rate of return (ROR) service will give you an estimate of the investment returns on any cash-value life insurance policy illustration. You simply send Mr. Hunt the policy illustration. And if you already have a policy, send in a current illustration. Contact James Hunt for details at 603-224-2805.

5. Work directly with a strong insurance company that employs salaried people to help you. I can recommend two companies: (1) Ameritas Life (with a Weiss Safety Rating of A–), 800-555-4655 or www.ameritasdirect.com, and (2) USAA Life (Weiss Safety Rating also A–), 800-531-8000. USAA Life is the only branch of USAA (www.usaa.com) that is not restricted to members of the military, so don't let their Web site or their ads prevent you from contacting them. Because the agents are salaried, there is much less concern about the motivation behind their recommendations.

YOUR FIRST AND LAST STEP: ALWAYS CONSIDER FINANCIAL SOUNDNESS

When you receive any kind of recommendation regarding life insurance, make certain you check the financial stability of the company through Weiss Ratings before you sign anything. After all, what good is life insurance if you outlive your insurance company? The same applies to every kind of insurance product–especially annuities, the subject of Chapter 10.

CHAPTER

10

ANNUITIES— THE PROS AND CONS

Annuities are invariably the investment most commonly recommended to folks over 50. However, many annuities lock up your funds and commit you to a single investment program—not always a good idea when things are changing so quickly. In these uncertain times, I believe the key to your success will be *flexibility*. Our financial markets are so volatile—even fragile—it's almost impossible to imagine a world without big surprises that upset our best-laid investment plans.

Take inflation and interest rates, for example. Almost every tax-advantaged financial product you buy today makes assumptions about these two key factors, usually assuming they'll remain pretty much where they are for the life of the plan.

But the reality is that no one knows what inflation and interest rates will be 10 or 20 years from now. We could have a return to double-digit inflation, or we could even have chronic *deflation*. Interest rates could decline more than anyone expects, and they could spike higher than anyone dreams possible. In either scenario, the dangers—and opportunities—could be enormous.

In this environment, you must keep a substantial portion of your money *liquid;* you must avoid, as much as possible, precisely the investments or programs that salespeople like to promote the most—the ones that lock you in. Try to:

- Steer clear of annuities and insurance policies that involve large start-up commissions or large surrender charges (cancellation fees).

- Avoid esoteric investments that are easy to buy, but hard to sell (e.g., limited partnerships, municipal bonds that rarely trade, penny stocks with low trading volume, "special" opportunities in start-ups or private investments in business deals, and so forth).

- Stick primarily with investments that are traded in large volume in open markets—that you can sell at any time, with no penalty.

Don't get me wrong. There *is* a place for a long-term plan that helps you build your wealth without the continuing drag and drain of taxes. Your money grows more quickly. You reach your goals sooner. You retire with more.

But tax deferral does not come without a cost. Nearly all tax-deferred investments require that you sacrifice liquidity. The IRS will hit you hard with penalties for early withdrawal of your funds before age 59½, and the insurance company charges additional penalties.

To begin with, don't put *all* your savings into tax-deferred investments. Use these vehicles only for a modest portion of your overall nest egg. This way, the bulk of your funds will stay completely liquid and under your direct and immediate control.

In addition, make sure that the money you do set aside for tax-deferred programs is money that you're reasonably sure will *not* be needed for living expenses and other needs.

Next, follow along with me as I help you ask—and answer—six key questions about annuities.

QUESTION 1: WHAT *IS* AN ANNUITY ANYHOW?

Insurers use statistics to make the odds. Then, they use those odds to determine how much you have to pay in premiums and what the payouts will be. You always bet against the house (the insurance company). No matter which side you want to be on–life or death–the house will take the other side.

Life insurance is actually a way for you to bet on death. It really should be called "death insurance," but the insurance industry decided long ago that such a name would not exactly be good for sales.

When you buy life insurance, the insurance company is betting–and hoping–that you will live longer. The longer you live, the longer they can put off paying the death benefits to your heirs, and the more they can earn on your money in the meantime.

Annuities are a vehicle for you to bet on your life–the reverse of life insurance. In effect, the insurance company is betting that you will die *sooner* than average. If so, *they* win the bet and make more. If you fool them and live longer, *you* win the bet and make more.

Why is an annuity a kind of insurance? Because it's *your protection against the risk that you might outlive your income*. What confuses most people is the fact that there are two entirely different kinds of annuities you can buy, and one of them isn't really an annuity at all.

Immediate Annuities versus Deferred Annuities

If you are near or at retirement age, you can buy an annuity immediately. So it's called an *immediate annuity*. This is the true annuity and functions exactly as described above. You pay a lump-sum premium *now* and start getting your monthly income checks right away.

The insurance company is, in effect, saying to you: "Give us your principal and we will give you a monthly check for as long as you live. If you live longer than average, you will receive more checks than those who don't live as long. If you die sooner, we pocket the difference."

If you are *not* yet ready to retire, but you want to start saving for that time, you don't need to put up all your money right away. You buy a *deferred annuity*. This is not insurance. It's not even a true annuity. Rather, it's an *investment-savings plan* in which you accumulate funds on a tax-free basis toward the *future* purchase of an immediate annuity.

Similarly, the insurance company that's selling you a deferred annuity isn't really acting as an insurance company. It's acting as an investment company that's competing directly with mutual funds and banks for your investment dollars.

Deferred annuities are not insurance. They're investments. The proof is that they come with the option to either (1) convert to an immediate annuity or (2) take the proceeds in a lump-sum settlement. If you take the lump-sum settlement, it's purely an investment from the first to the last day. You buy. Then you sell. End of story.

Indeed, many people who buy deferred annuities never intend to convert them into an immediate annuity. They use the deferred annuity as an investment vehicle and for its tax advantages. Then they simply take out the cash when they retire. Nothing wrong with that. Just make sure you recognize it for what it really is—an investment like any other.

Variable Annuities versus "Fixed" Annuities

When you buy a deferred annuity with an insurance company, you can either retain control over where your money is invested, or you can leave those decisions entirely up to the insurance company.

Variable annuities give you the control. You choose from a range of options (e.g., a mutual fund investing in stocks, a bond fund, or a money market fund), and you assume the investment risk. If the market value of your investments goes up, you reap the benefits. If it goes down, you suffer the losses.

In effect, you are investing in mutual funds affiliated with the insurance company—and with the additional advantage of tax deferral.

As with mutual funds, your investment is kept in separate

accounts that are segregated from the insurance company's general pool of assets. When you're ready to get your lump-sum distribution, you get your fair share of what's in those accounts, depending on the performance of the funds.

With *"fixed" annuities,* you let the insurance company make all the investment choices; and they assume a part (but not all) of the investment risk. Your money goes into a general pool. No matter what happens, the company guarantees you a certain bare-bones minimum result.

Two warnings: I put the word "fixed" in quotes for a reason. It's not really fixed. In addition, there's a big difference in the *safety* of variable versus fixed annuities. More on both of these in a moment.

QUESTION 2: DO I REALLY *NEED* AN ANNUITY?

No matter how attractive it might sound, and no matter what the salesperson may tell you, *buying an annuity is not a foregone conclusion.* Remember, when you invest in a deferred annuity, you are giving up some liquidity. When the time comes to buy the real thing, an immediate annuity, you are completely giving up your principal to the insurance company. It's irreversible and final.

There is another option: Instead of buying an annuity, you can direct your own retirement investments. To help you make this critical decision, let's take a closer look at how an annuity works and how it compares with other investments.

Let's say you put $100,000 in a deferred fixed annuity at age 50. And let's assume there are no front-end charges or maintenance fees. Further, let's assume the original crediting rate (yield) is 5 percent guaranteed for one year.

On the first anniversary of your policy, your account value will have grown to $105,000. So far, the account pays interest just like a certificate of deposit (CD), with the sole difference that you do not have to pay income tax on the $5,000 worth of interest income.

The problem is that the one-year guarantee period on your

crediting rate has now expired. So the insurer will reassess your rate. If interest rates are rising and their investments are performing well, they will probably raise your rate. But the company also has the option to lower your rates for the coming year if they feel a need to do so.

Sure, it is in the interest of the company to keep rates competitive, but if interest rates on competing investments are going down, theirs will probably go down, too. They can't drop your rate below their minimum guaranteed rate, but that's usually set pretty darn low. Then, each year thereafter, the company reassesses their investment performance and declares a rate for the coming year.

That's why the term *fixed annuity* is deceptive. I can't even count the number of people who have told me they didn't read the fine print and were shocked when their rate went down. They'd never let a mutual fund get away with a product name like that. The truth is that the rate is fixed for only one year at a time.

The growth in your account value will depend on the rate declared each year. For the purpose of illustration, let's say the rate is 5 percent in year two, and 6 percent in year three. Your $100,000 annuity would be worth $110,250 at the end of the second year and $116,865 after three years.

Now, let's say you need to withdraw some money. Under the terms of your contract, you are allowed to withdraw 10 percent with no surrender charges. That would be $11,686. If you need $20,000, you'd have to pay a surrender charge on the remaining $8,314.

Surrender charges for most policies start at 7 percent for the first year and decline by 1 percent each year (i.e., 6 percent in the second year, 5 percent in the third year, and so on), until you get down to zero charges in your eighth year and beyond.

So, if you are making a withdrawal during the fourth contract year, the charge would be 4 percent of $8,314, or $332. Your account balance now stands at $96,533.

You would also have to pay regular income taxes on the interest income portion of the funds that are being withdrawn plus a 10 percent tax penalty if you're under 59½. This is generally not as grievous as it sounds since you still have had the advantage of deferring the income taxes for the three years.

This is the most common example. And it's simple. But there are many policy features that can vary substantially from company to company and policy to policy that you should know about— surrender fees, other fees, and bailout rates.

Surrender fees. Although the most common surrender fees start at 7 percent and are scaled down to 0 percent after seven years, some companies charge more—9, 10, sometimes even 15 percent!

Even if you are fairly sure you will not need access to your money soon, don't even think about getting stuck in policies with such huge fees. Unexpected things do happen.

Bailout rates. While they are not as popular as they were several years ago, certain contracts offer a bailout provision in their annuity contracts. This provision allows you to withdraw all your funds without penalty if your interest rate drops below a set figure, such as 6 percent.

The bailout option will be especially useful if the rate decline is due to specific problems in the company's investments. However, if the rate drop is due to generally declining interest rates, you may not be able to find a comparable investment with a better return elsewhere.

Front-end load and other fees. Few policies now on the market carry either front-end loading fees (fees subtracted from your cash value when you first purchase the policy) or yearly maintenance fees. However, policies with between 1 and 3 percent in front-end loads and with yearly fees of $25 to $100 do exist. Avoid them.

Settlement options. Most policies provide at least two ways to use the proceeds of your deferred annuity when it matures. You can choose between two options:

1. *Lump-sum withdrawal.* You take out all of your accumulated cash values when the contract matures or at retirement.
2. *Annuitization.* You convert it into an income annuity, putting you in the same situation as someone who is buying an immediate annuity. This will typically pay out the

funds to you monthly for the rest of your life. The actual amount of the monthly check will depend on the investment climate at the time of annuitization. As a result, most policy illustrations will show both a guaranteed payout (the minimum the company will offer) and a current rate payout (the amount it would be if the current interest rate were in effect at the time of annuitization).

QUESTION 3: TO ANNUITIZE OR NOT TO ANNUITIZE?

The term of your deferred annuity is up, and you face a decision: Do I take all my money in a lump sum? Or do I annuitize (i.e., use the money to buy an immediate annuity)? Even if you don't have a deferred annuity, and you're at or near retirement age, your question is similar: Do I buy an immediate annuity, or not?

Whatever you decide, don't be overly influenced by insurance agents, stockbrokers, or financial planners who sell annuities. Two warnings include:

- A lot more depends on *your* individual circumstances than the salesperson may indicate. For example, if you feel you're healthier than the average person, or you come from a family of people who usually enjoy long life, annuities have an additional advantage to you, beyond the standard advantages. Otherwise, the annuity may have additional *dis*advantages for you.

- Many salespeople will push the annuity that will give them the largest commission, not necessarily the one that's best for you.

Aside from a short grace period (which may vary from 10 to 30 days, depending on each state's laws), once you've bought an immediate annuity, that's it. You're in for life.

If you can accept this disadvantage, the advantages are still worth considering:

Advantage 1: Loved ones can be provided for. You can purchase an annuity called a *joint and survivor annuity*. In that way, some or all of the annuity income will continue going to the survivor when the original annuitant dies. Also, with one of the most common contracts, called "10-year certain and life," monthly checks keep coming for a minimum of 10 years and for as long as you live thereafter. If you die before the 10-year period is up, the checks are sent to a designated beneficiary for the balance of the 10-year period.

Some companies may give you the option of buying a certain and life annuity that ranges between 5 and 20 years. The payout amounts differ from company to company, perhaps by as much as $60 a month on a $100,000 annuity. So compare monthly income payments carefully.

Advantage 2: Reduced income taxes. You may have to pay taxes on as little as one-third of your monthly check, depending on your contract and your age. If you're in a 28 percent tax bracket, for example, and your monthly annuity check is $400, you may only owe taxes on approximately $130. So all you'd owe Uncle Sam each month is about $36. (However, in some states you may have to pay premium taxes.)

Advantage 3: Favorable monthly cash flow compared with CDs. Assume a 70-year-old widow in the 28 percent tax bracket invests in a $50,000, 5-year CD yielding 5 percent. She makes about $2,500 per year in interest, leaving about $1,800 in after-tax income.

By contrast, if she bought a $50,000 immediate 10-year certain and life annuity, she could get a check for roughly $385 a month, or $4,620 a year. The key is that this includes both interest and principal. The interest portion is $143, which after taxes, gives her $103 per month, or $1,236 per year. Adding in the principal portion, the total money she receives comes to $345 month or $4,140 a year. That's a cash flow of 8.3 percent even after taxes.

Keep in mind that, with the CD, the bank will return your principal when the CD matures. In contrast, with the annuity, the insurance company keeps your principal and guarantees monthly checks.

Advantage 4: Annuity income for a lifetime. With other investments that pay out principal as well as interest (e.g., a Ginnie Mae bond), when you deplete your capital, the checks stop coming. With an immediate annuity, because of the insurance aspect, the payout of principal does not result in a cutoff of your monthly checks. You continue to receive the checks for the rest of your life.

The insurance company—which bases payouts on average life expectancies and the earnings on its investment portfolio—is, in effect, betting that the funds paid *in* will cover all the funds paid *out*. That's why it's so important to buy annuities from strong companies that can back up their promises with their own reserves if they miscalculate their earnings or their liabilities.

QUESTION 4: CAN YOU GIVE ME AN EXAMPLE OF A TYPICAL IMMEDIATE ANNUITY?

Let's assume the following:

- You're 65 years old.

- The immediate annuity costs $100,000.

- The payout is $850 per month.

- It has a provision called *10-year certain and life.* (This stipulates that payments are guaranteed for a minimum of 10 years and for as long as you live thereafter. In case of premature death, payments would go to your designated beneficiaries.)

Since the payout is $850 per month, your benefit amounts to $10,200 per year. After 10 years, you will have received a total of $102,000 and will have recouped your original $100,000 investment. In other words, the 10-year certain provision protects you against an outright loss of principal.

Now let's explore another route. Instead of putting your $100,000 nest egg in an annuity, suppose you put the money in a 10-year U.S. Treasury note.

If the average yield is, for instance, 5 percent, or $5,000, during the first year, your interest will be *less* than the $10,200 paid out by the annuity. But unlike the annuity, *you have not given up your principal.* You still have your original $100,000. So to maintain your income, you can simply withdraw the difference (i.e., $5,200) from your principal.

For the second year, your principal would be $94,800. Interest for the year would be $4,740, and you'll have to withdraw $5,460 to maintain your income level.

As your principal shrinks year after year, earnings will also diminish. To maintain your income level, you'll have to dip deeper into principal each year at an accelerating rate. *Eventually,* it will be reduced to nothing. For many people, however, losing their principal eventually is a lot better than giving it up immediately as with an immediate annuity.

Table 10.1 shows you what happens to your money. As you can see, your nest egg will be gone after 14 years. At age 78, you will either have to reduce your living standard or look for another income source. If you live beyond 78, you'd be better off with an annuity. If you don't live past 78, you'd be better off with a self-directed investment program.

(***Note:*** For this illustration, I have assumed that when you cash out your annuity, it has been in force for at least 10 years and you are at least 59½ years of age. If these conditions are not met, your proceeds may be subject to a substantial excise tax. Review the matter with your tax advisor.)

Table 10.1   The Disadvantage of a Bond Instead of an Annuity

Your Age	Principal at Beginning of Year	Interest	Withdraw Enough Principal to Equal	Principal at End of Year
65	100,000	5,000	10,200	94,800
66	94,800	4,740	10,200	89,340
67	89,340	4,467	10,200	83,607
68	83,607	4,180	10,200	77,587
69	77,587	3,879	10,200	71,267
70	71,267	3,563	10,200	64,630
71	64,630	3,232	10,200	57,662
72	57,662	2,883	10,200	50,345
73	50,345	2,517	10,200	42,662
74	42,662	2,133	10,200	34,595
75	34,595	1,730	10,200	26,125
76	26,125	1,306	10,200	17,231
77	17,231	862	10,200	7,892
78	7,892	395	8,287	0

This illustrates the one big *disadvantage* of putting your money in a bond instead of an annuity: As you draw down from your principal to cover expenses, its ability to generate interest for you will also diminish over time. The annuity helps insure you against this problem. But don't forget the big advantage of a bond: You retain control over the asset at all times. That means you can sell it at any time and pull out all the remaining cash. You can't do that with an annuity.

QUESTION 5: HOW CAN I MAKE SURE MY INSURANCE COMPANY DOESN'T DIE BEFORE I DO?

One of the greatest tragedies of our times is that many investors have gone through all the sacrifices of planning for retirement, only to find out that their insurance company has died before they do.

A few years ago, the phone rang at the home of Vincent Triglia in Jamestown, New York. A friendly salesman at a local bank said that he had noticed Triglia's money sitting in CDs, and was calling to suggest another investment: tax-deferred annuities.

Mr. Triglia said he didn't want to put one penny at risk. The salesman said the annuities were 100 percent guaranteed, just like bank deposits—only better, because up to $500,000 per account was covered.

So as each CD matured, Mr. Triglia shifted all $350,000 of his savings into annuities issued by one insurance company, Executive Life of New York. At that time, the company carried a high rating from all the established rating agencies.

But later, when Mr. Triglia tried to withdraw $58,000 to build a home, he found that his money was frozen in a moratorium. After formally applying in April 1991 for the cash, he received a letter telling him that the New York State Insurance Department had just seized the company, following the collapse of its affiliate, Executive Life of California.

Mr. Triglia wasn't the only victim. Nearly 2 million American households suffered a similar disaster.

Don't let this happen to you! Before you even consider a specific annuity, look at the longevity of the insurance company itself. What good is it to buy a product with high yield and great payout promise, if the company doesn't stick around to fulfill that promise? What good is it if you win that bet with your insurance company, living longer than they expect, but they don't pay up? There are two ways you can greatly reduce this risk:

1. *Always check the company's Weiss Safety Rating.* If it's B+ or better, the chances of a failure are greatly minimized. Of course,

this is no guarantee that some of the B+ companies won't eventually run into trouble. But the chances are small, and we are bound to downgrade them long before insolvency.

2. *You can use variable insurance products instead of fixed products.* In variable annuities (and also in variable life insurance policies), the funds you invest are kept in separate accounts, segregated from the insurance company's general pool of assets. If the company fails, there may be some inconveniences and annoyances. But unlike fixed annuities and whole-life or cash-value insurance, you will probably still be able to take your money out normally.

QUESTION 6: I KNOW THERE ARE RIP-OFFS OUT THERE. BUT HOW DO I AVOID THEM?

When you buy a fixed annuity, you can accumulate a nice nest egg, tax-deferred. And when you retire, the insurance company promises to either give you a lump-sum check or send you a monthly check for as long as you live. But it won't work for you unless you avoid the most common rip-offs.

Rip-off 1: More risk than you bargained for. In the early 1990s, many investors in Executive Life of California, Mutual Benefit Life, and other large insurance companies that failed lost up to half their principal. That wasn't so long ago. And if it happened once, it can certainly happen again.

The money you invest in fixed annuities is inseparable from the insurance company's general pool of funds. So if your insurer fails, you could meet a similar fate.

Rip-off 2: High surrender charges that lock you in. If you cancel during the first year, you will be hit with a surrender charge between 5 and 10 percent of your principal. That's a big loss just for changing your mind.

Although the charge typically diminishes by one point each year, it still means annuities are far from liquid. To avoid or reduce these charges, do the following:

- Make sure that you invest strictly funds that you definitely will not need in the short or medium term.
- Stick with annuities with surrender charges of 7 percent or lower.
- Favor annuities that will allow you to take out a portion of your funds, typically 10 percent each year, with zero surrender charges.
- Look for those annuities that will at least let you withdraw your money if you are hospitalized or confined to a nursing home for a certain period of time.

Rip-off 3: Front-end loads. Some companies advertise "no surrender charges." The implication is that you're free to cancel anytime you want. The catch is that, in order to get in the door, they charge huge *front-end* loads, which you sacrifice immediately, whether you cancel later or not. I found one with a front-end fee as high as 15 percent!

Rip-off 4: Teaser rates. Some companies lure investors with high first-year rates. Then they lock the door with steep surrender penalties, which continue even after the rate drops sharply.

You'd think these gimmicks would be the exception, not the rule. But New York City insurance consultant Glenn Daily found that two-thirds of the annuities that pay the highest rates at the outset fall to below-average rates after the renewal period.

Always ask: "What rate are your one-year-old policies paying right now?" But, remember, a rate that is too high may reflect higher risks.

Rip-off 5: Misleading policy illustrations. The problems here are similar to those described in the previous chapter. The illustrations may do the following:

- Exaggerate the real returns you can expect by making optimistic assumptions about the future level of interest rates.

- Disguise the fact that mortality charges and expenses can change, potentially draining the account value severely.
- Fail to disclose whether their policies have performed as well as their policy illustrations.

Shop around! There are hundreds of different annuity products available. There are over 100 companies with a Weiss Safety Rating of B+ or better. Bear in mind, though, that the safest companies don't always offer the best deals. Before you buy from them, always weigh the costs and the benefits, using the questions and answers in this chapter as a guide.

CHAPTER

11

THE CASE AGAINST TAX-EXEMPT BONDS

The great irony of megabillion-dollar scams by large, well-established financial institutions is that they can go on for years, even decades, before the public finally finds out about them. What's even more ironic is that industry insiders and regulators are often very aware of the hanky-panky, but they are afraid to say or do much about it. That's exactly what happened in the Great Stock Market Scam of the 1990s. The Securities and Exchange Commission (SEC) knew about the problem for years. They even reported the study, discussed in Chapter 1, showing that only 1 percent of Wall Street's ratings were "sell" ratings. Unfortunately, running studies is one thing–taking action is another.

The sad reality is that as long as stock prices kept going up and everyone was making money, no one seemed to care. It was all just one, big inside joke. Now, the truth is out and it's not funny. But it's too late–$5 trillion in destroyed wealth too late.

You saw very much the same pattern in the Great Insurance Cover-Up of the late 1980s. Huge life insurance companies, supposedly *protecting* policyholders from risk, were actually *taking* far more risk than policyholders themselves would ever dream of taking–by loading up with junk bonds and other risky investments.

Ironically, experts at the leading rating agency at the time, A. M. Best, knew all about the junk bond problem. They even wrote detailed, technical articles about the financial decline of the insurance industry in their own trade journal.[1] However, did they warn the public? No. They often didn't even issue warnings about the very insurance companies that were obviously the worst offenders, according to the General Accounting Office (GAO).

Experts at state insurance departments around the country also knew about the junk bond problem. They even set up a special office in New York City to monitor the safety of the bonds that life insurance companies were buying. But rather than expose the fact that some major life insurance companies were putting a large percentage of your money into junk bonds, they cooperated with an industry effort to cover it up. The truth finally came out. But again, by that time, it was far too late—6-million-policyholders-trapped-in-failures too late. I warned of these disasters before they happened. Now I warn you of another hidden danger.

THE HIDDEN DANGER IN TAX-EXEMPT SECURITIES

Like the junk bond debacle among the life insurers, and like the tech wreck on Wall Street, a danger has been lurking for years in an area of great importance to investors who are over 50: tax-exempt securities issued by municipal and state governments and related entities. It's only a matter of time before the truth comes out, and millions of American investors, especially retired, fixed-income investors, get the shock of their lives.

I can't say whether it will be as bad as the junk bond debacle or the tech wreck. Nor can I tell you when it will burst onto the scene. But as your author—and, in that sense, as your advisor—I feel obligated to point out the dangers of cover-ups like these that threaten you.

Right now, millions of investors yearning for tax relief have been told that tax-exempt bonds are the panacea. It's no wonder.

They feature not only exemption from local and federal income taxes, but they also provide all kinds of guarantees. Consequently, the tax-exempt bond market in the United States has grown dramatically—to 50,000 local governments and agencies, putting out more than one and a half *million* different issues, worth over $1.5 *trillion*, held by 5 million investors—mostly 50 and over.[2]

Tax-exempt bonds have been promoted more heavily by brokers than virtually any other type of fixed-income investment. They promote the tax exemption, the ratings, and the safety. They especially hype the insurance, which is supposed to protect you in the event of a default by the bond issuer.

What few people realize is that much of the tax-exempt market is built on a deception. It may be subtler and more complex than some of the other deceptions I've told you about, but it is no less deceptive.

HOW MUNICIPAL GOVERNMENTS CAN BUY A AAA RATING

It used to be that Wall Street rating agencies graded the tax-exempt bonds on their own merits. If a city or state was weak financially, its bonds got a weak rating. If it was strong, it got a strong rating. That made sense. But that's not how it's done today.

Let's imagine that you're the newly appointed finance officer for your city. You don't have much experience in this particular specialty, but you're determined to learn everything you possibly can.

On your first day on the job, you're told that your boss, the mayor, has a pet project. He wants to build a new, $10 million bridge, and the city council has agreed to go along with him. So your job is to raise the money by issuing some tax-exempt bonds.

The trouble is that your latest rating from Moody's and Standard and Poor's (S&P) is a low triple-B. It might even be on the verge of slipping to double-B, which would be considered junk. With that kind of a rating, your chances of raising any decent money in this market are not good. And even if you did get all the money you needed, you'd probably have to pay far too much in interest.

You've heard, however, that there's actually a way you can *buy* a top-notch, triple-A rating. All you have to do is sign up for municipal bond insurance. You call one of the leading insurance companies that specialize in this kind of insurance and probe for more details.

The conversation could go as follows: "Here's the deal," says the company's rep. "We guarantee the interest and principal to your investors, and then we pass on our own rating to your bond. Since our rating is triple-A, both from Moody's and S&P, you get a triple-A, too."

You respond with a mixture of delight and skepticism: "Let me get this straight. Moody's and S&P give *us* a lousy rating. But they give *you* a great rating. All I have to do is sign up with you, and my city gets to use *your* great rating instead of our lousy one?!"

"Exactly," responds the rep.

But you're still concerned. "Won't investors see our bad rating and start asking some embarrassing questions about this little arrangement?"

"No. Few investors will ever see your bad rating. They will only see ours. Our triple-A rating will be *your* triple-A rating. Period. You will be part of our family."

"Okay, but suppose we run into some financial difficulty and our own, *real* rating is downgraded to the junk-bond level. Then what?"

"Not to worry," says the rep reassuringly. "We stand behind you. Your bond rating will always be our bond rating. Our contract with you is binding for the life of the bond. We can never cancel. Even if your city goes bankrupt, your rating will always be our rating."

You think for a moment and then query: "Wait a minute. Suppose S&P and Moody's downgrades *your* company's rating? Then what?"

You hear a faint sigh. "Look," he says, "I don't know what your problem is. Our rating has *always* been triple-A, and always *will* be triple-A. We guarantee thousands of tax-exempt issues. If Moody's or S&P ever downgraded us, they'd be downgrading every one of those issues in one fell swoop. Can you imagine the chaos that would cause in the muni bond market? Every single investor holding those bonds would suffer a loss as their market prices plunged to reflect the downgrade—not to mention the shock to confidence in the entire muni bond marketplace."

Again a sigh, this time for emphasis, and then his concluding statement: "Moody's and S&P will never do that. They're not that dumb."

THE FUNDAMENTAL FLAWS OF MUNICIPAL BOND INSURANCE

When I first heard a similar pitch many years ago, I didn't just think they were dumb—I was downright dumbfounded. The idea that "they will never downgrade because it would result in chaos" assumes that *they* have godlike powers to control the underlying fundamental changes that naturally mandate those ratings downgrades. Obviously, they don't.

Indeed, when I dissected the arguments for municipal bond insurance, I uncovered the same kind of fiction as I uncovered in the Great Insurance Cover-Up of the early 1990s, and in the Great Stock Market Scam of the late 1990s: a thin veneer of feel-good ratings, on top of what could be a financial house of cards. Think through this and you, too, will see the following series of flaws in the system:

Flaw 1: As the investor, you are being given the wrong ratings. You're rarely told the underlying rating of the tax-exempt bond (i.e., the rating of the bond without the insurance or credit enhancement). Instead, the rating you get is strictly the rating of the municipal bond insurance company.

This is backward. You should *first* be given the actual rating of the municipal bond. *Then,* they should give you the rating of the insurance company, as secondary information. Instead, the real bond rating is suppressed and only the insurance company rating is cited.

This poor disclosure, in itself, is a source of serious concern. Just as you saw in the Great Stock Market Scam and in the earlier Great Insurance Cover-Up, it creates a *bubble of false confidence*. But when you least expect it, the truth always comes out, and the bubble pops. Investors panic. Markets collapse. Big players go broke.

One would think that Wall Street firms would have learned by now that it's wiser just to tell the truth up front and avoid big surprises down the road. Unfortunately, they haven't.

Flaw 2: A tax-exempt muni bond continues to keep its triple-A rating, even if it becomes a junk bond. Right now, the muni bond insurers don't cover many junk bonds. That could easily change, though, because these insurers *do* cover a large number of triple-B muni bonds—the ones that are just one grade above junk. In a deep recession, if the many triple-B municipalities fall on hard times, all it would take is one downgrade in their underlying ratings, and suddenly the municipal bond insurers would be guaranteeing the principal and interest payment on a vast number of junk munis.

Flaw 3: No way of accurately estimating long-term risks. As you saw, these insurance contracts are irrevocable for the life of the bond, which can be up to 30 years. The trouble is that a heck of a lot can happen in 30 years! The municipality, or the entire country, could fall onto hard times.

Suppose, for example, that we experience worldwide recession. And suppose the recession causes falling tax revenues in thousands of U.S. cities, leading to a wave of defaults on their municipal bonds. Would the municipal bond insurance companies have enough capital to cover it? No one knows—the last time there was a severe municipal crisis in the United States, there was no such thing as municipal bond insurance.

Flaw 4: Overrated bonds are overpriced bonds. Lower-grade municipal bonds of the same maturity and coupon naturally cost less than higher-grade municipal bonds.

Therefore, when a bond is downgraded, its market price immediately has to fall to reflect the downgrade. If you're holding on to the bond, you have two choices: Either (1) sell and accept the loss, or (2) hold and accept the risk that your bond could fall further and even default. I don't think you'd like either option very much.

Flaw 5: Incest–The bond rating agency and insurance rating agency are one and the same. The Wall Street agencies that rate the municipal bonds–S&P and Moody's–are the very same companies that rate the municipal bond insurers. This, in itself, is an incestuous situation that can bias their ratings process.

If S&P or Moody's downgrades just one municipal bond insurance company, they would have to immediately downgrade all the bonds that the company covers–like a row of dominoes. This would not only hurt the municipal bonds, but it would undermine their own business, which often depends upon the high fees charged to each municipal bond issuer seeking their ratings.

Fees for municipal issues range all the way from $2,000 to $55,000, depending on the size of the issue. Each municipal bond insurer covers up to $25 billion in par insured issues. If the rating agency lowers the grade on one of these insurers, it will automatically antagonize the hundreds of covered cities and states, which would also be downgraded. With a downgrade of just one institution, the rating agency would be jeopardizing millions in revenues.

In the Great Insurance Cover-Up, we saw the same situation. Apparently, A. M. Best and S&P were reluctant to downgrade obviously weak companies until it was too late. By that time, the companies had already failed, and investors were already trapped.

Flaw 6: More incest. The muni bond insurers not only *insure* municipal bonds, they also *invest* heavily in municipal bonds with their own money. If something happens to the municipal bond market, they'll be hit with a double-whammy: more claims and falling investments at the same time.

Flaw 7: Old, shaky theories. All three rating agencies (A. M. Best, Moody's, and S&P) base much of their bond insurance rating scheme on one single, unpublished Ph.D. dissertation: *The Postwar Quality of Municipal Bonds,* submitted by George H. Hempel at the University of Michigan in 1964, along with an update by the same author, titled *The Postwar Quality of State and Local Debt,* published in 1971.

I don't question the author's conclusion for that period of time. However, since then, we have seen some major changes in municipal bond finances, mostly for the worse. Specifically, in the 1960s and 1970s, the total amount of revenues received by state and local governments usually exceeded the total amount of debt they had outstanding. That was good. It meant that one year of revenues could theoretically pay off all of their debts. In the modern era, the reverse is true: The total debt outstanding of state and local governments has almost invariably exceeded their revenue.[3]

My conclusion is that tax-exempt bond insurance is largely a farce, and the insured bond industry is mostly a bubble.

WHAT ABOUT NONINSURED MUNICIPAL BONDS?

If insured municipal bonds are problematic, what about noninsured bonds? First, you should know that *the municipal bond market is the nation's least regulated securities market,* even though investors, the majority of whom are individuals over 50, hold a whopping $1.6 trillion worth of these debt issues.

If you invest in a stock, you can use the Internet to examine the quarterly and annual financial statements that public companies file with the SEC. However, when you invest in a municipal bond, it's a different story. The municipalities aren't required to disclose financial information more than once a year, often with as much as a six-month lag. That information can be hard for you to obtain because it isn't filed with the SEC. What's worse, some bond issuers fail to release any financial reports at all.

The Bond Market Association has formed a task force to help improve disclosure practices.[4] But because of the vast size of the market, ranging from villages looking to buy fire trucks to states funding power generators, it's going to be a long haul. Don't hold your breath.

Despite all this, the assumption has always been that investing in a government entity, no matter how small, is somehow safer than investing in a private corporation. The many disasters that have occurred over the years belie that notion.

New York City.   When the SEC investigated the city's fiscal crisis of the mid-1970s, the staff determined that the city had serious, undisclosed, financial problems, even while underwriters were distributing over $4 billion in short-term securities.

WPPSS.   A decade later, while investigating the default of securities issued by the Washington Public Power Supply System (WPSS), the SEC found that the Wall Street brokers who underwrote the issue failed to examine the issuer's disclosures to determine the accuracy of statements to investors. Wall Street blindly sold $2.5 billion in revenue bonds. Ill-informed investors purchased the bonds on the basis of an old prospectus. They were not told there was ongoing litigation regarding the bonds' backing. Nor were they told that Moody's had suspended its rating on the bonds, and that S&P had placed the bonds on its CreditWatch list. As a matter of fact, investors weren't even told that the construction on the utility projects supposedly being financed with their money had been terminated. Many investors wound up with only 41 cents on the dollar.[5] Can this happen again? Absolutely.

United Medical and Surgical Supply Corporation.   After $16 million in bonds were sold to finance the development and construction of a retirement center, the bonds defaulted. It was only then that investors found, to their horror, that they were never informed of several significant facts. They were not told that the developer had been unable to obtain private financing for the project or that the project's underwriters had an incredibly *bad* track record with municipal bond issues for health care facilities.

Furthermore, at the time the bonds were issued, their project's underwriters were involved in 36 bond issues that were either experiencing financial difficulties or were already in default. Of those issues, 30 were for retirement centers or nursing homes. Investors were blissfully unaware.[6]

Other disasters. More recently, investors lost 90 percent of their money with $21.3 million worth of bonds issued by a municipal authority in Texas in 1998 to finance a water park. They lost 75 percent in $18.5 million worth of bonds issued by a Mississippi county to finance a home for the elderly. They lost even more in hundreds of other defaults.[7]

COULD WE SEE A REPEAT OF THE 1930S MUNICIPAL BOND DEBACLE?

According to George H. Hempel, in the Great Depression, 15.4 percent, or $2.85 billion, of the total outstanding state and local debt had defaulted by 1932.

That was just during the first three years! By 1938, $5.5 billion defaulted, or about 30 percent of the total in muni issues outstanding. This number includes defaults that lasted only a few days, such as New York. It also includes defaults that lasted a lot longer, however, and that were never completely resolved.

Can this happen again? Wall Street will tell you no. They say the situation was far worse in the 1930s, when real estate companies fronted as municipal units and promoted bond issues to develop their own real estate holdings.

They argue that there are numerous safeguards in place (e.g., insurance and more attention paid to ratings) that will prevent a repeat of that scenario. However, as shown in this chapter, those safeguards are not only flawed, they're actually a large part of the problem. Moreover, there are four serious structural weaknesses in the municipal bond market that offset the strengths and cloud the picture:

Weakness 1: Big deficits even in the best of times. By 2001, we had a full decade of nearly nonstop prosperity in the United States. Cities and local governments had the best of times. They enjoyed rising tax revenues. They had dwindling welfare expenses. They had everything they could possibly dream of to improve their budgets.

Or did they? Only momentarily. They had a $50 billion surplus in the mid-1990s, but they immediately splurged the money and let the surplus slip through their fingers. Just a few years later, by 2001, the cities and local governments in the United States were running close to a $100 billion *deficit,* one of the largest in 100 years.[8] (See Figure 11.1.)

The burning question is this: If city and state governments are still running huge deficits after the longest period of nonstop prosperity in America's history, what will happen in a severe recession? Many might not be able to meet their debt obligations, and a chain reaction of defaults is a real possibility.

Weakness 2: An abundance of unrated issues, with rising failure rates. Between 1990 and 2001, there were 917 municipal issues that defaulted, with a total of $9.8 billion owed. Of those, 780, or 85 percent, were unrated issues.[9]

Weakness 3: Illiquidity. Unlike the market for U.S. Treasury securities, the volume of trading in individual municipal bonds is often small. If there is any kind of confidence crisis in municipal bonds, such as a reaction to a slew of downgrades, the decline in prices could be very disorderly, trapping most investors with losses. This is a concern not only for individual investors, but also for the institutions, including the municipal bond insurance companies, who hold large amounts of these bonds.

Ironically, the very investments that many people have selected for their insurance protection could be among the

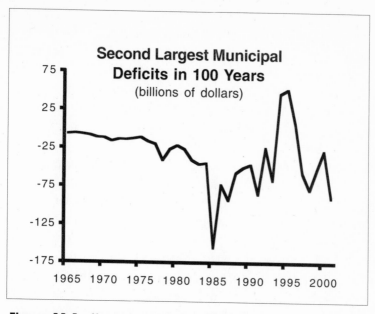

Figure 11.1 If you invest in tax-exempt bonds of state and local governments, a key question you should ask is: "What are they doing with my money?" This graph shows that most are *not* spending it prudently. As you can see, their finances have plunged from a $50 billion surplus to a $100 billion deficit, one of the worst in nearly 100 years. And this is *before* the decline in the economy! As these deficits increase, two things could happen: First, the cities and states will have to issue more bonds, creating an excess supply and possibly a decline in the market value of *your* bonds. Second, they are more likely to default on their interest and principal payments to you. The insurance companies that guarantee payment will probably have enough capital to cover individual defaults, but it is uncertain whether they will have enough to cover a sharp, nationwide increase.

(Source: "Flow of funds for the U.S.," Table F.211: "Municipal Securities & Loans," Section 36, Federal Reserve Statistical Release, Z.1.)

investments that suffer large declines. Many investors will simply not be able to get their money to safety in time.

Weakness 4: Ratings inflation. To avoid the dangers, investors rely heavily on ratings of municipal bonds. But the ratings themselves suffer from the following five deficiencies:

1. Insured municipal bonds automatically inherit the triple-A rating of the insurance company.
2. Rating agencies accept substantial fees from the municipal bond issuer to rate each bond. If they rate too many bonds poorly, they will lose lucrative business to the competition.
3. Most rating agencies give the issuers the option of suppressing the ratings if the issuer is not happy with the results.
4. Wall Street rating agencies seem to be making the assumption that the big operating deficits and other weaknesses affect only the unrated or low-rated issues. I disagree. Anything that weakens a substantial segment of the muni bond market also weakens the entire bond market. Any loss of investor confidence quickly spreads from one sector to the other. Price declines in unrated bonds force parallel price declines in rated bonds. There is no magic wall that separates the bad issues from good issues.
5. In recent years, we've seen several periods when the average ratings went up while the finances of the average municipality were going down. This is evidence of ratings inflation of the worst kind.

My overall conclusion is this: It *may* be true that most investment-grade tax-exempt bonds are not as dangerous today as they were before and during the Great Depression. However, I can say unequivocally that they are *far* more dangerous than most Wall Street firms would have you believe.

How to Buy Municipal Bonds

Brokers will tell you: "This bond is triple-A. It's insured. So don't worry about it." The main point of this chapter is that you *should* worry about it. The brokers are getting their money out of the deal now. But will they be around to help you get your money out if these bonds go sour?

You suffer the worst losses when a city or state defaults. But the situation doesn't have to reach that extreme before it begins to cause damage to your portfolio. Any downgrades will force down the market value of your bonds.

Suppose you need the money for an emergency. Suppose you want to use it for a better investment. Or suppose you want to get out precisely to avoid the possibility of a default down the road. Regardless of the reason, you may have to take a severe loss to do so.

How do you buy tax-exempt bonds? Well, if you feel you must have some in your portfolio, here are five steps that I recommend:

Step 1: Avoid all unrated municipal bonds. Don't fall for the argument that the extra yield on a "diversified portfolio of unrated bonds" will cover the extra default risk. This is the same argument that was made about junk corporate bonds. But then junk bond default rates surged, and they were proven wrong.

Step 2: Avoid all low-grade municipal bonds. Although I believe that the rating agencies may often be biased toward giving higher ratings than the municipalities deserve, there is still a value in considering the ratings. This is because, despite any bias, there is still a correlation between grade and quality. In other words, on average, a triple-B bond will indeed be inferior to a triple-A bond. I recommend only double-A or higher for uninsured bonds.

Step 3: If you own an insured bond, find out the underlying rating without the municipal bond insurance. Few people will tell you this, but you *can* find this information. Call Moody's at 212-553-0300 or S&P at 212-438-2000 and ask for the public finance ratings desk. Explain that you would like the rating of your issue without the credit enhancement. Be sure to have the exact name, maturity, and coupon of your issue. It would also be helpful to have its "cusip" number. Or, you can also get up to five ratings by e-mail, including the same information and sending it to ratings_desk@standardandpoors.com.

If the underlying rating is A, or better, this is okay; otherwise, look for an opportunity to liquidate. Remember, though, that many of these issues are illiquid. Unlike a stock, you can't just call your broker, say "sell," and expect to get out right away at a good price. Wait for rallies in the municipal bond market. Give your broker time to work your order and get the best prices for you.

Step 4: Two investments you can switch to. (1) Highest-grade short-term municipal issues, or short-term municipal issues covered by the strongest insurers, and (2) short-term Treasury securities or equivalent money funds. (See Chapter 4.)

Step 5: Stay on the alert for major buying opportunities. The best time to pick up bargains–and lock in high yields with safety–will be precisely when all of the weaknesses detailed in this chapter come out in the open.

A friend of Dad's, Ed Ball, was once able to pick up muni bonds in Florida during the 1930s for 10 cents on the dollar. When the market recovered just halfway, he made profits in excess of 400 percent in a very short period of time. Even if the next municipal bond crisis is only half as bad, you are bound to enjoy major buying opportunities. For the bulk of your money, I suggest you wait. Don't let the lure of tax exemption drag you into investments that may be fundamentally unsound.

FOR MORE INFORMATION ON MUNICIPAL BONDS

www.investinginbonds.com.

www.bondmarkets.com/ gives comprehensive daily updates as well as regulatory information. The site has a great Gateway links section, which gives an outline of all bond markets and how they work, as well as further links to other institutions.

You should check out the ratings agencies for industry updates at:

www.fitchratings.com/corporate/index.cfm

www.standardandpoors.com/index.html

www.moodys.com/cust/default.asp

Another great link for authoritative and regulatory links can be found at www.bondtrac.com/info/infoLinks.html.

The Municipal Securities Rulemaking Board has a site at www.msrb.org/.

CHAPTER

12

HEALTH INSURANCE DECISION FOR SENIORS: HMO OR MEDIGAP?

My father was a vegetarian from age 13 on and started his own daily routine of exercises at age 17. Seven decades later, he was still eating only fruits and vegetables and still doing his routine at 7:00 A.M. every day. At age 88, however, he began to have recurring, debilitating bladder infections. After some great effort, I persuaded him to go to the hospital for tests, and since he seemed so weak, they decided to keep him overnight.

Unfortunately, the hospital was under some financial strains and had just cut back on night staff. Dad called out repeatedly for help in the wee hours of the morning but no one responded. He finally said, "the heck with this," got up on his own, started walking toward the nurse's station, fell in the corridor, and broke his hip.

That was the beginning of the end for Dad. Despite emergency hip surgery, he could no longer exercise. He weakened, got more infections, and died several months later.

I should have known. Indeed, when I had started rating managed care providers a few years earlier, my whole thesis was that financial strains can lead to dangerous cutbacks in the quality of health care. Health maintenance organizations (HMOs) were among the most susceptible, with the highest failure rate of any financial or health care sector in America.

It's already been four years since Dad died, and I still haven't gotten over it. He was almost 89, and I'm 55–certainly beyond the midpoint of life. I am continually asking myself: What would it have taken for him to be around just a few years longer? When will my day come?

So in my world, nothing is more important than health. The only time money *does* rise dramatically in importance to me is precisely when it has the potential to impact the present or future health care of my family. I don't want them to get into a situation in which they have to depend on a doctor in a dark suit to decide whether they can see a specialist, or some folks in Washington to decide what prescription drugs they can buy.

Likewise, I don't want their health care costs to wipe them out, leaving next to nothing for their last years. Here's what I do want for them:

- A good chunk of medical bills covered. It doesn't have to be 100 percent. We can chip in a portion from savings.

- Protection against catastrophic, financially debilitating illness.

- Good quality of care now, and especially in their later years.

- Choice–if we don't like a doctor or a hospital, we want the right to go elsewhere.

Where and how can we get all this? I doubt it will be with an HMO.

The story I'm going to tell you is mostly about seniors, 65 years or older. But even if you're still a decade or more away from that age bracket, read carefully. The hard lessons that seniors are learning today are very relevant to decisions that you may have to make right now.

WHY MOST HMOS HAVE BEEN A DISASTER FOR MOST SENIORS MOST OF THE TIME

Don't get me wrong. There are some good HMOs providing wonderful service to most patients. At the same time, there are some patients who swear by their HMO, even though it may be among the worst. But my own personal experience, plus the overwhelming statistical evidence, shows that HMOs are best when handling standard, well-known, common illnesses, and when dealing with patients under 50.

If you're among the millions who have an uncommon illness, or even some combination of *common* illnesses, the chances are high that you will fall through the cracks of even the best HMO system, a situation that becomes more probable over age 50. If you're 65 or older, you're probably *unwanted,* period.

That's a pretty strong statement, so you're naturally going to want me to back it up with evidence. Here it is: Over 2 million seniors have been unilaterally dropped from their HMOs since 1998.

You see, back in the mid-1990s, when HMOs ran out of hot new profit areas to grow into, they figured the next pot of gold would come from seniors on Medicare, a program they called "Medicare Plus." As it turned out, though, the HMOs' foray into the Medicare world was even more blunderous than the life insurance industry's expansion into the investment world.

The HMOs' advertising pitch to seniors was pretty strong: "Sign your Medicare over to us. You'll get unlimited attention from our doctors. We'll cover everything Medicare covers plus much more. You'll never have to spend an extra dime, and you'll get much better care."

Their pitch to the doctors to join their network was equally strong, but it brought home the *opposite* point: "Sign up with us and we'll guarantee you a fixed monthly payment per head, called "capitation." But don't worry, the actual amount of time and care you'll have to give your patients will be very limited."

From one side of their mouths, they told seniors they'd get virtually unlimited care just by signing over their Medicare checks, and from the other side of their mouths, they told the doctors the payment would be capped, and the care very limited. As it turned out, neither was true. Seniors got lousy service, and doctors got taken for a ride.

The advertising was powerful and the HMOs signed up Medicare Plus patients by the millions. However, the product was a disaster. The entire system was doomed to collapse from the out-set, and in the late 1990s, it did just that: The HMOs began to pull out–abruptly and en masse.

To this day, they won't tell us precisely *why* they decided to pull out. It could have been the uproar from patients and the growing fear that Congress would crack down on the HMOs as a result. Maybe it was the backlash from doctors. I think the most likely cul-prit is bad profit margins for the HMOs, *despite* the fact they were squeezing both the patients and the doctors.

Regardless of the cause, if you were a Medicare Plus patient in the late 1990s, one day, to your great surprise, you may have found a terse letter in your mailbox from your HMO, stating simply that your membership would not be renewed the next January.

In 1998 and 1999, about 700,000 seniors received these Dear John letters; in 2000, another 934,000. By year-end 2001, another 536,000 got Dear John letters for a grand total of over 2.1 million seniors who were unilaterally dropped from their HMOs.[1]

"What did I do wrong?" asked seniors. More important, "What do I do *now?*" Unfortunately, not much advice was forthcoming.

Most HMOs simply suggested that the patient find another HMO. But that advice backfired as soon as the *next* HMO joined the lineup of HMOs dumping Medicare patients. As a result, some seniors found themselves forced to switch not just once, but two or three times.

At Weiss Ratings, we sent out a special press release with advice for seniors being dropped. We told them not to sign up with another HMO. Among the 237 HMOs we reviewed that opened their doors to Medicare beneficiaries in recent years, 147 had fully or partially abandoned the business by year-end 2000. That left only 90 HMOs that were continuing to maintain their current Medicare business.

Among those remaining HMOs, 37 were losing money, and only 22 had earned a Weiss rating of B– ("good") or better. So even if you could join another HMO, you'd most likely wind up getting dropped again, or worse, getting stuck with an HMO that was under financial pressure to cut corners on the quality of care it pro-vided. Seniors dropped by their HMOs suddenly found them-selves in a difficult predicament: Many were forced to pay substantial amounts for out-of-pocket bills that Medicare failed to cover. Or, worse, if they couldn't afford to pay, they wound up with substandard health care under some form of welfare.

MEDICARE SUPPLEMENT INSURANCE (MEDIGAP)

Medigap is one of the few brainchilds of the insurance industry that had a sordid beginning but a relatively happy ending, thanks to the intervention of the U.S. Congress.

When it was first launched in the 1980s, thousands of insurance agents fanned out around the country with the mission to sell as many policies as they could. The pitch was simple and compelling: "Medicare covers only 80 percent of standard charges. In addition, doctors and hospitals are now charging a lot more than what Medicare allows. So even if you're on Medicare, you're at risk of paying an arm and a leg for quality health care. Buy our policy and we'll cover the gap between what they charge you and what the government will reimburse. Plus, we'll cover many expenses that Medicare won't even touch."

The trouble was that no insurance company covered the entire gap, and each company offered a different policy with different twists, turns, bells, and whistles.

An agent would come knocking on the door of a 70-year-old widow living alone and persuade her to buy one Medigap policy that covered prescription drugs. Then another agent would come along and sell her another policy that duplicates all the coverages of the first, *plus* adds some coverage for hospital stays in Ouagadougou, West Africa. Each time, the woman would buy more policies from all those "nice, friendly young men."

The abuses got so bad that, in 1992, Congress stepped in and did something it had never done before: It established 10 standard plans, with standard benefits. Every insurer offering insurance in every state (except Massachusetts, Minnesota, and Wisconsin, which already had their own standards) had to abide by these standards—from the no-frills Plan A to the top-of-the-line Plan J.

This was very unusual, because the federal government doesn't have jurisdiction over insurance. It's strictly a state-regulated industry. Once, many years ago, the Federal Trade Commission (FTC) had an insurance division. But as soon as it started to poke into some of these abuses, the insurance lobby reacted fiercely, twisted the arms of a couple of congresspeople, and persuaded Congress to shut down the FTC's insurance division. However, Congress found a way into Medigap via Medicare. This was a product that was linked directly to a federal program. They figured they had a right to intervene.

The abuses promptly disappeared and Medigap grew into one of the most successful products for the insurance industry, with millions of policyholders nationwide.

All of the Medigap plans offer basic coverage, which is what you get with Plan A:

- If you stay in the hospital for longer than 60 days, but less than 90 days, Plan A covers the Medicare Part A coinsurance amount of $194 per day (in 2000) for each benefit period.

- For each Medicare hospital reserve day you use, Plan A pays the $388-per-day (in 2000) Medicare Part A coinsurance amount. *Hospital reserve days* are 60 nonrenewable hospital days that Medicare provides you and that can only be used once in a lifetime.

- After all Medicare hospital benefits are exhausted, Plan A will cover 100 percent of Medicare Part A eligible hospital expenses.

- If the need arises, Plan A covers costs for the first three pints of blood or equivalent quantities of packed red blood cells received each year in connection with Medicare Parts A and B covered services. Once you have met this three-pint blood deductible under Medicare Part A, it does not have to be met again under Part B.

- After your $100 annual Medicare Part B deductible is met, Plan A will cover the coinsurance amount for Medicare-approved medical services, which is generally 20 percent of the approved amount.

Plans B through J add a series of other benefits incrementally, with Plans H, I, and J being the only ones that provide some prescription drug coverage. But the drug benefits are limited and add a lot to your premium costs. Table 12.1 outlines all 10 plans with their benefits.

You Can Save a Small Fortune On Your Medigap Insurance

With these neatly designed and universally followed standards, you'd think the premiums from company to company wouldn't vary all that much. Medigap plans are like standard unleaded gasoline, medium-grade, and high-test. If the Exxon gas station on the corner of Olive and Main charges $1.56 per gallon, the Mobil station across the street can't get away with charging $2.99 for what is essentially the same product. Obviously.

Unfortunately, that's not what happened with Medigap insurance. Although the product specs were just as standardized as American gasoline, the prices have forever been *all over the lot*. The simple reason is that the industry's penchant for secrecy took over, and they failed to make their prices widely available to consumers to compare.

Since consumers can't readily compare prices, they can't shop around. And since they can't shop around, it is easy for insurers to charge pretty much whatever they please. Some insurers slash prices on a couple of Medigap plans to help bring in new customers for their other higher-profit products. Other insurers really didn't want to offer many of the Medigap plans in certain markets, but keep them on their shelf at outrageous prices, just in case some uninformed consumers might bite for them anyhow. So the price discrepancies are huge, as you can see from the following examples taken from the Weiss Ratings' database on Medigap pricing.

Assume, for example, the following scenarios: in June 2001, a 65-year-old man living in Fort Myers, Florida, goes to his agent and asks for the top-of-the-line Plan J. The poor man practically

Table 12.1 Medigap Insurance: You Get What You Pay For (Benefits of Plans A through J)

Benefits	Plans									
	A	B	C	D	E	F	G	H	I	J
Basic										
Part A Hospital (Days 61–90)	X	X	X	X	X	X	X	X	X	X
Lifetime Reserve Days (91–150)	X	X	X	X	X	X	X	X	X	X
365 Life Hosp. Days—100%	X	X	X	X	X	X	X	X	X	X
Parts A and B Blood	X	X	X	X	X	X	X	X	X	X
Part B Coinsurance—20%	X	X	X	X	X	X	X	X	X	X
Additional										
Skilled Nursing Facility Coinsurance (Days 21–100)			X	X	X	X	X	X	X	X
Part A Deductible		X	X	X	X	X	X	X	X	X
Part B Deductible			X			X				X
Part B Excess Charges						100%	80%		100%	100%
Foreign Travel Emergency			X	X	X	X	X	X	X	X
At-Home Recovery				X			X		X	X
Prescription Drugs								X	X	X
Preventive Medical Care					X					X

There are 10 standard Medigap plans—from the no-frills Plan A to the top-of-the-line Plan J. All Medigap insurers offer these same exact policies (but may not offer all 10 plans). The goal: to cover a portion of what Medicare doesn't. Here's how to use the chart: Starting at the top, run down the list of benefits and ask yourself: "Is this something I must have? Is this something I would *like* to have if it doesn't add significantly to my cost? Or is this a benefit I can easily do without?" The answers will help to guide you toward picking the right plan. *Warning:* The prescription drug coverage is very limited and expensive. Not worth it!

falls out of his chair when he hears the cost–$3,667.18 per year, with Physicians Mutual Insurance Company. He walks out frustrated and resigned to pay his extra medical bills out of his Social Security checks.

Too bad. Because if he could shop around, he would have found that he could save nearly $1,000 for an identical policy, also available to him in Fort Myers, from United Healthcare Insurance Company through AARP.

No one tells him that he probably doesn't need Plan J. Nor does anyone tell him that the extra prescription drug coverage of Plan J is mostly responsible for the higher premiums. He can save an even bigger amount simply by dropping down to Plan F or Plan G.

A 65-year-old man, living in Las Vegas, Nevada, has a similar experience. Premiums are a lot lower in Las Vegas, but he's still taken aback by his agent's quote of $1,543 for Plan G with United American. If he only knew that USAA Life would charge him less than half that ($778) for the same exact policy. His agent might be glad to tell him, but probably doesn't have the information handy.

For some people, a few hundred dollars a year may not be a big deal. But when you get older, and you consider the cost for both spouses, the dollars start piling up quickly. A 75-year-old husband and wife living in Tucson would pay a combined rate of $5,953.20 for Plan F with Reserve National Insurance Company, but only $3,479.60 with American Family Mutual Insurance Company. If only they had the access to the needed pricing information to compare these identical policies, they could save almost $2,500 a year. Over 10 years, that comes to $25,000, not including compounded interest.[2]

Give me a break. These policies are identical, plain-vanilla products that should vary only slightly in price. Unfortunately, it is very difficult for consumers to get the pricing information they need to shop for Medigap policies, making it possible for insurers to rip off consumers month after month.

When I first started telling consumers and the press about this years ago, the industry's response was that the policies aren't *truly* identical because of the different ways a company can raise rates for existing policyholders in future years. Some companies base their premiums on *attained-age* pricing, which automatically goes up as a policyholder grows older. So these are supposed to be lower in the first year but higher in future years.

Other companies base their premiums on *issue-age* pricing, which are promised *never* to rise for an individual unless they are raised for everyone in a particular group. So these are supposed to be higher up front, but less expensive in future years.

It sounds logical. But, in reality, some attained-age policies are actually more expensive than issue-age policies for the same individual and the same plan. For example:

- A 65-year-old male living in Dayton, Ohio, would pay $1,254.38 with Continental General Insurance Company for Plan A using attained-age pricing, but only $771.40 from Nationwide Life Insurance Company using issue-age pricing. One would expect the attained-age policy to be less expensive up front because of the greater likelihood of future premium hikes, but it's actually more expensive.

- Similarly, in McAllen, Texas, World Insurance Company charges $1,911.07 for an attained-age Plan F policy, but Christian Fidelity Life Insurance Company charges only $1,220.00 for the same exact Plan F using issue-age pricing.

- A 70-year-old male living in Morrisville, Pennsylvania, would be charged $2,075.80 by Guarantee Trust Life Insurance Company for an attained-age Plan C policy, but only $1,454.76 by Philadelphia American Life Insurance Company for an issue-age Plan C.

YOUR STEPS

If you have been dropped from your HMO this year, here's what to do:

Step 1: Don't resign from the plan until the end of the year. Stick with your existing HMO until December 31. If you drop out sooner, your withdrawal will be considered voluntary, and you will immediately forfeit certain kinds of guaranteed coverage for next year.

Step 2: Start checking into alternatives immediately. To avoid any coverage gaps, you will want to enroll before December 31 in a new policy that will take effect as of January 1.

Step 3: Avoid HMOs. Most HMOs have already started dropping their Medicare patients, and more are bound to follow. Among the remaining HMOs serving Medicare patients, many are financially unsound.

Step 4: Switch to Medigap. Provided you've received a letter of cancellation and don't withdraw until December 31, you are guaranteed eligibility for a Medigap policy *regardless of your health status*. Under this guarantee, you can choose among four different Medigap plans: Plans A, B, C, and F. Depending on your health, you may also be eligible for six other Medigap plans available. With Medicare and Medigap, it is unlikely you will ever get dropped again. Plus, you will have more freedom to choose your provider or hospital, and will benefit from better access to specialists. *Warning:* Your last day to take advantage of this guarantee is 63 days after your HMO coverage ends.

Whether you've been dropped from an HMO or not, I suggest you follow steps 5 through 8.

Step 5: Shop around for the least expensive Medigap policy that meets your needs. The cost of Medigap insurance can vary drastically by insurance provider, even for identical plans offering the same benefits in the same location. If the policy that your agent quotes for you is too expensive, don't give up. There could be much cheaper policies available with the same benefits. Urge your agent to find you the least expensive quotes.

Step 6: Don't overbuy. You may be able to meet most of your needs adequately with a lesser plan that does not have all the frills of Plan J. For example, Plan F, one of the most popular in the country, may be sufficient.

Step 7: Don't necessarily rely on your agent to get all the information you need. It is very difficult for agents to get quotes from all the providers in your area. If you have access to the Internet, go to www.medicare.gov. Then, in the upper left of your screen, click on "Search Tools." Next, select "Medigap Compare." If you enter your zip code, you will get a list of the companies that offer Medigap policies in your areas. However, this source will not give you the *prices* that would be offered to you, which vary depending on your location, age, and gender.

Step 8: Contact Weiss Ratings (800-289-9222). To help you shop for the least expensive and most financially stable Medigap policies, we offer the the *Consumer Guide to Medicare Supplement Insurance* ($49 per person). We will ask you to provide your age, gender, zip code, and county of residence. Then, we will generate a custom, 45-page report for you that gives you a personal shopping guide, unique for you, with all of the actual premium rates that are available to you for each of the 10 Medigap plans in your area.

Remember that the federal Medicare program will cover no more than half to three-quarters of your medical expenses. That's why private Medicare supplement insurance, or Medigap, makes sense. Its goal is to cover a portion of what Medicare doesn't. But in order for Medigap to make sense for you, you need to find the right policy, from the right company, for a reasonable price.

CHAPTER

13

WHAT ABOUT YOUR LONG-TERM CARE? DO YOU NEED INSURANCE? WHAT KIND? WHEN? HOW MUCH?

My first experience with nursing homes was the day I visited my grandmother at a home for the elderly in New Haven, Connecticut. It was a top-notch facility, cheerfully decorated, supposedly very well staffed. But I was both shocked and depressed. No matter how much they sugarcoated the facts, the harsh reality was that the institution had, in effect, taken Grandma's home, sold all her things, and carted her off to live with strangers.

Although she accepted her fate graciously, she absolutely *did not* want to be there. She participated unenthusiastically and sporadically in all the "glorious" activities, got almost no exercise, and died of heart failure several months later. And this was a nursing home paradise in comparison to the thousands of lesser or substandard facilities, where violations of federal standards have *quintupled* in the last five years.

Grandma and I were far apart in years—almost three-quarters of a century. But we had one thing in common that distinguished us from the rest of the family: We both came of age in less advanced, family-centered cultures where nursing homes were virtually unknown. Her village in nineteenth-century Russia was not all that different from the town in rural Brazil where I spent many years as a child–the same time-worn cobblestones on the main avenues, the same street trolleys, and the same custom of caring for the elderly at home.

I have seen both home and institutional care. I know the difference firsthand, and I can tell you, point-blank: Assuming access to medical facilities when needed, *there is simply no comparison in the quality of care.* Care involving dedicated family members is usually vastly superior; care in even the best-intentioned, best-equipped institutions can often be fatally inferior. Yet, for over a century, the focus of care for the elderly in America had been to build more and larger nursing homes.

Fortunately, now at the beginning of the third millennium, this is changing for the better. I'm pleased to see that new, alternative styles of long-term care have emerged in the United States, offering more opportunity for personal independence and family participation. I'm delighted to see that the options you and I have available today are both broader and more flexible than ever before.

- You can get *custodial care*–personal assistance with your everyday life. You remain in a residential setting and you continue to live independently. But you also have the advantage of some continuing oversight. If you need it, you can get assistance in your daily life–from shopping and cooking to getting out of bed, walking, eating, and bathing.

- You can step up to *intermediate care.* At this level, you'll get some supervision by skilled medical personnel–such as occasional nursing and rehabilitative care, plus basic medical procedures that are required on and off. But don't expect on-site, around-the-clock attention.

- That kind of 24-hour service is only available with *skilled care,* or *acute care*–the highest level and, as you might expect, the most expensive. This care is prescribed by a doctor and involves full-time supervision by a skilled nurse or therapist. The cost can be very high, but don't fret. Even among the 2.25 million Americans in nursing homes, only 5 percent require skilled care.

Not only do you have several choices for the level of care you will receive, you also have several choices of *where* you will receive that care:

- *At home.* This is my personal preference and, I trust, yours as well. I want to stay in my own home as long as I possibly can, and fortunately, that's going to be a lot more feasible today than it was during my grandmother's final days. Skilled care at home may be prohibitively expensive for you. But if you plan carefully, you can be among the millions of Americans who can be able to afford custodial and intermediate care at home strictly with Medicare and your own savings. Add in a Medicare Supplement policy and it should become even more affordable (see Chapter 12).

- *In adult day care centers.* If you've ever dropped your children or grandchildren off at a child day care center, you know exactly how this would work. It's the same concept, but for adults. Someone—it could be your daughter, your son, a grandchild, or even a transportation service provided by the center—would drop you off at the facility in the morning. There, you'd spend the day participating in activities. You'd get the therapies you need. And (hopefully!) they'd give you food that you could actually enjoy eating. The idea is that your family member can take care of you at home, while still keeping a full-time job.

- *In assisted living facilities.* No, it's not the same as your own home. But you can make it feel almost like your own condo. The idea is to give you immediate access to help when you need it. And if you don't need it, fine. As a rule, no one will be hovering over you or telling you what you can or cannot do. On the other hand, if you *want* (and can afford) *extra,* personal, VIP attention beyond what the facility typically provides, that's okay, too. You can have them arrange for your own private-duty nurse to come to the facility. Or you can hire one separately.

- *Through hospice care.* This is provided in your home or in a facility. The exclusive goal is to manage pain and symptoms of terminal illness. It is, no doubt, one of the most needed and most underappreciated services in this country. But beware that insurance companies and health maintenance organizations (HMOs) are coming under increasing financial pressures to cut short the large cash drain they suffer from caring for elderly patients with chronic diseases. And, sadly, one of the "most efficient" ways some have found to cut the expense quickly is simply by referring borderline patients to a hospice sooner than necessary. Needless to say, if the patient is not terminally ill, the simple act of referring the patient to a hospice is more than enough to *make* the patient terminal with great dispatch and speed.

- *Continuing care retirement communities.* This is a new option. These types of communities give you a combination of housing, health care, and social services. The setup can be similar to an independent living facility, a nursing home, or something in between. You can choose from various levels of care. And you can opt for different payment plans (e.g., all-inclusive, pay-for-service, and other such plans).

- *In nursing homes.* If you reached age 65 in the early 1990s, chances are less than 1 in 10 that you'll live in a nursing home for five years or more. If you reach 65 before 2010, the chances will be even lower. Clearly, spending your final years in a nursing home is not the sure thing that some people say it is.

That's good. Despite all the knowledge and technology we have nowadays, the overwhelming majority of the 17,000 nursing homes in this country are not doing a great job. They say they're understaffed and overworked. True. But with a few notable exceptions, I think a key problem is also the attitude of the administration. The patients need—and deserve—tender loving care. They're not getting it.

There are no federal standards for most long-term-care facilities, except for nursing homes that participate in Medicaid or Medicare. The trouble is that over half the nursing homes fall below the bare-bones minimum standards. This means "residents don't get fed enough. They don't get turned to prevent bedsores. They end up in the hospital much more often than they should."[1] And, *the number of government-imposed fines has quintupled in the last five years.* So what good are these standards? Not much, I'm afraid.

The good news is that you can get a government evaluation on almost any nursing home that's subject to federal standards. On the Internet, go to www.medicare.gov. Then click on the section "Nursing Home Compare." Also be aware that nursing homes vary greatly in quality and cost. There are two commonly recognized categories:

- *Skilled nursing facilities.* This is where registered nurses give you 24-hour service. You get more medical care, and you have better access to all kinds of therapies (e.g., physical, restorative, occupational, and so on).
- *Intermediate care facilities.* Here, the stress is on social and rehabilitative services. It includes some intensive care by registered nurses, but mostly lighter care by practical nurses.

Overall, this wider range of choices, despite obvious deficiencies, is a welcomed change. But no matter which option you choose, it doesn't come without a price tag. For example, ponder these shocking stats: Nine million Americans need long-term care right now, paying an average of $55,750 per year. And by 2060, the number of Americans needing the care will swell to 24 million, paying over $250,000 per year.

I told you that the chances of being in a nursing home for five years or more are low. But if you're 65 years old, chances are three in four that you'll use some kind of formal home care during your lifetime. *Those costs can exceed the cost of a nursing home.* This is especially true if the care extends over several years and covers more than a few hours a day. This raises some urgent questions, which are discussed next.

HOW ARE YOU GOING TO PAY FOR LONG-TERM CARE? CAN YOU AFFORD TO BUY A LONG-TERM-CARE POLICY? CAN YOU AFFORD NOT TO?

Will you be able to rely on family members for most of the care that you'll need? Will you be able to cover the balance of the costs from your savings?

It's easier to plan if you have a fixed retirement income. Assuming inflation doesn't pop up again between now and then, a fixed income helps you know ahead of time if you can cover the premium payments. Otherwise, you could wind up paying premiums on a policy for years, be forced to stop when you can't afford it any longer, let the policy lapse, and risk losing everything you've paid into it.

The same rules of thumb I gave you for life insurance also apply here: If you have to use your savings or make significant lifestyle changes to pay the premiums on a long-term-care policy, don't do it. It probably means you can't afford it.

How much should you have? On average, figure $25,000 to $35,000 in annual income and $75,000 in assets *per person* (not per household, and that does not include your home or car). Above that level you should be able to afford long-term-care insurance. Below it, Medicaid will probably absorb the costs.

To find out, call 202-690-5742 to get the toll-free number of your local Medicaid office. Or, if you have access to the Internet, go to www.hcfa.gov/medicaid/obs5.htm. Or check the Medicaid information page at www.hcfa.gov/medicaid/mcaicnsm.htm.[2]

NAVIGATING THE MAZE OF LONG-TERM-CARE INSURANCE

When you shop for long-term-care insurance, you are bound to be confused by the wide array of policies available. If so, you're not alone. When I first looked into this new industry a few years ago, I was confused too.

But it's not your fault or mine. In fact, I honestly believe that most insurance companies don't *want* you to compare one company with another or one product to another. That's one of the reasons they make every policy different from every other policy, and are continually adding new wrinkles and complications.

Some insurance agents will help you navigate this maze, whereas others may pull a different kind of wool over your eyes. These agents will tell you that long-term-care insurance is the "only way" to prepare for the unexpected needs that you may face in your later years.

These insurance agents either don't know what they're talking about, or they're deliberately misleading you. *Long-term-care insurance is just one of several options.* To find your way to the best solution *for you,* follow a series of easy, but detailed steps. Don't rush through them, and don't expect this process to be short. Take each step carefully and one at a time.

BEFORE YOU CONSIDER LONG-TERM-CARE INSURANCE

Step 1: Find out what Medicare will cover. Agents often spend a lot of time telling you what Medicare does *not* cover, and I can't deny they have a point. But they don't tell you much about what it *does* cover [e.g., 100 percent of the first 20 days of skilled nursing care (under certain conditions), the full amount of home health care expenses (under certain conditions), hospice care in your home, and more].

Step 2: Seriously consider Medigap (Medicare supplement insurance). This insurance was designed to help fill in the gap between what Medicare pays and what hospitals and doctors actually charge you. Unlike long-term-care insurance, you can easily compare one Medigap policy to another, thanks to standards mandated by Congress. But, like Medicare, it does not extend into nonmedical needs. Medigap can cover your prescription drugs, preventive screening, foreign travel emergencies, and other benefits, but it still does *not* cover types of services beyond those covered by Medicare.

For more on Medicare and Medigap, see Chapter 12. You can get an outline of exactly what medicare and Medigap cover by ordering a free copy of the *Guide to Health Insurance for People with Medicare* from Medicare at 800-638-6833. There is also an outline of what Medicare, Medigap, and long-term-care insurance cover in Appendix E.

Step 3: Try to avoid relying on Medicaid if you can. Medicaid *will* cover your long-term-care expenses, but only if your assets and income are below a certain level defined by your state. I don't normally recommend Medicaid because the quality of care is usually substandard. And even standard care can often be disappointing.

Nevertheless, many people jump through hoops to qualify for Medicaid. If they don't qualify because their assets are valued above the cutoff level, some people will "spend down" their assets, or transfer them to someone else.

If you have no other alternative, I cannot stop you from pursuing this strategy. But before you do, make sure you have *all* the info you need.

First, check out the facilities covered by Medicaid in your areas. Many are bound to be substandard. But maybe you'll be fortunate and find an exceptional situation.

Second, recognize that you'd be using up funds you could put to better use later to help cover some of your long-term-care expenses.

Third, for a certain period of time, you could wind up stuck in limbo, with too much money to qualify, but not enough money to finance your basic needs. In general, I feel *it's simply not a good idea to deplete all your assets.*

Fourth, if you are going to transfer assets, you have to do it well ahead of time, which could be a lot sooner than you'd like. You can't do it at the last minute and expect to qualify right away. Depending upon the type of asset transfer, the lead time required can vary.

Maybe you don't have to deplete your assets to qualify for Medicaid after all! If you're married, the amount you're allowed may be a lot higher than you think. It varies from state to state, so check with your local senior counseling center.

If you live in Connecticut, Indiana, New York, or California, you can participate in a Partnership Program. This program will let you buy approved long-term-care insurance and still qualify for Medicaid. It's set up so that the insurance policy is your first line of defense, and once you've exhausted its benefits from the policy, *then* Medicaid takes over.

Another advantage of living in these states is that you don't have to use your own assets or spend down to go on Medicaid. If you reside in one of these states, refer to Appendix G for numbers you can call for Partnership Program information.

CHOOSING A PLAN FOR LONG-TERM CARE THAT'S RIGHT FOR YOU

To assist you with the steps that follow, I have also provided the Long-Term-Care Planner in Appendix F.

Step 1: Don't buy long-term-care insurance too soon, or too late. Insurance agents are in business to sell you a policy now—not years from now. Many insurance agents will tell you that regardless of your age, you need a long-term-care policy *right now.* And they will argue that "the sooner you buy, the less it will cost you." But this pitch is both incomplete and misleading.

Sure, your premium will go up with age, but there's a lot more to this than meets the eye. Let's say *you* start paying premiums every month for 20 years before you start collecting your benefits. And let's say *I* pay premiums for only 10 years. Who's going to pay more in total—you or I? Even if the monthly premium you pay is significantly lower, the total amount I pay could be a lot less.

At Weiss Ratings, we studied this issue very carefully, and we found that the key questions at stake is: At approximately what age will your premiums be most likely to really start going up at a fast pace? On average, premiums rise gradually until you are in your early 60s, and then begin to take off at around the mid-60s. Table 13.1 and Figure 13.1 tell the story.

Table 13.1   Long-Term-Care Premiums Rise Most Rapidly after Age 60

Age	Average Premium
50	$736.00
55	$877.00
60	$1,169.00
65	$1,704.00
70	$2,646.00
75	$4,466.00
80	$7,280.00

Source: Weiss Ratings, Inc., Palm Beach Gardens, FL, based on year 2000 annual premium data provided by long-term-care insurers directly to Weiss Ratings.

At age 50, you'd pay an average of $736.00 for a comprehensive policy covering nursing home care, community-based care, and home health care with a 0-to-30-day deductible period, and a $100 daily benefit, for life. At 60, the price would go up, but not dramatically—you'd pay an average of $1,169.00 per year. But that's when the cost really begins to skyrocket. By age 70, you can expect to pay, on average, $2,646.00, or more than *double* the amount you'd pay at age 60 for the exact same policy.[3]

Strictly in terms of cost, it's clear that you should not feel a pressing need to buy a long-term-care policy until your early or mid-60s. It's equally clear that until that age, the longer you wait the better. The reason is simple: You're aiming at a moving target. You're trying to plan now for a set of circumstances in the future that are hard to predict. The longer the time between the day you buy the policy and the day you start collecting benefits, the greater the chance you will miss the target. Consider all the things that can change:

First, your needs. There are no guarantees, but as a rule it's going to be a lot easier for you to anticipate your needs when you're approaching retirement than when you're in your 40s or 50s.

Don't buy long-term-care insurance too early.
The best time for most people: when they're in their early 60s.

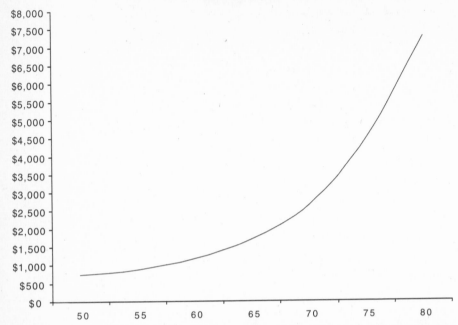

Figure 13.1 Most insurance salespeople will try to persuade you to buy long-term-care insurance regardless of your age. But buying too early has several disadvantages, as explained in this chapter. As you can see in this graph, on average, premiums begin to go up rapidly when you reach your mid-60s. So the best time to buy is usually in your *early* 60s.

(*Source: Weiss Ratings, Inc., Palm Beach Gardens, FL.*)

Second, the facilities. A major pitfall of long-term-care insurance is that *future long-term-care facilities may not fit the criteria of present long-term-care policies.* Indeed, the long-term-care industry is undergoing relatively rapid change. If you buy a policy, for example, at age 50 but don't use it until age 70, the types of facilities defined in your policy may no longer match what's available in your area or in the country as a whole.

Third, inflation. Economists and financial planners try to predict inflation. But it's more of a game than a science. They really have no way of knowing how quickly the cost of long-term care will rise. They don't even know for sure if we will have inflation in the years ahead (we could have deflation instead).

Taking all of this into consideration, my advice is simple: Unless you anticipate an unusual situation (such as declining health), start shopping for long-term-care insurance when you're in your early 60s (see Figure 13.1).

If you're younger now, it certainly is a good idea to learn all about it, but don't be in a hurry to buy. If you are already older, don't panic. Go through all of the steps I recommend, but do try to buy within, say, the next six months or so.

Warning: If you will need care within the next two years, the premium will be prohibitively high and the policy is also likely to include a long list of situations that are *not* covered (so-called exclusions).

If you decide that long-term-care insurance is right for you, do your utmost to buy a policy *before* the need arises.

Step 2: Recognize the importance of shopping around! The cost of long-term-care insurance can vary, even for the same person living in the same place, and you won't always know why. Sometimes the price differences are simply because the benefits are different. That's understandable. Often, it's just a reflection of the company's desire to increase or decrease its market share in a particular area, or of flaws in a company's pricing method.

The first rule in shopping around is: You usually get what you pay for, and you have to pay more if you want more. (More on this in the steps that follow.) The second rule is: If you shop around, you may very well be able to get essentially the same benefits for less.

To give you an idea of the range of price variation, our staff at Weiss Ratings conducted a survey of 17,625 premium quotes by 25 long-term-care insurers. As our standard, we compared policies with comprehensive coverage of nursing home care, community-based care, and home health care, a three- or four-year benefit period, a 0-to-90-day deductible period, and a $100 daily benefit. The premiums you would pay vary from state to state, but we took the national averages of all policies offered by each company. Our conclusion? *Some insurance companies will charge you as much as four times more for seemingly similar policies.* (See Table 13.2.)

Some of the price differences can be due to subtle differences in the policies. Some companies offer one price for a core policy with riders charged separately for additional features, while others offer higher-priced policies that automatically include the extra features.

**Table 13.2   Similar Long-Term-Care Policies but Vastly
Different Rates**

Company Name	Premium at Age 65 ($) as of 6/4/2001	Weiss Safety Rating*
United American Ins (Delaware)	1,366.60	A–
Conseco Senior Health Ins (Pennsylvania)	1,265.00	C–
Cincinnati Life (Ohio)	1,170.00	B
Continental Casualty (Illinois)	1,150.00	C+
Guarantee Trust Life (Illinois)	1,015.55	B–
IDS Life (Minnesota)	980.00	B
United Security Assurance of Pennsylvania	960.00	C–
Fortis Benefits (Minnesota)	902.00	B

Each of the plans in this chart offers similar levels of coverage, but at vastly
differing prices. So you can see the importance of shopping around! The core
benefits of each policy are: (1) Comprehensive coverage including nursing
home care, community-based facility coverage, and home health care
coverage; (2) four-year maximum benefit period; (3) a minimum daily benefit
of $100 or monthly equivalent for nursing home care, community-based facility
coverage, and home health care coverage; and (4) tax-qualified status.

*A = excellent, B = good, C = fair, D = weak, E = very weak.

Source: Weiss Ratings, Inc., Palm Beach Gardens, FL, based on third-quarter
2000 data filed with state insurance regulators, as well as some data provided
by the companies directly to Weiss Ratings.

For example, both UNUM Life's "Advantage I" policy and Pyramid Life's "Comprehensive Long-Term Care" policy include certain extra benefits such as a waiver of premium for facility care and bed reservation. However, each of the other policies also includes benefits excluded by the other. (More on the extra benefits follows.)

The price differences can also be because some companies are more competitive. Such is the case of Penn Treaty whose Personal Freedom policy is consistently less expensive than most of the competition. This is despite the fact that it offers some extra benefits, including an in-home family member benefit, a family member training benefit, a bed reservation benefit, and restoration of benefits.

Even nearly identical policies can vary widely in price. For example, comparing long-term-care policies offered to a 65-year-old in at least 10 states, we found that United American Insurance (Delaware) offers the most expensive policy at $1,366.60, while Equitable Life & Casualty Insurance (Utah) had the least expensive policy at $834.00. Both policies include the same core benefits and coverage of nursing home care, community-based facilities, and home health care.

Step 3: Reduce your cost by buying only what you think you'll need. Start by determining what type of care you think you will need *beyond* the assistance that your own family members may be able to provide–custodial care, intermediate care, or skilled care.

I know it's often hard to anticipate your future needs, but try your best. Remember that *custodial care* is provided by someone without medical training who helps you with daily activities. *Intermediate care* includes occasional nursing and rehabilitative care supervised by skilled medical personnel. *Skilled care* includes 24-hour care provided by a skilled nurse or therapist.

Step 4: Do your best to decide where you would most likely be receiving the care. Your choices include in-home care, nursing care, adult day care, or an assisted living facility. Most people prefer in-home care. However, if you have no family members to help you at home, in-home care could be prohibitively expensive, especially if it requires skilled care.

Nursing homes are designed for 24-hour care and are best used for short-term stays. Adult day care is an option, but will probably require someone, such as a family member, who can drop you off and pick you up daily.

Assisted living facilities are increasingly popular, offering a good balance between independence and assistance. Other types of care could include hospice care (for the terminally ill) or respite care (temporary assistance to help relieve family members).

Step 5: Check out the facilities in the area in which you plan to live, make sure you're comfortable with them, and find out how much they cost. The type of coverage you need will depend, among other things, on your health, your finances, and assistance you can expect from friends or family members. Check out the cost of facilities and services in the area in which you will be living. If you can narrow down the coverage and facility options, you will find yourself a long way through the maze.

For care within your home, contact a home care agency and ask them about the going rates for home nurses and therapists. Also consider costs associated with any modifications that may be needed for your home (e.g., wheelchair accessibility, handicap rails, and so on).

Step 6: Try to estimate how much of the long-term-care expenses you will be able to pay on your own per month. Your financial planner may be able to give you an estimate of your retirement income that would be available for health care costs. However, even a good estimate can be off the mark, so make sure your policy covers enough to avoid being financially strapped by long-term-care expenses. Later, make sure your agent takes this information into consideration, limiting your out-of-pocket expenses to what you have specified.

Step 7: Try to arrive at a reasonable guess regarding when you might start using the benefits. If you're in good health and you have a family history of longevity, set your date further into the future than average. In contrast, if you're already suffering from chronic health problems, you may need the benefits sooner rather than later. If you don't anticipate needing the benefits until more than 10 years from now, you can buy a long-term-care policy with an optional inflation protection feature to help protect against the rising cost of health care. This can add significantly to the cost, but you get what you pay for.

WORKING WITH A QUALIFIED INSURANCE AGENT

Step 1: Find a good, competent, and specialized insurance agent. Before you can purchase a policy, you need to find a good agent. That means interviewing several before selecting the one that's right for you. Some tips include:

- Do not limit your choices to those you happen to know about or who are associated with your broker. Shop around.

- Make sure the agent is *specialized* in long-term care. This is a very complex field, and you need someone who can clearly explain all the ins and outs.

- Listen carefully and make sure the agent's explanations are not limited to the policies he or she sells. If they are, look for another agent.

Step 2: Check my Consumer Guide to Long-Term-Care Insurance (800-289-9222). This report is not free, but so many people over 50 have asked me for help, I decided to create a consumer shopper's guide for comparing a large number of long-term-care policies with the actual premium you would be charged, based on your age and location. Or, ask your agent for the names of at least three different policies, from different insurers, so that you can compare. Unfortunately, there is *no standardization* among policies. This means you must read the policies carefully to determine exactly what will qualify you to receive benefits.

Step 3: If you're not using our report, have your agent check the safety rating for each company. It may be a long time before you begin to submit claims. Therefore, you will want to make sure your insurance company will still be viable at that time. If you use the Weiss Safety Ratings, you should favor companies with a rating of B+ (good) or higher, and you should avoid companies with a rating of D+ (weak) or lower.

Step 4: Favor companies that have more experience with long-term-care insurance. This shouldn't be a deal breaker, but favor companies that have been selling long-term-care insurance for 10 years or longer. You're better off with a company that has been offering long-term care policies for a while and has never raised rates for existing policyholders. In contrast, companies that are new in long-term care—or that have a history of raising rates on existing policies—are more likely to raise your rates in the future.

Warning: Claims of "no rate hikes" may be misleading. Insurance company literature often contains phrases such as: "We will not raise the premiums for your policy unless we raise the premiums for all policies in your class." Unfortunately, many companies and state regulators have no precise definition of a *class*. This allows the companies to manipulate the definition of class, giving them ample leeway to raise premiums at almost any time.

If you ask your agent: "Has the company ever raised the premiums on this policy?" you are likely to get a resounding no. But don't be satisfied with that answer. Typically, when a company applies to its state regulators to raise the premiums on a policy, it will also change the identification number of the policy. This technically makes it a new policy, even though it is nearly or exactly the same as the previous policy (except for the higher premium).

Given that the company or its agent can technically tell you that the premiums have never been raised on the existing policy, how do you make sure you don't get caught in such a ruse? Instead, ask: "Has this company ever raised premiums on this *type* of policy?" In addition, insist on literature with wording such as: "We will not raise the premiums for your policy unless we raise the premiums for all policies in your state." That's a big difference: Instead of all policies in your *class,* it should be all policies in your *state.*

Step 5: If you're considering buying a policy with your spouse, check how you qualify for a spousal discount. If both you and your spouse or significant other (not all companies cover significant others–make sure to ask and see it in writing) purchase a policy from the same company, some companies will give each of you a discount on your annual premium. Most companies require the policies to be exactly the same. However, men usually have different long-term-care needs than women, since women tend to live longer and be alone in their later years. If the company you are considering provides a discount when your policy is different from your spouse's, it's worth considering, as Table 13.3 illustrates.

Be sure you find out how to qualify for a spousal discount and how the discount is actually applied. At General Electric Capital Assurance Company, for example, the 20 percent discount is applied to each policy, and the two policyholders do not have to be married. At Equitable Life & Casualty Insurance Company, the 10

Table 13.3 Major Savings When You Buy Two Policies under Spousal Discounts

Company (State of Domicile)	Two Policies Bought Separately from Same Company	Two Policies Bought under the Spousal Discount	Discount (%)
AIG Life Ins Co (Delaware)	$1,710	$1,539	10%
Bankers Life & Casualty Co (Illinois)	$1,840	$1,564	15%
Continental Casualty Co (Illinois)	$2,047	$1,638	20%
Equitable Life & Casualty Ins Co (Utah)	$1,500	$1,350	10%
General Electric Capital Asr Co (Delaware)	$1,820	$1,456	20%
Physicians Mutual Ins Co (Nebraska)	$1,905	$1,762	7.5%
Pyramid Life Ins Co (Kansas)	$2,254	$1,784	50%*

Long-term-care polices aren't cheaper by the dozen, but they *are* cheaper by the couple. If both you and your spouse are ready to buy a long-term-care policy, or at least close, be sure to ask your agent about special discounts. The chart reflects "Total Base Premiums" (excluding inflation protection, etc.) for two individuals at the ages of 65 and 60 (whether female or male). It includes: comprehensive coverage of nursing home care, community-based care, home health care with a four-year benefit period, a 30-to-100-day deductible period, and a $100 daily benefit. They are national averages. So your actual premium will vary, depending on the state you live in.

*Discount is applied to the lower premium only.

Source: Weiss Ratings, Inc., Palm Beach Gardens, FL. based on year 2000 annual premium data provided by long-term-care insurers directly to Weiss Ratings.

percent discount is applied to both policies as a unit, and the benefits must be exactly the same.

Step 6: If you're not using our custom report, ask your agent for quotes on the monthly premiums. Make sure the quotes are based on the preferences and needs that you outlined in earlier steps.

Step 7: Find out exactly what each policy covers in addition to the basics that you require—in terms of custodial, intermediate, or skilled care. The actual policies that your agent has suggested may differ somewhat from your wish list of benefits, including some that you did not ask for, or excluding others that you wanted. This may help explain some, but not all, of the price differences.

Step 8: Ask your agent to give you a list of the types of facilities that are included and how they are defined. Facilities may include nursing home care, in-home care, adult day care, hospice care, assisted living facilities, and other options. *Warning:* There are no national standards for most long-term-care facilities. The precise definition of these facilities can vary greatly from policy to policy and from state to state. Consequently, if you buy a policy in one state and then retire to another, there may be no facilities in your new state that meet the precise definitions in your policy.

Step 9: Find out the basic terms of coverage and reimbursement.

Basic term 1: The elimination period. This is akin to the deductible on your other insurance policies. The difference is that the elimination period is measured in days rather than dollars. Just like other deductibles, you get to choose among several options, such as 0, 60, or 100 days. An elimination period of 60 days means that you pay for services for 60 days before your long-term insurance starts to pick up the tab.

There are two important tips: (1) Find out if the elimination period is separate and distinct for different coverage types, and (2) inquire as to exactly *how* the elimination period is satisfied. Are the days added consecutively as soon as you have triggered benefits? Or do only those days in which you incur expenses count toward the elimination period?

Confused? Then consider this example: Suppose you need care on days 1, 4, and 10. With some policies, that would be counted as only *3* days toward your elimination period. With other policies, it would be counted as *10* days, which would mean you'd start collecting the benefits much sooner.

How do you decide which elimination period is best for you? It depends entirely on your financial situation and how long you can afford to pay for your own care without depleting your assets. The shorter the elimination period, however, the higher the premium you have to pay on the policy.

Basic term 2: The benefit period. This is the length of *time* the policy will pay benefits. This can typically range from two to five years, and some may even have an unlimited lifetime period. Some policies, however, use a *maximum* total value of the benefits instead of a period of time.

Figuring out exactly the benefit period that you will need can be a complex exercise, but you can arrive at a rough estimate. First, try to anticipate how long you might stay in a nursing home or in whichever facility you anticipate needing.

Consider the national stats: The average length of stay in a nursing home is from 2½ to 3 years. Among the people 65 or older who entered nursing homes in 1990, only 21 percent lived there for five years or more. But use these stats only as a starting point. You are bound to differ from the national average, depending on your health and your personal circumstances. Your safest bet is to aim for a policy that pays for lifetime benefits. Then, if the cost is too high, cut it back from there.

Basic term 3: The daily benefit. This is the amount the policy will pay for each day of covered services. Choosing a daily benefit is not a simple issue, because the second part of the question is: What is the cost of the daily benefit you *would like* to have? And the third issue is: Can you afford it?

The best way to determine what you will need is to contact local nursing homes, assisted living facilities, and home health agencies, and ask them what their average daily cost is. Make sure you are checking with facilities that you would consider using. If you want to use nicer, upscale facilities, be sure to check into the cost of those.

Because this is not a simple equation, some plans give you more flexibility by offering a daily benefit reimbursable on a weekly or monthly basis. For example, if you selected a daily benefit of $100 reimbursable on a weekly basis, you would be reimbursed for up to $700 dollars per week in expenses no matter how much you incurred on any one day.

Step 10: Determine if the policy is a pool-of-money contract or not. Most current policies will actually give you more time to collect the benefits than indicated by the benefit period. For example, in a four-year policy, if you need care on and off, you may not use up all your benefits in that four-year period. So you could continue to collect those unused benefits in subsequent years as well. These are called *pool-of-money* contracts. (To calculate your pool, just multiply the total number of days by the daily benefit.) Other policies will actually end at the end of the four years, no matter what. Try to avoid these.

Step 11: Check into the requirements needed to activate the policy.   Before your policy begins to cover your long-term-care expenses, you have to meet what are referred to as *benefit triggers,* and these can vary from policy to policy. Under most policies, you will be qualified for benefits when you meet certain conditions: (1) the inability to perform activities of daily living (ADLs), which typically include bathing, dressing, transferring, toileting, eating, continence, and taking medication on your own; and (2) cognitive impairment.

But here's the all-important wrinkle: Some plans require you to satisfy *either* condition 1 or 2. Some require that you satisfy *both* conditions. Still others also allow for a third trigger, often referred to as *medical necessity.* This means that a doctor determines if you need care due to an injury or sickness. Make sure you find out the precise requirements of each policy. Clearly, the most liberal triggers, which allow you to qualify most easily, are the best.

Step 12: Find out the true cost and benefit of any other features that are included (or can be added by a rider) to the policy.   Extra features that you truly will need and use are fine. But when an agent persuades you to spend more money on bells and whistles that you're unlikely to take advantage of, he or she is doing you a disservice. Make sure your agent carefully explains each additional feature that he or she is recommending, and gives you the option to reject it or choose another policy that does not include this feature. The agent may tell you that it doesn't cost extra. Believe me, it does. Some commonly offered features include:

Inflation protection.   As with anything, the cost of long-term care will probably increase at least as rapidly as the cost of living.

If you're buying long-term-care insurance in your early 60s, you will probably not need this feature. But if you're buying the insurance 10 or 20 years in advance, then you may need the inflation protection.

You can choose between a *simple* and *compound* benefit increase. Under a simple increase, your benefit will go up by a specific percentage of your *original* daily benefit each year. With a compound increase, your benefit will go up by a specific percentage of your *previous year's* benefit each year. The percentage is usually 5 percent.

Assuming the current rates of inflation continue, the average annual cost of nursing home care is expected to increase from $42,000 in the year 2000 ($115 per day) to $80,000 ($220 per day) in 2010. If the policy provides a $100 daily benefit now, it would rise to $163 in 10 years.

This protection doesn't come cheap, however. On average, a 65-year-old who wants to buy a typical comprehensive policy (four-year benefit period, a 30-to-100-day deductible period, with a $100 daily benefit) would pay a yearly premium of $2,015 with the inflation protection feature. For the same exact policy *without* the inflation protection, the price would drop to an average of $1,125.

Warning: If we experience deflation in the years ahead, the extra premiums that you've paid for inflation protection will have been wasted. Also, premiums that include the inflation protection feature can also vary widely. Shop around. Check out the examples in Table 13.4.

Waiver of premium. After you receive long-term-care services for a designated period of time, some policies waive payment of your premiums while you receive benefits. Other companies waive your premium forever once you've been in a nursing home for a certain period of time, even if you completely recover. Many companies break this benefit down between nursing home care and home care services. This is an excellent feature. But it costs, and it's often bundled into a policy whether you want it or not.

Nonforfeiture. Suppose it turns out you don't need the benefits provided by your long-term-care policy. Or suppose you decide that the premiums are too high. You may want to stop paying the premiums. Well, some policies will give you a partial refund of your premiums. Other companies reduce your benefit period or benefit amount if you cancel because of increased premiums. Again, this nonforfeiture feature is a nice benefit to have.

Table 13.4   The Cost of Inflation Protection Is Very High

Company	Domicile State	Total Premium with Inflation Protection	Total Premium without Inflation Protection
AIG Life Ins Co	Delaware	$1,670	$1,010
Bankers Life & Casualty Co	Illinois	$2,047	$1,073
Bankers United Life Asr Co	Iowa	$1,950	$1,054
Equitable Life & Casualty Ins Co	Utah	$1,251	$834
General Electric Capital Asr Co	Delaware	$1,930	$1,070
Physicians Mutual Ins Co	Nebraska	$1,798	$1,097
Pyramid Life Ins Co	Kansas	$2,859	$1,313
United American Ins Co	Delaware	$2,561	$1,366

The amount that your long-term-care insurance policy will pay for your care is fixed at a maximum figure, even if the cost of care goes up with inflation or for any other reason. The only way you can protect yourself is by paying extra for inflation protection. Unfortunately, plans including this protection can be prohibitively expensive.

Source: Weiss Ratings, Inc., Palm Beach Gardens, FL, based on year 2000 annual premium data provided by long-term-care insurers directly to Weiss Ratings.

But it does boost your cost. If you have done your homework and bought only the benefits you will really need and can truly afford, you shouldn't have to spend the extra money for this feature.

Restoration of benefits.   If you can avoid using any benefits for a period of, for example, six full months, some policies will restore your full benefit period. Let's say, for example, that you have a policy with a three-year benefit period. And let's say you've spent one year in a nursing home. With this feature, if you spend the next six months without any care, your full three-year benefit period would be restored. But this particular situation is actually very unusual, so I certainly wouldn't make my decision to buy or not to buy based on this feature.

Other features. There are many additional features that can be included in a long-term-care policy. Sometimes they are included in the policy or need to be added with a rider. Familiarize yourself with these options, weigh their benefits against their costs, and of course make sure the definitions are clear.

Your agent will explain the details of each policy. I repeat: Just make sure that you actually need these additional benefits, because they can add substantially to your total costs.

Step 13: Learn more!   This is the most complete review I can fit into this space. I feel confident I have given you *almost* everything you need. But, alas, there's *still* more to learn—especially with respect to the specifics of your state. So contact the helpful organizations listed in Appendix G.

If you suffer from information overload and get confused, just come back to this chapter and review the steps. Or for the latest information we have on long-term-care insurance, check www .WeissRatings.com. Remember, we are not in the business of selling insurance. We have no relationship with anyone who does. The same goes for the 30,000 banks, brokers, mutual funds, and stocks we rate.

No matter whom you deal with, protect your wealth and your health with information that is free of any conflicts of interest.

CHAPTER

14

"HELP! THIS IS THE FIRST TIME I'VE HAD TO MAKE MY OWN INVESTMENT DECISIONS! WHAT DO I DO?"

You have always relied on someone else to make financial choices—the bank you used, the life and health insurance you bought, or the investments that would sustain you through retirement. Now, due to divorce, death, or some other unforeseen happenstance, the full decision-making burden has suddenly fallen on your shoulders. You're confused but afraid to reveal your ignorance. You're afraid, but anxious to portray an air of confidence. Where to go? Whom can you trust? What to do?

You have time to answer these questions. You don't have to rush to conclusions. But you will have to confront them squarely without too much delay. Don't let the emotional upheaval you are feeling lead to a financial upheaval you will regret.

A scary fact: According to the U.S. General Accounting Office (GAO), 80 percent of women living in poverty were not poor before their husbands died. One of the most common reasons was that the women were not involved in the bookkeeping and financial decisions of their family. For widowers, the statistics are not as severe, but they can also be vulnerable to a similar plight. But there's good news, too. It's not nearly as hard as you may think, and I will prove it to you.

Put all your concerns aside for a short while, and join me as we visit a fictional mall of a special variety: a money supermall where all varieties of investment products are sold. You're not going to buy anything. You're not going to spend a dime. You're just going to peruse the possibilities—to touch and feel every product that catches your interest, talk directly to every person who'd be responsible for your money, ask any question you may want, and, you hope, always get straight answers.

As we walk to the mall from the parking lot, I give you some basic instructions. "Look," I say, "everyone in there is going to want your money. But remember, don't buy anything yet. Instead, at each store you visit, and for each product the shop offers, just get some basic answers to some simple questions." You will put each through the following tests:

- If you change your mind, can you get your money back?
- Is there a warranty?
- What's the price? Is it on sale—is it a good value?

You nod knowingly, but your attention is distracted by a commotion coming from a store with bright flashing lights and a giant, wall-to-wall video screen. A large crowd of shoppers is jockeying for position for what appears to be a high-tech magic show by young fashion models. As it turns out, it's actually a sales presentation for a small, upstart Internet company.

A share in the company, originally priced at $85, has now been marked down to just $14.75. It's a fire sale! But when you ask about getting your money back, you realize there are two problems:

1. The company is losing money. So there's nothing to stop the share price from getting slashed to $9, $6, or even just $2.
2. Since it's such a small company, not many people own its shares. If you buy and then change your mind, you may have an awfully tough time finding a buyer.

Your response: Not interested! They don't even pass the first test. We move along and stop at a juice stand for a drink. While we're getting our change, we realize that this little business is also for sale. The owner says it's a prime location and he's clearing about $20,000 a year after all salaries and costs. He wants $100,000 for the franchise.

Is it worth it? When I buy a private business like that, I want to make my original investment back in about three years, maybe four at the most. But at a price of $100,000 with $20,000 of yearly profit, you'd have to wait a full five years. That's too long. No deal.

At the store across the way, classy mahogany molding and deep burgundy carpeting exude stability and longevity. The company's a national high-end furniture maker with its own chain of a couple of hundred stores. It seems like it might be a bit pricey, but the reps offer two different alternative products:

- You can buy shares of stock and you become a part owner in the company.
- Or, you can buy bonds (i.e., you loan them money and they give you the bond certificates as a guarantee of repayment).

They try to sell you on the stocks first. They tell you that since it's a big company with a lot of buyers every day, you'd have no trouble selling back the shares at whatever the market price is at the time. Right now, each share costs about $100.

Is that cheap or expensive? To get an idea, we can use the same logic we used with the juice stand. We find out the company makes a profit of $2 per share. (It makes $200 million a year, and there are about 100 million shares; ergo $2 per share.) And we discover that the earnings are pretty steady from year to year.

"I don't believe this!" you exclaim. "This is much worse than the juice stand. They're telling me I'd have to plop down one hundred bucks just to buy one share!? Then, all they'd make is two bucks every year?! Doesn't that mean I'd have to wait fifty years before the company earns back my investment?"

You're a fast learner. That's precisely the concept. Since it's a large, established company, and since you could easily sell its shares to someone else, it might make sense to pay more than just three years of earnings. You might pay up to 10 or even 15 times earnings. But 50 times earnings? For a plain-vanilla furniture company? That's definitely way too expensive.

You turn to walk out, but another rep beckons. "Wait," he says, "don't you want to talk about our bonds?"

"Okay, what's the deal?"

"You loan us, for instance, ten thousand dollars for thirty years. We give you a bond certificate, with the equivalent of sixty coupons—two for each year. Then, every six months, you effectively clip off a coupon, and we send you an interest check. What's the APR? It's right there on the coupon—eight percent fixed rate. Every year you collect eight hundred dollars in interest. Then, when the bond reaches maturity at the end of the thirty years, we give you your ten thousand dollars back."

You shake your head. "Thirty years? There's no way I can wait that long. Suppose I want my money back after ten years?"

The rep gives you a wishy-washy answer. So I step in to explain: "You probably could sell it to someone else, but the price you'll get is uncertain. Let's say I'm the buyer. And let's say that ten years from now, interest rates have doubled. Since competing interest rates have doubled, the company has to sell its new bonds for about double too—suppose, a coupon yield of sixteen percent. If that's the case, I'm going to say: 'Why should I buy your old bonds paying only eight percent when I get new bonds paying me sixteen percent?' I'd have to be insane to do that."

"Okay, but . . ."

"But here's what I *can* do for you: Instead of paying you the full, original price for your old bonds, I'll pay you about half—five thousand dollars. That way, when I collect the eight hundred dollars interest per year, I'll still be earning the same sixteen percent on my investment that I could have been earning with the new sixteen percent bonds. So sell it to me for half price, or no deal." This is why the market price of a bond automatically goes down when interest rates go up.

"What if interest rates go *down* in ten years?" you wonder out loud. "To four percent, for example?"

"In that case, the market price of your bond will go *up*. If new bonds are offering just four percent, I'd be willing to pay you a pretty premium for your older, eight percent bonds."

"Sounds interesting," you say to the rep. "Let me think about it."

The next store is quiet and tucked away in the corner. What catches your eye is an official emblem of the U.S. government on the door. You're curious: "What's Uncle Sam doing in this mall?" You're surprised to find that it's the size of a major department store. The atmosphere is sedate, like a bank, but with more activity than a central post office.

One department, representing the United States Treasury, is offering bonds similar to the furniture company's, but paying only six percent. You challenge the salesperson with this question: "Why should I buy your long-term bonds with a coupon yield of six percent, when I can get eight percent from the company down the corridor?"

His answer: "You're talking about the furniture company, aren't you? I know them. I figure they could go broke and cease to exist between now and twenty thirty-two. Even Wall Street, which has been known to be overly optimistic, says it's a shaky company–they give it a low rating. Now, do you think the United States government is going to go broke and cease to exist? Even during the Civil War, we never missed a payment on our Treasury securities. When you buy one of our securities, you're loaning your money to the United States Treasury Department. We guarantee that we will pay back every single penny of principal and interest, with not a moment's delay, and that guarantee is backed up by our ability to collect taxes or borrow money from hundreds of millions of people and companies."

"But suppose interest rates go up? Won't the value of my Treasury bond go down?"

"Yes," says the salesperson from the Treasury Department, "but you can almost always sell Treasury bonds. The market is one of the biggest in the world. There are millions of buyers. The Treasury's price guarantee, though, is valid strictly when the bonds mature. So if you don't want to wait too long for our guarantee, we offer you a whole range of shorter Treasury securities to choose from. You can buy other Treasury bonds, which mature in ten years or more. You can buy Treasury notes, which mature in one to ten years."

"What's the difference?"

"No difference, except the notes are medium-term and the bonds are long-term. Plus, you can buy Treasury bills, which are short-term. We can sell you three-month Treasury bills, six-month Treasury bills, or twelve-month Treasury bills. The shorter the term, the less chance the market price will decline. Even if the market price does go down a tiny bit, you can always wait a few months until it matures and we give you back the full amount. We guarantee you'll get one hundred percent of your money back one hundred percent of the time. And there's no limit to our guarantee. You can invest one thousand, one million, or even one billion."

"And these Treasury bills are the same as Treasury notes and Treasury bonds, I presume."

"Uhm . . . no," says the rep. "They're slightly different. You see, for just a few months, it doesn't make sense for us to give you a batch of coupons. So we just discount them right up front for you. Let's say you want to invest ten thousand dollars in a one-year Treasury bill with a rate of four percent. You just pay nine thousand six hundred dollars. Then, when it matures, you collect the ten thousand dollars. In effect, the four-hundred-dollar difference is your interest."

"Same difference," you say with a sigh of impatience.

"No, wait a minute," he retorts. "It's an important difference. Since you get the four hundred dollars right away, you can earn another four percent on the four hundred dollars. That gives you an extra sixteen dollars to put in your pocket. So the coupon-equivalent yield (calculating it the same way we would for a coupon-type bond) is actually 4.16 percent. It may not sound like a big difference, but it adds up. And when you're comparing it with other safe investments, like a bank CD, it can be important. Plus, you don't have to pay state or local income taxes on the 4.16 percent. On a CD, you do."

You count out the benefits. "Okay. I always get all my money back. The price is stable. It's guaranteed by the U.S. Treasury Department. I pay no local income taxes. Any disadvantages?"

"Just one. The rate is low compared with what you can make on other investments. And if interest rates go down, the rate will be still lower. On the other hand, if interest rates go up, you'll get the new, higher rates as soon as your Treasury bill matures and you roll it over into a new Treasury bill."

As we head toward the exit and back to the car, we pass at least a half-dozen departments in the government store, representing a list of government agencies, each selling their own notes and bonds–the General National Home Mortgage Association (nick-named Ginnie Mae), plus others like Sallie Mae and Freddie Mac. We also pass scores of other stores in the mall selling stocks and bonds.

One company is ranting and raving about a new cancer drug it's about to launch. The company is selling for only 10 times earnings and has the potential to double its earnings based on this one drug alone. If you consider those future earnings, it would actually be selling for only five times earnings. You'd have a well-established company, with plenty of willing buyers, and all you'd have to wait is five years for it to earn back its share price. That's cheap, and it's a good value.

Another company is a leading maker of software with virtually no competition. Because of the bust in the tech stocks, investors have been dumping their shares in nearly *all* software companies– whether good or bad. They've been throwing out the baby with the bath water, and this company is one of those babies. Due to all the selling, the company's shares have fallen dramatically. But it's still a darn good company. Based on its earnings, it's probably worth $100 per share. Right now, though, it's selling for only $30 per share. You can scoop it up for a song, wait for it to bounce back, and double your money or more.

Still another one is a gas utility. They have no competition. Their earnings are very steady year after year. And they almost always pay out a portion of their profits to shareholders–a regular dividend.

But you've seen enough for the day. On the drive home, you start jotting down some notes of what you've learned just from this brief trip:

1. You can never seem to get safety and high return in the same investment. When you prioritize safety, you have to sacrifice how much you can make. And when you prioritize how much you can make, you sacrifice safety.

2. Based on this alone, you begin to form a notion of what you might want to invest in–maybe something very safe for some portion of your money (despite a low yield) and maybe something with great value and a promising future for some

other portion of your money (despite some risk). In your situation, and given the big ups and downs that we've seen in the markets, you decide you want to lean mostly toward safety.

3. U.S. Treasury securities are the safest in the world.

4. There are three kinds of Treasury securities: (1) Treasury bills, which range from 3 to 12 months; (2) Treasury notes, which are from 1 to 10 years; and (3) Treasury bonds, which are 10 years or more. The notes and bonds work the same way. They pay you interest every six months. But with the bills, the method is a bit different. You buy them at a discount and, in effect, you get your interest up front.

5. It's best to buy the short-term bills if you may need your money back very soon. But if you can afford to wait for your money, it might not be a bad idea to buy some of the medium-term notes or even some long-term bonds.

6. Right now, you can probably get the most interest on the longest bonds. But not many people can wait a long time until maturity. Yes, you can also sell them at almost any time to someone else, but if
   - Interest rates go up
   - You change your mind and decide to sell them before they mature

   then you could suffer a significant loss. To avoid any such risk, the shortest-term Treasury securities (Treasury bills) are the safest kind.

7. Interest rates and the market price of existing bonds move in opposite directions. When interest rates go up, bond prices go down. When interest rates go down, bond prices go up. That's true of all bonds—whether they're issued by the government or by a corporation.

8. It's also true of the medium-term variety—the notes, but not quite as much. And with bills, the price changes are the smallest. So the shorter the maturity, the less the risk of a price decline.

9. The bonds you buy from a corporation—corporate bonds—usually offer more interest but involve another kind of risk:

They could have financial troubles, miss some interest payments, or even go out of business. If the company is solid with a high rating, and you can wait until maturity, okay. But if there's a relatively high chance the company may go under, you want to avoid them.

10. With stocks, there is almost always a risk of losing money—sometimes *a lot* of money. But they can offer much better returns. Instead of just 4, 6, or 8 percent, you could make 20, 30, even 100 percent. They are worth considering, provided that:

   - The stocks have plenty of willing buyers and you can sell out at almost any time.
   - The company has a good chance of earning back the share price within a reasonable time.

11. Different people seem to have different views of what's reasonable. Depending on the kind of company, you might be willing to wait a longer time. But as a general rule, 15 years is a limit to consider for safety-conscious investors.

You're also intrigued by other possibilities—other agencies of the government, perhaps safer stocks. But as soon as you get home, you remember you still have many unanswered questions: What about all the various investments my spouse or family member left me with? Should I sell? Should I hold? Which ones? I don't even know what half of them are! What do I do?

The following steps are directly applicable to you if you've recently been widowed. But if you're divorced, most of the steps will still apply. Just skip over those that don't. You'll see right away which ones they are.

Step 1. Assemble any information your spouse or family member may have written down regarding an accountant and/or attorney that he or she used. Then call them to get an update on what they know about your assets. You can decide later whether you want to continue using their services. For now, just go forward with the assumption that you will.

Step 2. Make a list of all your assets and accounts. Your spouse may have a file in which all of the records were kept. If you can't find one, look through personal items and drawers for:

- Credit cards
- Membership cards
- Statements from a bank, brokerage firm, insurance company, or mutual fund
- Bills—paid and unpaid.

Include on your list every account you can find, including the company name and phone number, along with account number and balance.

Step 3. Go through each item one by one. If it's a credit card that's only in one name, call the company, and ask for instructions. If the card is in both your names, have your spouse's name removed. Follow the same steps for membership cards.

Step 4. If you have one or more bank accounts, go to each bank with your latest statement (if you have it) and talk to the customer service representative.

Step 5. If you find a life insurance policy on your spouse, call the company named in the policy and ask them if it is in force. (You can usually find the phone number on the policy.) Then have them send you a claim form. If you need to get advice, get it from your accountant. If you want to get basic information from the insurance agent, that's fine. But don't use the agent as an advisor.

Step 6. If you have health insurance, you probably have your own card. Call the company and notify them of your spouse's passing so that the premiums can be reduced immediately. It's very possible your health insurance is Medicare supplement insurance. If so, the insurance company can also give you information on how to go about notifying Medicare. If they can't tell you, look at your latest Explanation of Benefits form. There should be a phone number to call. Also, refer to Appendix G in this book.

Step 7. Review checkbook entries for the last three or four months to see what your spouse has been paying. If there are recurring payments, then you should be aware that they may be coming due shortly.

If you find something in your spouse's records that you're not familiar with, call the company and ask about it. Don't be embarrassed if you don't understand. Just continue asking questions until you *do* understand completely.

Step 8.   Don't forget Social Security. If you were married for at least nine months before your spouse died, you are eligible for Social Security benefits. Contact the Social Security Administration to file your claim at your local office, at 800-772-1213, or at www.ssa.gov). Some possibilities include:

- If you are widowed before your spouse's Social Security payments would have begun, you can receive a widow's or widower's benefit at age 60.

- If you are disabled, you can collect as early as age 50.

- If you are widowed after Social Security payments have begun, and you were receiving spousal benefits, you will continue to receive the higher of the two benefits: yours or your spouse's, but not both.

- If you choose to remarry, your benefits will continue. Congress made that possible in 1984, after noting the number of seniors who were living together in order to maintain their benefits.

The amount of your monthly benefit depends on your age when you start collecting and the amount your spouse was, or was entitled to, receiving. The amount of your benefit ranges from 71½ percent of your spouse's benefit amount if you begin receiving them at age 60, all the way up to 100 percent of the amount if you begin receiving them at 65.

These are just the basics. There are several other options and conditions for the widow's or widower's benefit to which you are entitled. So *do* speak with the Social Security department to determine exactly what you are eligible for.

Step 9.   Now, it's time to start making some investment decisions. Arrange a face-to-face meeting with your accountant and take your list along. If you don't have an accountant, don't fret. You can go straight to an accountant with proven investment training. Your main requirement should be that your advisors never make money from selling you something. They should charge you strictly an hourly fee. If you want to invest some portion of the money later with someone who charges you, for example, 1 percent of your assets, okay. But don't let anyone charge you 1 percent on *all* of your money. If you're earning only 4 percent on a large portion of your funds, you'd be giving away 25 percent of your income!

Step 10.   Before you review your list of assets, think about what you'd do if you were starting with a clean slate. For starters, take the Risk Self Test in Appendix A.

Step 11.   With the assistance of your accountant or advisor, look over the recommendations I make immediately following the test. Use it as a guide to help put together an investment plan that best fits your needs. Unfortunately, there's no such thing as a money supermall, and buying investments directly from the institutions is often either cumbersome or impossible. You usually have to go through an intermediary—a broker or a mutual fund.

Step 12.   Now take out your list of investments, accounts, and other assets to review which items fit into your investment plan. Check off the ones that fit. Mark with an *X* the ones that don't fit. These may include high-risk investments similar to the first three you saw at the mall. Don't be surprised if there are a lot of them.

Remember the furniture company that was selling for 50 times earnings? Well, if you think that was too high, consider some of the high-tech companies I told you about in Chapter 1. Even when Wall Street was still hotly promoting them, many were selling for 100 times earnings, 200 times earnings, even 1,000 times earnings.

By the way, in case you're interested, these numbers are what they call the *p/e ratio* (i.e., the ratio of the stock's price to its earnings).

With one Wall Street favorite, the p/e ratio was 1,500—you would have to wait 1,500 years before it earned back its share price. Can you believe that? If you could have bought it back in the ninth century when the Crusaders were marching toward the Holy Land, today, you'd still have to wait a few hundred years before you earned your money back. Wall Street's rationale is that these companies are going to grow their earnings by leaps and bounds. But often, it doesn't quite work out that way. In fact, by mid-2001, the 4,200 companies listed on the Nasdaq exchange had lost so much money, they'd wiped out every last dime of profits they'd made between 1994 and June 2000.

If you have these kinds of investments on your list, mark them off with a giant *X* in red ink.

You also may own them indirectly—through a high-tech mutual fund. You can usually tell by the name of the fund. But don't go by that alone. In Chapter 5 (approach 3, step 2), I give you instructions on how to figure out how risky each fund is. If it's a high-risk fund, mark it off with a giant red *X*, too.

Step 13.   Time to start selling and getting to safety! The first items to sell are those that have a liquid market—with plenty of buyers willing to take them off your hands. That doesn't guarantee you'll get a great price. But it does mean you can probably get out promptly and efficiently.

I can't tell you exactly when or how much to sell. As a general rule, though, if the price has been going down sharply in recent days or weeks, it's wisest to sell half right away and hold the rest in the hope of a temporary rebound. Then, when the rebound comes, even if it's a bit disappointing, sell the rest.

Step 14.   The next items to sell are those that do *not* enjoy a liquid market—perhaps some municipal bonds issued by a small town, maybe some stocks in small companies. This may take some time, and even if you're anxious to get rid of them, it's usually not a good idea to rush. The broker who's been handling your spouse's account can usually help you. Just don't let the broker talk you into keeping them.

Step 15.   The hardest things to get rid of are investments or insurance policies that charge you a big penalty for exiting. Ask yourself: "What's worse: The risk of staying or the cost of leaving?" The answer depends on three things:

1. *How much risk you're willing to take.*   The Risk Self-Test should help you there.

2. *How much it costs to get out.*   You can get that information directly from the company or your broker. (If it's a mutual fund, you may avoid the penalty by switching to a safer fund offered by the same mutual fund company or family. So explore those alternatives first, before exploring funds outside the family.)

3. *How risky the investment really is.* On this aspect, I can probably help you myself. My company, Weiss Ratings, rates the risk of thousands of stocks and mutual funds. I have given you some ratings in this book, but to fit them all would require a hundred books. So check with your public library. If they don't have our guides, they may be able to order them. Or, for many companies or investments, you can get some information on the risk from other sources, with the instructions I've given you in earlier chapters.

The final decision is yours. Only you can weigh the risk versus the cost and make up your own mind. If I were you, though, I'd err on the side of more safety and less risk. Missing out on a profit opportunity may be a bit frustrating. But losing your nest egg will be devastating—a disaster from which you may never recover.

Step 16. Where do you sell? There are three possibilities:

1. Some of the items on your list may be held at the brokerage firm. You should have its name. Don't worry about changing brokers right now. Just use the same one.

2. Other items may have been bought through an insurance agent. So just contact the agent.

3. The rest were probably purchased directly from the institution, such as a mutual fund. Call the fund directly. They all have toll-free numbers you can get from the toll-free information operator, 800-555-1212.

Step 17. You suspect the broker was the one who got your spouse into a lot of your losing investments in the first place. Should you switch to a different broker? Not necessarily. Promise yourself that you will use the broker strictly to buy and sell what *you* want to buy and sell. As long as you follow that prescription, your broker's expertise in picking investments, or lack thereof, is irrelevant. Concentrate instead, on picking a broker who is honest and works for a stable firm. For further instructions, see Appendix B.

Step 18. Recently divorced? Then also consider the steps in the accompanying box.

ARE YOU RECENTLY DIVORCED? THEN CONSIDER THESE STEPS AS WELL . . .

Cicily Maten, CFP, author of *For Women by Women*, has written a great chapter on this subject, which I paraphrase here.

Step 1. Your natural inclination will be to get the most you can from any settlement. But when considering assets such as stock options, investments, IRAs, and even homes, don't assume that getting them is always better than *not* getting them. There are some other facts regarding the transfer of ownership that you must understand in order to make the most informed decision. For instance:

- Some assets have a built-in tax liability. You may get stuck with a huge tax bill.
- Others are best transferred *before* the divorce rather than after.

Step 2. Find an accountant or advisor who is an expert in divorce. Your divorce lawyer may also be very helpful. Part of their job is to be up to date on the changes in tax law and how your choices now will affect your life in the future. So get as much help from them as you can.

Step 3. Consider whether to keep or sell your house. In the past, especially in more traditional marriages where the wife was the homemaker and caregiver, it was the norm for the house to be awarded to the wife. This made sense inasmuch as women were being awarded the one asset that meant the most to them emotionally. But it was potentially a problem if they did not have the financial income to maintain that asset, and that could lead to a decline in their standard of living. (Naturally, for the divorced husband, it was also a problem if he didn't have alternative living arrangements.)

In any case, before agreeing to accept the house in the property division, I recommend calculating its long-term financial impact on you. Whether you are a long-term home-maker, a mother with young children, or a wage earner, you don't want to wind up with any unwanted financial surprises long after the divorce is over. It could turn what was meant to be an equitable distribution into a financial burden.

To help you decide, reread what my concerns are regarding real estate values (Chapter 7). Then, also consider your *cash flow.* In other words, make sure there will be enough money coming in to cover all of your expenses, including the mortgage, real estate taxes, assessments, homeowner insurance, as well as repairs and maintenance. If you can easily cover those expenses, great.

Determine the terms of the existing mortgage and make sure the lender will allow you to assume the mortgage on your own. Be careful not to take over a mortgage with a balloon payment due in one or two years unless you *know* that you will qualify to get a new mortgage.

When you sell your home, you may have to pay a big tax on the profit—a capital gains tax. But the Taxpayer Relief Act of 1997, which provided substantial relief for divorcing couples, states that you are permitted up to a $250,000 exclusion (if you are filing individually) from capital gains tax from the sale of your principal residence (where you've lived for at least two of the five years prior to the sale).

This corrects a major problem for divorcing individuals who have moved out of the principal residence and who still had an ownership interest in the home. Before this tax law change, the home had to be the principal residence *at the time of the sale.* Now, even if you haven't been living there for quite a while, you can still exclude $250,000 of gain when the house is sold.

Do get professional help in assessing your situation and deciding which strategies might be appropriate for you. Also, call the IRS or go to their Web site at www.irs.gov to get a copy of IRS Publication 523, "Selling Your Home."

(continued)

Step 4. If your settlement involves a pension, get a copy of all of the paperwork as soon as possible. There are two main types of pensions:

1. *Defined benefit pensions.* These pay a benefit at retirement based on a formula, such as years of service and average wages for a specific number of years. These are usually *paid for by the employer.*

2. *Defined contribution.* These are pension plans that are held in the name of the individual wage earner and are accumulated from *voluntary contributions from the wage earner,* and perhaps also some contributions from the employer.

To transfer pension benefits you have to correctly complete a Qualified Domestic Relations Order (QDRO) once your divorce and property settlement have been granted. This form states that you are an alternate payee of the pension plan. Then, the QDRO must be signed by the court and accepted by the administrator and/or custodian of the pension plan to enable the administrator of the pension to transfer your award to you. Ask the administrator for a prototype of a QDRO ahead of time to make certain it is in acceptable form.

If your spouse has a 401(k) pension and profit-sharing plan, you can receive some or all of the money in the plan as part of the settlement in the divorce. Many plans allow the money to be transferred directly into a rollover IRA in your name and invested for the future, so that when you are $59\frac{1}{2}$ you can begin drawing out money to live on.

I wish I could give you everything you need to know right here. But, unfortunately, there are an infinite variety and combination of pension plans, profit-sharing plans, employee savings plans, stock ownership plans, and so on, with a few important differences and opportunities with each. For more details, call the IRS or go to www.irs.gov for a copy of IRS Publication 575, "Pension and Annuity Income."

> **Step 5.** The splitting of an IRA or an SEP does not require a QDRO. A letter of transfer signed by both the owner of the IRA or SEP and the alternate payee will be enough, as long as the transfer is included as part of the property settlement. Any money rolled over into the payee's IRA continues to grow tax-deferred. The only time you will have to pay taxes is if the rollover occurs before the divorce.

Step 19. Above all, never stop learning. Never let anyone intimidate you with cryptic stats and theories. The investing world is a real-life drama that's usually less complex than many of your favorite plays or novels you probably know like the back of your hand. Moreover, some of the most sophisticated actors in the investment world have turned the drama into a comedy of errors that only they still fail to comprehend. You probably have a better sense of what's appropriate—and what's not—than many of them do. All you need is straight answers to simple questions.

Get your money to safety now. Then, start considering some of the programs I've recommended in this book to help grow your wealth.

WHERE TO GET MORE HELP

Whether you're male or female, contact the Older Women's League in Washington, D.C., at 202-783-6686, and ask for their educational pamphlets and audiotapes on income security. For free legal advice, call the Women's Legal Defense League in Washington, D.C., at 202-986-2600.

In addition, here are three more books you will find helpful: *The Savage Truth on Money* by Terry Savage; *The Financially Confident Woman* by Mary Hunt; and a book with specific instructions for widows—*Every Woman's Guide to Financial Security* by Ann Z. Peterson and Stephen M. Rosenberg.

Best wishes and good luck!

APPENDIX A

Risk Self-Test

Use this test to evaluate your risk tolerance, and to decide how to allocate your funds. Each person approaches his or her investment decisions from a unique perspective. A mutual fund or stock that is perfect for someone else may be totally inappropriate for you due to factors such as:

- How much risk you are comfortable taking
- Your age and the number of years you have before retirement
- Your income level and tax rate
- Your other existing investments and personal net worth
- Your expectations about investment performance

The following quiz will help you to quantify your tolerance for risk based on your own personal life situation. As you read through each question, circle the letter next to the single answer that you feel most accurately describes your current position. Keep in mind that there are no correct or incorrect answers to this quiz—only answers that are helpful in assessing your investment style. Don't worry about how your answer might be perceived by others; just try to be as honest and accurate as possible.

Then at the end of the quiz, use the point totals listed on the right side of the page to compute your test score. Once you've added up your total points, refer to the corresponding investor profile for an evaluation of your personal risk tolerance.

The table is also designed so you can share it with younger family members or associates who may be further from retirement age.

	Points	Your Score
1. I am currently investing to pay for:		
a. Retirement	0 pts	_____
b. College	0 pts	_____
c. A house	0 pts	_____
2. I expect I will need to liquidate some or all of this investment in:		
a. 2 years or less	0 pts	_____
b. 2 to 5 years	5 pts	_____
c. 5 to 10 years	8 pts	_____
d. 10 years or more	10 pts	_____
3. My age group is		
a. Under 30	10 pts	_____
b. 30 to 44	9 pts	_____
c. 45 to 60	7 pts	_____
d. 61 to 74	5 pts	_____
e. 75 and older	1 pt	_____
4. I am currently looking to invest money through:		
a. An IRA or other tax-deferred account	0 pts	_____
b. A fully taxable account	0 pts	_____
5. I have a cash reserve equal to 3 to 6 months' expenses.		
a. Yes	10 pts	_____
b. No	1 pt	_____
6. My primary source of income is:		
a. Salary and other earnings from my primary occupation	7 pts	_____
b. Earnings from my investment portfolio	5 pts	_____
c. Retirement pension and/or Social Security	3 pts	_____

	Points	Your Score

7. I will need regular income from my investments now or in the near future.

    a. Yes   6 pts   _____

    b. No   10 pts   _____

8. Over the long run, I expect my investments to average returns of:

    a. Less than 8% annually   0 pts   _____

    b. 8 to 12% annually   6 pts   _____

    c. 12.1 to 15% annually   8 pts   _____

    d. 15.1 to 20% annually   10 pts   _____

    e. Over 20% annually   18 pts   _____

9. The worst loss I would be comfortable accepting on my investment is:

    a. Less than 5%. Stability of principal is very important to me.   1 pt   _____

    b. 5 to 10%. Modest periodic declines are acceptable.   3 pts   _____

    c. 10.1 to 15%. I understand that there may be losses in the short run, but over the long term, I hope that higher-risk investments will offer highest returns.   8 pts   _____

    d. Over 15%. You don't get high returns without taking risks. I'm looking for maximum capital gains and understand that my stocks or mutual funds can decline substantially.   15 pts   _____

10. If the stock market were to suddenly decline by 20%, which of the following would most likely be your reaction?

    a. I should have left the market long ago, at the first sign of trouble.   3 pts   _____

    b. I should have substantially exited the stock market by now to limit my exposure.   5 pts   _____

    c. I'm still in the stock market, but I've got my finger on the trigger.   7 pts   _____

    d. I'm staying fully invested so I'll be ready for the next bull market.   10 pts   _____

	Points	Your Score

---

11. The best defense against a bear (down) market is:

   a. A defensive market timing system that avoids large losses. — 4 pts — _____

   b. A potent offense that will make big gains in the next bull market. — 10 pts — _____

---

12. The best strategy to employ during bear markets is:

   a. Move to cash. It's the only safe hiding place. — 5 pts — _____

   b. Short the market and try to make a profit as it declines. — 10 pts — _____

   c. Wait it out because the market will eventually recover. — 8 pts — _____

---

13. I would classify myself as:

   a. A buy-and-hold investor who rides out all the peaks and valleys. — 10 pts — _____

   b. A market timer who wants to capture the major bull markets. — 7 pts — _____

   c. A market timer who wants to avoid the major bear markets. — 5 pts — _____

---

14. My attitude regarding trading activity is:

   a. Active trading is costly and unproductive. — 0 pts — _____

   b. I don't mind frequent trades as long as I'm making money. — 2 pts — _____

   c. Occasional trading is okay, but too much activity is not good. — 1 pt — _____

---

15. If the S&P 500 advanced strongly over the last 12 months, my investment should have:

   a. Grown even more than the market. — 10 pts — _____

   b. Approximated the performance of the broad market. — 5 pts — _____

   c. Focused on reducing the risk of loss in a bear market, even if it meant giving up some upside potential in the bull market. — 2 pts — _____

	Points			Your Score

	Exten-sive	Some	None	
16. I have experience (extensive, some, or none) with the following types of investments:				
a. U.S. stocks or stock mutual funds	2 pts	1 pt	0 pts	_____
b. International stocks or mutual funds	2 pts	1 pt	0 pts	_____
c. Bonds or bond funds	1 pt	0 pts	0 pts	_____
d. Futures and/or options	5 pts	3 pts	0 pts	_____
e. Managed futures or commodity pools	3 pts	1 pt	0 pts	_____
f. Real estate	2 pts	1 pt	0 pts	_____
g. Private hedge funds	3 pts	1 pt	0 pts	_____
h. Privately managed accounts	2 pts	1 pt	0 pts	_____

17. Excluding my primary residence, safe investment represents ____% of my investment holdings.

	Points	Your Score
a. Less than 5%	10 pts	_____
b. 5 to 10%	7 pts	_____
c. 10.1 to 20%	5 pts	_____
d. 20.1 to 30%	3 pts	_____
e. More than 30%	1 pt	_____

TOTAL

Add up your score and follow the advice in this chart. Then, follow the advice that corresponds to your score. When calculating your portfolio allocations, exclude real estate and other assets that you are unable or unwilling to sell. However, do include real estate and other assets that you are able and willing to liquidate for cash. Until you do sell them, estimate their approximate value.

Under 58 pts **Very conservative.** You appear to be almost totally risk-averse, and capital preservation is your primary, or even sole, goal. So nearly all stock market investments—including stock mutual funds and individual stocks, whether common or preferred—are probably too risky for you, especially in a turbulent market environment such as we've already been experiencing in the early twenty-first century. Real estate you are not occupying or that you consider to be primarily an investment is also risky. Even some bonds and bond funds could involve too much risk for you. Instead, you should begin by putting nearly all your taxable funds in a safe place that gives you immediate access to your money at all times, with no penalty for withdrawals. I believe that should be a Treasury-only savings and checking program like the one described in Chapter 5. If you don't want to use a Treasury-only money fund as your primary checking account, you can still use it for the bulk of your savings.

In your 401(k) and other tax-protected investments, they will probably *not* have a Treasury-only money fund available. In that case, use the next safest money market or bond fund, as described in Chapter 5. For more information on the relative safety of money market and bond funds, refer to the Weiss Ratings' *Guide to Bond and Money Market Mutual Funds,* available at many public libraries.

If you are unable or unwilling to sell your stocks, your stock mutual funds, or any other risky assets you may have, protect your wealth with one of the crash protection or crash insurance programs recommended in Chapter 7. But you should recognize that the investments required for these programs are, themselves, volatile and risky. So limit these programs to a maximum of 5% of your assets.

If you wish to purchase annuities, life insurance, tax-exempt securities, or other investments covered in this book, you may draw the needed funds from your Treasury-only savings and checking program, or equivalent keep-safe account. However, try to limit your investment to no more than 10% of your total liquid investments. Plus, *read carefully the warnings in Chapters 7 through 11.*

To cover your future health costs, your best protection is to continue to build your nest egg of safe, liquid funds under your direct control—such as in a program like the Treasury-only savings and checking. However, depending on your personal situation, it may also be wise to spend some money on Medigap insurance and long-term-care insurance. Try your best to cover the premiums on these policies with your current income, and without pulling funds away from your savings. But if you feel you can afford to pull some funds from savings without jeopardizing your financial security, that is also acceptable. Plus, *be sure to read all the warnings in Chapters 12 and 13.*

58 to 77 pts

Conservative. Based on your responses, it is clear that you are more concerned about minimizing the risk to your principal than you are about maximizing your returns. I recommend that you begin by following the same recommendations I give for very conservative individuals for 80% of your money. In addition, if you are willing to accept some risk, allocate up to 20% of your money to mutual funds that can provide you with a higher overall return, using one of the four approaches described in Chapter 5. However, be sure not to exceed the 20% maximum.

For the best results, follow approach 4 in Chapter 5. If you follow approach 2, favor the mutual funds that offer strong returns with very little volatility. As a starting point, I recommend that you choose top-performing funds that have a Weiss Risk Rating of B ("good") or better. (See the Weiss Ratings' *Guide to Stock Mutual Funds,* available at many public libraries.)

If you wish to invest in individual stocks, do not allocate additional funds beyond the 20% you have already allocated to mutual funds. Instead, shift some portion of your 20% mutual fund allocation to individual stocks. In this way, your *total* allocation to mutual funds and stocks will still be 20% of your money.

78 to
108 pts

Moderate. Judging from your responses, it appears that you are prepared to take on some added risk to enhance your investment returns. However, I feel that in today's volatile environment, you should still err on the side of caution by starting with the same advice I give for very conservative investors for 60% of your money.

If you are sure you are willing to accept some risk, allocate up to 40% of your money to mutual funds that can provide you with a higher overall return, using one of the four approaches described in Chapter 5. However, be sure not to exceed the 40% maximum.

For the best results, follow approach 4 in Chapter 5. If you use approach 2, favor the mutual funds that offer strong returns with, at worst, average volatility. As a starting point, I recommend you choose top-performing funds that have a Weiss Risk Rating of C ("fair") or better. (See the Weiss Ratings' *Guide to Stock Mutual Funds,* available at many public libraries.)

If you wish to invest in individual stocks, do not allocate additional funds beyond the 40% you have already allocated to mutual funds. Instead, shift some portion of your 40% mutual fund allocation to this area. That way, your *total* allocation to mutual funds and stocks will still be 40% of your money.

The more you invest in stocks and stock mutual funds, the more you will need to be concerned about protecting those assets. So if you are using approach 2 to mutual funds, or you are investing in individual stocks, consider pulling a modest amount of the funds away from the 40% allocation to finance the crash protection or crash insurance programs described in Chapter 7.

109 to 129 pts

Aggressive. Double-check your test and your score. If you are 50+, you should be more concerned with safety and protection than you appear to be. If this is because you feel the assets you have are insignificant or insufficient, this alone should not be grounds for taking a more aggressive approach. Taking more risk with your money may merely compound any financial shortfallings you have.

Even if you have double-checked your score and you are confident that you are willing to take a lot more risk, for a portion of your assets, you can still benefit from the advice I give to very conservative individuals. Follow it for at least 40% of your money.

Allocate the remainder of your money (up to 60%) to mutual fund investing. But even though you are willing to take more risk, do not exceed the 60%.

For the best results, follow approach 4 in Chapter 5. If you use approach 2, favor the mutual funds that offer strong returns. As a starting point, I recommend you choose the fund with the highest Weiss Performance Ratings. But continue to consider the Weiss Risk Rating as an important factor in your decision making. (See the Weiss Ratings' *Guide to Stock Mutual Funds,* available at many public libraries.)

If you wish to invest in individual stocks, do not allocate additional funds beyond the 60% you have already allocated to mutual funds. Instead, shift some portion of your 60% mutual fund allocation to this area. That way, your *total* allocation to mutual funds and stocks will still be 60% of your money.

The more you sink money into stocks and stock mutual funds, the more you will need to be concerned about protecting those assets. So if you are using approach 2, or you are investing in individual stocks, consider pulling some funds away from the 60% allocation to finance the crash protection or crash insurance programs described in Chapter 7.

**Over
129 pts**

Very aggressive. Something seems to be wrong here. Double-check your test and your score. If you are 50+, you should not have a score of 129 points or more. If you are under 50, it is possible, but you are still much more aggressive than the average investor. In normal times, you could do very well. But in today's environment, I feel you are asking for trouble because you are multiplying *two* risk factors: (1) a volatile market *plus* (2) an aggressive approach to that market. Yes, if your timing is good, and you also make ample use of investments that profit from a market decline, you can do extremely well.

However, even if you are 100% sure you want to be that aggressive, you can still benefit from the advice I give to very conservative individuals above for a portion of your assets. I suggest you follow it for at least 30% of your money.

Allocate the remainder of your money (up to 70%) to mutual fund investing. Even though you are willing to take more risk, do not exceed 70% of your money.

For the best results, follow approach 4 in Chapter 5. If you use approach 2, favor the mutual funds that offer strong returns. As a starting point, I recommend you choose the fund with the highest Weiss Performance Ratings. But continue to consider the Weiss Risk Rating as a secondary factor. (See the Weiss Ratings' *Guide to Stock Mutual Funds,* available at many public libraries.)

If you wish to invest in individual stocks, do not allocate additional funds beyond the 70% you have already allocated to mutual funds. Instead, shift some portion of your 70% mutual fund allocation to this area. That way, your *total* allocation to mutual funds and stocks will still be 70% of your money.

The more you sink money into stocks and stock mutual funds, the more you will need to be concerned about protecting those assets. So if you are using approach 2, or you are investing in individual stocks, pull some funds away from the 70% allocation to buy the investments described in Chapter 7 under crash protection or crash insurance. You may even consider some of those same investments for purely speculative purposes.

APPENDIX B

How to Avoid a Broker That Will Break You, and Find One That Can Truly Help You

If you are reading this section, I assume that you have followed steps 1 through 5 in Chapter 6 and that you have picked out a brokerage firm that is (a) financially sound and (b) reasonably inexpensive.

Now, the question is: How to avoid an unethical or dishonest broker. Unfortunately, there is no foolproof method. Fortunately, however, no matter who your broker is, your risk is limited because *you will not be following advice from your broker.* You will be getting your advice from independent sources and using your broker strictly to help you with the mechanics of buying and selling, plus some basic information. To reduce the risk of winding up with the wrong individual, follow these 14 steps:

Step 1: Question your broker. Whether you are looking for a new broker or working with one you already know, it's extremely important that your broker learn that you are an active, businesslike, and informed participant in the investment process. If you show that you're savvy, a broker is going to think twice about trying to pull the wool over your eyes. To let your broker know that you are on top of things, you should have a five-minute telephone conversation where you ask a specific group of questions. By following this simple step, your broker will know that you're no fool. Remember, your broker works for you. You have the right to certain information—just as you would if you were hiring an accountant or a new employee. Here are some questions to ask:

- Are you a registered broker? With whom? For how long?
- What licenses and financial designations do you hold?
- What is your supervisor's title, name, and phone number?
- When I contact the National Association of Security Dealers (NASD) and the Central Registration Depository (CRD), will I find that either you or your supervisor has had any disciplinary history?

If you don't get satisfactory answers to any of these questions, find another broker. (For more guidance on how to interview a broker, go to www.sec.gov. Then, under "Investor Information," click on "Check out Brokers and Advisors.)

Step 2: Learn about the CRD. Fortunately, there's a large database of information on every registered broker that just might answer your important questions. Using this database, you can find out:

- If he or she has broken a regulation or the law—and has been caught
- Even if he or she has dodged the legal bullets but had a history of client complaints

It's essential that you protect your hard-earned assets by checking the background of your broker before entering into a relationship or making any transactions.

Vital information on all registered brokers is maintained on a broker database called the *Central Registration Depository* (CRD). The CRD contains such items as a broker's 10-year employment history, their reasons for termination, registrations held, licensing test dates and scores, customer complaints (including any large monetary settlements), disciplinary actions, arbitration awards, court judgments, criminal convictions, bankruptcy filings, and tax liens.

Here's what to do:

- Go to the home page of the NASDR (www.nasdr.com), under the heading "Broker/Advisor Information."
- Click on "Check Broker/Advisor Info."

- Click on "NASD Regulation Public Disclosure Program."

- Click on "Perform an Online Search."

- Click on "Agree."

- If you are interested in a particular broker, select "NASD Registered Representative" as requester type; then select "Broker."

- If you are interested in a particular firm, select "NASD Member Firm" as requester type; then select "Firm." (You will need to enter at least three of the items, such as the broker's first name, last name, and firm name.)

If you don't have access to the Internet, just call the NASD's Public Disclosure Hotline at 800-289-9999 and they will mail you the requested information.

While pending claims may not be listed, any NASD disciplinary histories *are* public.

Step 3: Search for enforcement actions online.   Go to their Web site at www.nasdr.com. Then, scroll down to the bottom of this page and click on "Recent Enforcement Actions." Or you can go right to the NASD's "Recent Enforcement Actions" at this address: www.nasdr.com/2700.asp. Then

- Once at the page for the NASD's "Recent Enforcement Actions," on the left side of the page, click on the button for "Search."

- Next, enter the last name of the individual or the first words in the company's name, and click on "Search."

- Check the results of the search until you find the name of the individual. Remember, there are many other people with similar-sounding names. Make sure you've found the correct one.

Step 4: You may also want to check out the Web site of the Securities and Exchange Commission (SEC).   Log on at www.sec.gov. Click on "Administrative Proceedings," under the heading "Litigation."

- When you go to this page, you will see a lot of brokers and other firms. Whether you are using Microsoft Internet Explorer or another browser program, in the menu at the top of your screen, click on **E**dit and then click on **F**ind.

- A box will pop up so that you can enter the broker's name. If it's an individual, we suggest you enter the last name only. If it's a company, enter the first two words in its name.

- Referring to the first name and/or initials, make sure this is *not* someone else with a similar name. If it is, just click on "Find" again, and do so as many times as you need until you find the right person. If you do not find the broker and get the message "Finished searching the document," make sure you have entered it correctly in the "Find" box.

- When you find the broker or corporation, you will see a list of cases. Click on "File number" and you will get the details on this case.

- These are strictly actions for the most current period. You may have to repeat these steps for the earlier actions. To do so, scroll down the page to the bottom, where you will find earlier time periods. I wish there were a more efficient way to find the cases. But I know of none available to consumers.

Warning: The fact that the individual or firm is listed in these databases does not automatically mean that they are guilty of offenses. They may have been cleared, or the offenses may not have been significant. So read the details carefully.

Step 5: Optional.   Sometimes, to get good, additional information a better alternative is to contact your state securities regulator. Most states view the information on the CRD database as being public information. Not all states release every bit of detail, but they may disclose more than the NASD. You can locate your state securities regulator by calling 888-846-2722 and pressing "0" for an operator.

Step 6: Decide whether you want to do business with this broker.   I cannot make that decision for you. Nor can I give you blanket rules to follow. A lot will depend on the nature of the offense and your relationship with the broker. But I do want to remind you of one fact: There are many other brokers who are not on these lists and who would be glad to get your business.

Step 7: If your brokerage firm is listed, don't jump to conclusions.   Many good brokerage firms with strong Weiss Safety

Ratings have employed a few errant individuals. Indeed, the larger the firm and the more customers they have, the more likely it is for them to receive complaints. Call the brokerage firm to ask them how they have dealt with that specific situation and what safeguards they have put in place to make sure the problem does not happen again. If you are still not satisfied with their answers, again, there are many other firms that would be glad to have your business.

Once you've selected a broker and opened an account, there are additional steps you can take to avoid problems.

Step 8: Whenever possible, use limit orders. *Limit orders* are orders to buy or sell an investment at a specific price or better. The word *better* refers to better for *you*, the customer. For example:

- If you tell your broker to buy 100 shares of a stock at "$50 or better," he or she will not go ahead with the transaction unless he or she can get you the shares for $50 or *less*.

- If you tell your broker to *sell* 100 shares of a stock at "$50 or better," he or she will not go ahead with the transaction unless he or she can get you $50 or *more* for your shares.

Limit orders are important when you are buying or selling stocks that are very volatile or that do not trade in large volume. They are also very important for any options that you might buy for the crash insurance program discussed in Chapter 7.

Even if you are using an honest broker, a market order can sometimes be like giving your brokerage firm or its traders on the exchange a license to steal. It may not sound like much when we're talking about transactions that cost you fractions of a point–but double them for both buy and sell orders and then multiply that by hundreds of shares and dozens or more transactions each year, and it can add up to hundreds, even thousands, of dollars of unnecessary costs. Instead, use limit orders, which force your broker to buy or sell only at your specified price.

Step 9: Make sure your free cash is always swept into a money market account. I prefer a Treasury-only money market account, to accomplish two goals: (1) It keeps your money safe and secure–guaranteed by the full faith and credit of the U.S. government–while it's in between investments. (2) It puts your free cash balances one step further away from your broker. If your broker does not have a Treasury-only money market fund available, consider a government-only money market fund. And if that is not available either, use a money market fund of your choice.

Step 10: Spot-check your broker with "time & sales" reports. These are daily reports of the trading activity in any listed stock, broken down to the minute and second in which trades occur. Note the time you place your order with your broker. Then, after your trade has been executed, ask for a time and sales report for the period 10 minutes before you placed your order up to the time you received your fill information. You'll see every trade that went by.

If the price you got for a purchase is much higher than the prices available at that time, something is wrong. Likewise, if the price you got for a sale is much lower, that's a similar problem. And even if it all looks fine, you've still sent your broker the message that you're monitoring his or her or the firm's activities.

Step 11: Never purchase an investment pitched to you by someone you don't know, especially a phone solicitor. Chances are it involves a scam. When you get this type of call, quickly hang up the phone–it's that simple. While I don't recommend you listen to the sales pitch, if you do, here are the questions that the North American Securities Administrators Association (NASAA) suggests be answered before you invest a nickel:

- Is the investment registered with the SEC and my state securities agency?
- How long has the company been in business? What is its product or service? Is it profitable? Who are the managers of the company, and have they made money for investors in the past?
- Will you send me the latest reports that have been filed on this company? How can I get more information?
- Where does the stock trade and how do I get information on its trading price?
- How easily can I sell this investment–and what price would I get if I sold it immediately?
- What are the costs to buy, hold, and sell this investment?
- How does this stock match up with my investment objectives?

- What is the risk that I could lose the money I invest?
- Is the broker licensed to do business in your state?
- Is the investment registered?
- Does the broker or the broker's firm have any complaints or a disciplinary history?

If you suspect fraud, get the caller's name, company, and phone number. Then call your state regulatory agency.

Step 12: If needed, get more help from these sources:

AMEX
American Stock Exchange
86 Trinity Place
New York, NY 10006-1881
212-306-1000

NYSE
New York Stock Exchange
20 Broad Street, Fifth Floor
New York, NY 10005
212-656-2772

PHLX
Philadelphia Stock Exchange
1900 Market Street
Philadelphia, PA 19103
800-THE-PHLX; 215-496-5000

NASD
NASD Ombudsman
Box 9492
Gaithersburg, MD 20898-9492
888-700-0028; 301-212-2515
You can also call the NASD at 800-289-9999 for the address of the district.

Step 13: Learn more!   Check Appendix D, "Other Resources for Investors."

APPENDIX C

Investment Watchdog Agencies

Alabama
Securities Commission
770 Washington Street
Montgomery, AL 36130
(334) 242-2984
Joseph Borg, Director
Susan B. Anderson, Deputy Director/General Counsel

Alaska
Division of Banking, Securities and Corps
P.O. Box 110807
Juneau, AK 99811-0807
(907) 465-2521
Debby Sedwick, Commissioner
Franklin T. Elder, Director
For Fedex delivery:
150 3rd Street, Suite 217
Juneau, AK 99801

Arizona
Corporation Commission
1300 West Washington, Third Floor
Phoenix, AZ 85007
(602) 542-4242

Mark Sendro, Director of Securities
Brian C. McNeil, Executive Sec.
Carl J. Kunasek, Chairman
William A. Mundell, Commissioner

Arkansas
Securities Department
201 East Markham, Third Floor
Little Rock, AR 72201
(501) 324-9260
Mac Dodson, Commissioner
Ann McDougal, Deputy Commissioner

California
Department of Corporations
Securities Division
300 Market St., Suite 300
San Francisco, CA 94105
(415) 705-2500
Helane Morrison, District Administrator

Colorado
Division of Securities
1580 Lincoln, Suite 420
Denver, CO 80203
(303) 894-2320
Fred J. Joseph, Commissioner

Connecticut
Department of Banking
Division of Securities
260 Constitution Plaza
Hartford, CT 06103
(860) 240-8230
John P. Burke, Banking Commissioner
Ralph A. Lambiase, Director,
Division of Securities

Delaware
Department of Justice,
Division of Securities
820 North French St., Fifth Floor
Wilmington, DE 19801
(302) 577-8424
James Ropp, Securities Commissioner
Peter O. Jamison, Assistant Attorney General

District of Columbia
Securities Commission
810 First St. N.E., Suite 701
Washington, DC 20002
(202) 727-8000
Larry Coates, Acting Director of Securities

Florida
Office of Comptroller
Attn: Investigations
Division of Securities & Finance
101 East Gaines Street,
Tallahassee, FL 32399
(850) 410-9805
Robert F. Milligan, Comptroller
Don Saxon, Director, Division of Securities

Georgia
Secretary of State, Securities and Business Regulation Division
2 Martin Luther King Jr. Drive
Suite 802, West Tower
Atlanta, GA 30334
(404) 656-3920
Cathy Cox, Secretary of State,
Robert D. Terry, Commissioner of Securities

Hawaii
Department of Commerce and Consumer Affairs
P.O. Box 40

Honolulu, HI 96810
(808) 586-2740
Ryan Uchijima, Commissioner of Business Registration
Patricia Moy, Senior Securities Enforcement Attorney

Idaho
Department of Finance
Securities Bureau
700 W. State Street, Second Floor
Boise, ID 83702
(208) 332-8004
Gavin M. Gee, Director
Marilyn T. Scanlan, Bureau Chief

Illinois
Secretary of State
Securities Department
520 South Second St., Suite 200
Springfield, IL 62701-1722
(217) 782-2256
Jesse White, Secretary of State
Tanya Solov, Director, Securities Department

Indiana
Secretary of State
Securities Division
302 W. Washington St., Room E-111
Indianapolis, IN 46204
(317) 232-6681
Sue Ann Gilroy, Secretary of State
Bradley W. Skolnik, Securities Commissioner

Iowa
Insurance Division
Securities Bureau
340 E Maple St.
Des Moines, IA 50319
(515) 281-4441
Craig A. Goettsch, Superintendent of Securities
Jeanie Vaudt and Chantelle Smith, Assistant Attorney General

Kansas
Securities Commissioner
618 S. Kansas Ave., Second Floor
Topeka, KS 66603
(785) 296-3307
David R. Brant, Securities Commissioner
Rick Fleming, General Counsel

Kentucky
Department of Financial Institutions
1025 Capital Center Dr., Suite 200
Frankfort, KY 40601
(502) 573-3390
Colleen Keefe, Director, Division of Law and
    Regulatory Compliance
Ken Pennington, Deputy Commissioner and General Counsel

Louisiana
Securities Commission
3445 N. Causeway Blvd., Suite 509
Metairie, LA 70002
(504) 846-6970
John Travis, Commissioner of Financial Institutions
Harry C. Stansbury, Deputy Securities Commissioner

Maine
Department of Professional and Financial Regulation
121 State House Station
Augusta, MA 04333
(207) 624-8551
Christine A. Bruenn, Securities Administrator
Judith A. Dorsey, Enforcement Supervisor

Maryland
Division of Securities
200 St. Paul Place
Baltimore, MD 21202
(410) 576-6360
Melanie Senter Lubin, Securities Commissioner
Dale E. Cantone, Deputy Securities Commissioner

Massachusetts
Secretary of the Commonwealth, Securities Division
1 Ashburton Place, Room 170
Boston, MA 02108
(617) 727-3548
William Francis Galvin, Secretary of the Commonwealth
Mathew J. Nestor, Acting Director, Securities Division

Michigan
Securities and Land Development Bureau
P.O. Box 30701
Lansing, MI 48909
(517) 241-6350
Ron Jones, Chief Deputy Director
Frank Fitzgerald, Commissioner

Minnesota
Department of Commerce
133 East Seventh Street
St. Paul, MN 55101
(651) 296-2594
James Bernstein, Commissioner of Commerce
Gary LaVasseur, Deputy Commissioner

Mississippi
Secretary of State, Securities Division
Attn: Nancy Thompson
P.O. Box 136
202 N. Congress Street, Suite 601
Jackson, MS 39205-0136
(601) 359-6371
Eric Clark, Secretary of State
William E. Chapman III, Assistant Secretary of State, Business
    Services

Missouri
Secretary of State
Division of Securities

600 West Main Street
Jefferson City, MO 65101
(573) 751-4136
Rebecca McDowell Cook, Secretary of State
Douglas F. Wilburn, Commissioner of Securities

Montana
Office of the State Auditor
Securities Department
840 Helena Ave.
Helena, MT 59601
(406) 444-2040
Mark O'Keefe, State Auditor and Securities Commissioner
Rusty Harper, Deputy State Auditor and Deputy Securities
  Commissioner

Nebraska
Department of Banking and Finance
Bureau of Securities
1200 N Street, Suite 311
Lincoln, NE 68508
(402) 471-3445
Samuel Baird, Director of Banking and Finance
Jack E. Herstein, Assistant Director of Banking and Finance

Nevada
Secretary of State,
Securities Division
555 E. Washington Ave., Suite 5200
Las Vegas, NV 89101
(702) 486-2440
Dean Heller, Secretary of State
Donald J. Reis, Deputy Secretary of State

New Hampshire
Department of State
Bureau of Securities Regulation
107 N. Main St.
State House, Room 204

Concord, NH 03301
(603) 271-1463
William M. Gardner, Secretary of State
Peter C. Hildreth, Director of Securities Regulation

New Jersey
Bureau of Securities
153 Halsey Street, Sixth Floor
Newark, NJ 07102
(973) 504-3600
Franklin L. Widmann, Bureau Chief
Richard Barry, Enforcement Officer

New Mexico
Regulation and Licensing Department Securities Division
725 St. Michaels Drive
Santa Fe, NM 87505-7605
(505) 827-7140
William J. Verant, Director
Michael J. Vargon, Deputy Director

New York
Department of Law
Bureau of Investor
Protection and Securities
120 Broadway, 23rd Floor
New York, NY 10271
(212) 416-8200
Elliot Spitzer, Attorney General
Eric Dinallo, Assistant Attorney General in Charge

North Carolina
Secretary of State
Securities Division
300 North Salisbury Street, Suite 100
Raleigh, NC 27603
(919) 733-3924
Elaine F. Marshall, Secretary of State
Rodney S. Maddox, Chief Deputy Secretary of State

North Dakota
Securities Commissioner
State Capitol, Fifth Floor
600 E. Blvd Avenue, Dept. 414
Bismark, ND 58505-0510
(701) 328-2910
Syver Vinje, Securities Commissioner
Harold P. Kocher, Securities Examiner

Ohio
Division of Securities
77 South High St., 22nd Floor
Columbus, OH 43215
(614) 644-7381
Debbie Dye, Commissioner
Dale A. Jewell, Broker-Dealer Supervisor

Oklahoma
Department of Securities
120 N. Robinson, Suite 860
Oklahoma City, OK 73102
(405) 280-7700
Irving L. Faught, Administrator
Melanie Hall, Deputy Administrator

Oregon
Division of Corporate Securities
350 Winter Street, NE, Room 410
Salem, OR 97301-3881
(503) 378-4387
Richard Nockleby, Administrator

Pennsylvania
Securities Commission
1010 North Seventh St., Second Floor
Harrisburg, PA 17102-1410
(717) 787-8061
Robert M. Lam, Chairman
A. Richard Gerber, Commissioner

Rhode Island
Department of Business Regulation
233 Richmond Street, Suite 232
Providence, RI 02903
(401) 222-3048
Marilyn Shannon McConaghy, Director
Maria D'Alessandro Piccirilli, Superintendent of Securities

South Carolina
Attorney General, Securities Division
1000 Assembly Street
Columbia, SC 29201
(803) 734-9916
Charles M. Condon, Attorney General and Securities Commissioner
Tracy Meyers, Assistant Attorney General Securities

South Dakota
Division of Securities
118 West Capitol Ave.
Pierre, SD 57501-2000
(605) 773-4823
Gail Sheppick, Director

Tennessee
Department of Commerce and Insurance, Securities Division
500 James Robertson Pkwy., Suite 680
Nashville, TN 37243
(615) 741-2947
Ann Pope, Commissioner of Commerce and Insurance

Texas
State Securities Board
208 East 10th Street, 5th Floor
Austin, TX 78701
(512) 305-8300
Denise Voight Crawford, Securities Commissioner
John Morgan, Deputy Commissioner

Utah
Division of Securities
P.O. Box 146760
Salt Lake City, UT 84114
(801) 530-6600
Douglas C. Borba, Executive Director
Anthony Taggart, Director

Vermont
Division of Securities
89 Main Street, Door 20
Montpelier, VT 05620
(802) 828-3420
Elizabeth R. Costle, Commissioner
Blythe McLaughlin, Deputy Commissioner

Virginia
Division of Securities and Retail Franchising
P.O. Box 1197
Richmond, VA 23218
Attn: Garland Sharp
(804) 371-9051
Ronald W. Thomas, Director
Thomas M. Gouldin, Deputy Director

Washington
Department of Financial Institutions
Securities Division
210 11th Ave. SW, Room 300
Olympia, WA 98504
(360) 902-8760
Deborah R. Bortner, Administrator
Michael Stevenson, Audit and Enforcement

West Virginia
State Auditor, Securities Division
State Capitol, Bldg. 1, Suite W-114
Charleston, WV 25305

(304) 558-2257
Glen B. Gainer, III, State Auditor and Commissioner of Securities
Chester Thompson, Deputy Commissioner of Securities

Wisconsin
Department of Financial Institutions
Division of Securities
P.O. Box 1768
Madison, WI 53701-1768
(608) 261-9555
Patricia D. Struck, Administrator
Randall E. Schumann, General Counsel

Wyoming
Secretary of State, Securities Division
State Capitol Building
Cheyenne, WY 82002
(307) 777-7370
Joseph B. Meyer, Secretary of State
Thomas Cowan, Assistant Securities Administrator

APPENDIX D

Other Resources for Investors

The Securities and Exchange Commission (SEC). The SEC Web site (www.sec.gov) offers a wealth of additional information and hints. Although these may not always coincide with my advice, they are valuable nonetheless. At the site, you get a list of:

- Questions to ask before investing in stocks
- Questions to ask of brokers and other salespeople before investing
- Questions to ask about the progress of your investments
- What to do if you run into problems with your investments
- How to handle problems with your broker

You can also download a number of useful forms and publications, such as:

- A complaint form against your broker
- Instructions for interviewing your broker
- "Invest Wisely: Introduction to Mutual Funds" (www.sec.gov /investor/pubs/inwsmf.htm)
- "Invest Wisely: Advice from Your Securities Industry Regulators" (www.sec.gov/investor/pubs/inws.htm)

■ Complaints and inquiries (www.sec.gov/investor/pubs /howoiea.htm)

and many others.

Go to www.sec.gov. Then, under "Investor Information," select "Online Publications." Or if you do not have access to the Internet, contact:

Securities and Exchange Commission
450 Fifth Street NW
Washington, DC 20549-0213
Useful SEC phone numbers:
(202) 942-4040 (Publications Unit)
(202) 942-7040 (Investor Assistance and Complaints)
1-800-SEC-0330 (Investor Information Service–to obtain free publications and investor alerts, learn how to file a complaint, and contact the SEC.)

The New York Stock Exchange (NYSE). The NYSE provides an excellent glossary of terms you may encounter when making investment decisions. Go to www.nyse.com and, at the bottom of the screen, click on "Glossary." In addition, you may find answers to some of your basic questions if you click on the green box in the lower left of the screen "Getting Started."

The Chicago Board of Options Exchange (CBOE). The CBOE is probably the best place to learn about options, especially if you click on "Learning Center."

APPENDIX E

Medicare, Medigap, and Long-Term Care: Piecing the Puzzle Together

Follow these steps to get the best-fit amount from (a) your Medicare coverage, (b) your Medigap insurance policy and (c) any long-term care policies.

For Skilled Nursing Care

Step 1: Consider what Medicare will cover.   100% of the first 20 days of skilled nursing care provided that . . .

- You have spent three consecutive days in the hospital (not including the day of discharge) for the same condition before entering a skilled nursing facility that is certified by Medicare.
- Care (for the same condition you were hospitalized for) is administered in a certified facility.
- Care is administered within 30 days of your discharge from the hospital.
- A medical professional has certified that you need skilled nursing care or rehabilitation services on a daily basis.

Medicare Part A pays all expenses for the first 20 days you stay in a skilled nursing facility. Then for the next 80 days, you must pay a daily coinsurance amount. After those 100 days, you are personally responsible for all charges.

But, Medicare does *not* pay for any services beyond 100 days, nor does it pay for services in a skilled nursing facility or nursing home that are primarily personal care or custodial (e.g., bathing, eating, and dressing). These, unfortunately, are the services most needed by elderly Americans.

Step 2: Supplement the coverage with Medigap insurance (Chapter 12). Medigap Plans C, D, E, F, G, H, I, and J will pay the daily coinsurance amount for skilled nursing facility care for the 21st to the 100th day that you are in a skilled nursing facility.

Step 3: Consider long-term-care insurance to cover:

- Nursing care needs beyond the 100th day
- Nursing care that is unrelated to a hospital stay

For Home Health Care Coverage

Step 1: Consider what Medicare will cover. Medicare Part A covers the full amount of home health care expenses only if:

- Intermittent skilled nursing care, physical therapy, or speech therapy is needed
- You are confined to the home
- You are under a physician's care
- You receive services from a Medicare-certified home health agency

Important: All four of those conditions must be met in order to qualify for home health care. You do not have to pay a deductible or coinsurance, and no prior hospitalization is required before receiving home health care benefits. Medicare also covers a portion of the cost of durable medical equipment that is provided and supervised by a physician, such as wheelchairs and hospital beds.

Medicare also covers hospice care *if it is in your home.* Hospice care is a program in which terminally ill patients are cared for. Caregivers make no attempt to cure the illness or disease but, instead, provide pain management and counseling services. Medicare Part A pays for all hospice care provided in the home by a Medicare-approved hospice including:

- Physician services

- Nursing care

- Medical appliances and supplies

- Drugs (for pain and symptom management)

- Short-term inpatient care (a maximum of five days' respite care to relieve the primary caregiver)

- Medical social services

- Physical therapy, occupational therapy, and speech/language pathology services

- Dietary and other counseling

You pay no deductible for hospice services. The only copayments required are a maximum $5 payment for each prescription drug and a daily charge of approximately $5 (depending on the area of the country) for respite care in the hospice facility.

Step 2: Supplement the coverage with a Medigap policy. Medigap Plans D, G, I, and J augment the Medicare coverage by providing $40 per visit for at-home recovery following an illness or injury, but only if a physician orders the follow-up care. Typically, you can get this coverage for up to seven visits a week for a maximum of eight weeks after your Medicare-covered home health care visits stop. To qualify for the at-home recovery benefit, you must receive Medicare-covered home health care services after an illness, injury, or surgery, and the services covered by the Medigap policy must be ordered by your doctor. The maximum benefit per year is $1,600.

Step 3: Consider a long-term-care policy to cover non-medical care. This includes care such as custodial or personal care. You have sole responsibility for the cost of any assistance you receive that is not provided in conjunction with skilled medical care. Some examples include: light housekeeping, meal preparation, laundry, and the services of a home care aide who acts as a companion or homemaker on a short- or long-term basis. You are also responsible for the modification of your home so that you can live comfortably there without having to go to a nursing home.

For Community-Based Care

Step 1: You should know that Medicare offers no coverage for community-based care.

Step 2: Same for Medigap. No coverage for community-based care.

Step 3: If you want community-based care covered, and you do not have other alternatives (your own savings or help from family, then long-term-care insurance is probably your only alternative. Long-term-care insurance covers facilities such as adult day care centers, continuing care retirement communities, assisted living facilities, and hospice care.

APPENDIX F

Long-Term-Care Planner

Use this worksheet to navigate through the maze of long-term care and select the policy that is truly best for you. For a detailed explanation of each step, see Chapter 13.

CHOOSING A PLAN FOR LONG-TERM CARE THAT'S RIGHT FOR YOU

Step 1. Are you younger than 59? If so, see my advice in Chapter 13.

Step 2. Do you have access to the information you need to shop around? For more information on paying for long-term care, contact the *United Seniors Health Cooperative* by calling 202-393-6222, and request their free report, "Long-Term Care Planning: A Dollar and Sense Guide." Also, see our lists, "Helpful Organizations" and "Helpful Publications" in Appendix G.

Step 3. To buy only what you really need, try to determine, ahead of time, what type of care you think you will need from others beyond the assistance your own family members may be able to provide:

	Yes	No
Custodial care	☐	☐
Intermediate care	☐	☐
Skilled care	☐	☐

Step 4. Decide where you would most likely be receiving the care.

	Yes	No
In-home care*	☐	☐
Nursing home*	☐	☐
Adult day care	☐	☐
Assisted living facility	☐	☐
Other _____	☐	☐

*Typically available with all three levels of care—custodial, intermediate, and skilled.

Step 5. Check out the facilities in the area in which you plan to live, make sure you're comfortable with them, and find out much how they cost:

Estimated Costs

In-home care	_____
Nursing home	_____
Assisted living facility	_____
Adult day care	_____
Other	_____

Step 6. Try to estimate how much of the long-term-care expenses you will be able to pay on your own: $_____ per month.

Step 7. Try to arrive at a reasonable guess regarding when you might start using the benefits. _____

WORKING WITH A QUALIFIED
INSURANCE AGENT

Step 1. Find insurance agents in your area that specialize in long-term-care policies:

Agent Name	Phone Number	Specialization in LTC?	Name of Insurance Company
		(Y/N)	
		(Y/N)	
		(Y/N)	
		(Y/N)	

Step 2. Ask your agent for the names of at least three different policies, from different insurers, that you can compare.

	Policy A	Policy B	Policy C
Insurance company name			
Policy name /number			

Step 3. Have your agent check the safety rating for each company.

Safety Rating

Policy A: _____

Policy B: _____

Policy C: _____

Step 4. Favor companies that have more experience with long-term-care insurance.

	Years of Experience with Long-Term Care	Have They Ever Raised Rates for Existing Policyholders?
Policy A:	_____	(Y/N)
Policy B:	_____	(Y/N)
Policy C:	_____	(Y/N)

Step 5. If you're considering buying a policy with your spouse, check how you qualify for a spousal discount.

Policy A: _____

Policy B: _____

Policy C: _____

Step 6. Ask your agent for quotes on the monthly premiums. Make sure the quotes are based on the preferences and needs that you outlined in steps 1 through 6.

	Single Policy Premium	Combined Policy Premium	% Savings
Policy A:	_____	_____	_____
Policy B:	_____	_____	_____
Policy C:	_____	_____	_____

Step 7. Find out exactly what each policy covers in addition to the basics that you require:

	Policy A	Policy B	Policy C
Custodial	(Y/N)	(Y/N)	(Y/N)
Intermediate	(Y/N)	(Y/N)	(Y/N)
Skilled	(Y/N)	(Y/N)	(Y/N)

Step 8. Ask your agent to give you a list of the types of facilities that are included and how they are defined. Facilities may include nursing home care, in-home care, adult day care, hospice care, assisted living facilities, and other options.

Policy A

_____

_____

_____

Policy B

_____

_____

_____

Policy C

_____

_____

_____

Step 9. Find out the basic terms of coverage and reimbursement: the elimination period, the benefit period, and the daily benefit.

Policy A: How the company calculates elimination period:

_____

Facility of Care	Elimination Periods	Benefit Period	Daily Benefit
In-home care:	_____	_____	_____
Nursing home	_____	_____	_____
Assisted living:	_____	_____	_____
Adult day care:	_____	_____	_____

Policy B: How the company calculates elimination period:

_____

Facility of Care	Elimination Periods	Benefit Period	Daily Benefit
In-home care:	_____	_____	_____
Nursing home	_____	_____	_____
Assisted living:	_____	_____	_____
Adult day care:	_____	_____	_____

Policy C: How the company calculates elimination period:

_____

Facility of Care	Elimination Periods	Benefit Period	Daily Benefit
In-home care:	_____	_____	_____
Nursing home	_____	_____	_____
Assisted living:	_____	_____	_____
Adult day care:	_____	_____	_____

Step 10. Determine if the policy is a "pool of money" contract.

	Pool of Money?
Policy A:	(Y/N)
Policy B:	(Y/N)
Policy C:	(Y/N)

Step 11. Check into the requirements needed to activate the policy.

Policy A: _____

_____

Policy B: _____

_____

Policy C: _____

_____

Step 12.   Find out what other features are included or can be added by a rider to the policy.

	Policy A	Policy B	Policy C
Waiver of premium	(Y/N)	(Y/N)	(Y/N)
Nonforfeiture	(Y/N)	(Y/N)	(Y/N)
Restoration of benefits	(Y/N)	(Y/N)	(Y/N)
Alternate care plan	(Y/N)	(Y/N)	(Y/N)
Bed reservation	(Y/N)	(Y/N)	(Y/N)
Guaranteed renewable	(Y/N)	(Y/N)	(Y/N)
Inflation protection	(Y/N)	(Y/N)	(Y/N)

Step 13.   Learn more! Contact one or more of the organizations listed in Appendix G, as needed.

APPENDIX G

Helpful Organizations, Publications, and Programs

ORGANIZATIONS

American Association of Homes and Services for the Aging
901 E Street, N.W. #500
Washington, DC 20004-2037
202-783-2242 or 1-800-508-9442

American Association of Retired Persons
601 E. Street, N.W.
Washington, DC 20049
202-434-2277

American Health Care Association
1201 L Street, N.W.
Washington, DC 20005
202-842-3860

Assisted Living Federation of America
10300 Eaton Place #400
Fairfax, VA 22030
703-691-8100

Health Care Financing Administration
7500 Security Boulevard
Baltimore, MD 21244-1850

Medicare Hotline
1-800-638-6833

Health Insurance Association of America
555 13th Street, N.W. #600E
Washington, DC 20004-1109
202-824-1600

Medicare Rights Center
1460 Broadway
New York, NY 10036-7393
1-800-333-4114

National Adult Day Services Association
c/o The National Council on the Aging, Inc.
409 Third Street, S.W. #200
Washington, DC 20024
202-479-1200

National Association for Home Care
228 Seventh Street, S.E.
Washington, DC 20003
202-547-7424

**National Association of Professional Geriatric Care
    Managers**
1604 North Country Club Road
Tucson, AZ 85716
602-881-8008

National Consumers League
1701 K Street, N.W. #1200
Washington, DC 20006
202-835-3323

National Hospice Organization
1901 North Moore Street #901
Arlington, VA 22209
1-800-658-8898

United Seniors Health Cooperative
409 Third Street, S.W., 2nd Floor #200
Washington, DC 20024-3132
1-800-637-2604

HELPFUL PUBLICATIONS

A Shopper's Guide to Long-Term Care Insurance
State Department of Insurance or the National Association of
    Insurance Commissioners
120 W. 12th Street, Suite 1100
Kansas City, MO 64105-1925

Long-Term Care Planning: A Dollar and Sense Guide
United Seniors Health Cooperative
409 Third St., S.W.
Washington, DC 20024-3132
1-800-637-2604

STATE PARTNERSHIP PROGRAMS

California Partnership for Long-Term Care
Consumer Information: 1-800-434-0222

Indiana Long-Term-Care Program
Senior Health Insurance Information Program (SHIIP) offers a
    complete list of companies participating in the program at
    1-800-452-4800.

New York State Partnership for Long-Term Care
Office of Medicaid Management offers the "Consumer Book-let–Affordable Financing for Long Term Care" at 1-888-NYS-PLTC.

State of Connecticut's Partnership Program
Consumer Information: 1-800-547-3443

ENDNOTES

Introduction

1. According to the U.S. General Accounting Office (GAO), this was a common occurrence for A. M. Best & Co. The GAO reported that, for the six largest insurance companies that failed in the early 1990s, "Best assigned a 'vulnerable' rating before [failure] in only one of six cases and this was only six days before the [failure] occurred. In one case, Best stopped rating the insurer and never assigned a 'vulnerable' rating. In the remaining four cases, it assigned a 'vulnerable' rating only after the [failure]."

2. The GAO study, *Insurance Ratings: Comparison of Private Agency Ratings for Life/Health Insurers* (September 1994) can be found on the Weiss Ratings Web site at www.weissratings.com/gao. To order a free copy directly from the GAO, write to U.S. General Accounting Office, Box 37050, Washington, DC 20013; call 202-512-6000; fax to 202-512-6061; or visit www.gao.gov and request report GAO/GGD-94-204BR.

3. Ibid.

4. According to industry observers, Best, Fitch, Moody's, and Standard & Poor's generally charge $25,000 or more per year, per rating. In contrast, organizations seeking to protect consumers refuse to accept any compensation whatsoever from the rated companies.

5. This is no secret. A. M. Best & Co. clearly states in its 1995 *Insurance Reports,* p. xv: "NA-9 Rating (Company Request): Assigned to companies eligible for ratings, but which request that their rating not be published because *they disagree* with our rating." [Italics added.] Beginning with its 1996 *Insurance Reports* (p. xiv), Best changed its NA-9 category to NR-4, but the definition is very similar. With this mechanism, ratings that might otherwise have served as warnings to the public are removed from public view, with disastrous consequences for consumers. Thus, in its 1994 report (GAO/GGD-94-204BR), the GAO states that in

4 out of 30 cases rated by both Best and Weiss, "Best never actually assigned a 'vulnerable' rating. Instead, Best changed these ratings from 'secure' to one of its 'not assigned' categories. And in a follow-up report using the same methodology as that used by the GAO, entitled *Performance Review of Insurance Ratings Agencies,* Weiss found that, subsequently, there were another 16 companies in Best's NR category that failed. In each case, Best's standard operating procedure was to cooperate with the companies, remove the bad ratings from circulation, and hide the financial weaknesses from the public. And in each case, the companies failed, causing severe hardships to consumers.

6. *Barron's* (October 30, 1995); *New York Times* (January 5, 1991); *Esquire* (April 1996).

Chapter 1

1. For specific instructions on how to duplicate this research, see Chapter 6. Or, if you have a mathematical inclination, just use this formula: Absolute value [(quarterly net income minus quarterly operating cash flow) divided by total assets] is greater than or equal to 4 percent.

2. The companies find a handy rationale for this gimmick in the Financial Accounting Standards Board's (FASB's) FAS 121, which encourages them to review assets yearly and write them off if they have become "impaired." However, the companies are going far beyond the original intent, using this as an excuse to wipe goodwill off the books and exaggerate future earnings.

3. Since then, the FASB has eliminated this method of accounting. See "FASB Enacts Standards Prohibiting 'Pooling' in Mergers," *Wall Street Journal* (July 6, 2001).

4. Option costs must be carefully disclosed in footnotes to financial statements, according to guidelines set forth in FAS 123. However, very few companies include them in their compensation costs, reporting instead deceptively high earnings to investors.

5. Daniel Murray, "Employee Stock Options: The Fed Joins In," *Smithers & Co., (London) Report,* no. 142 (January 20, 2000).

6. For an excellent review of how companies circumvented accounting standards to manipulate earnings reports, see D. Henry, "The Numbers Game," *Business Week* (May 14, 2001). See also P. Elstrom and D. Henry, "Today Nortel, Tomorrow . . . ," *Business Week* (July 2, 2001).

7. "SEC Chairman Arthur Levitt, Concerned That the Quality of Corporate Financial Reporting Is Eroding, Announces Action Plan to Remedy Problem," September 28, 1998. www.sec.gov/news/press/pressarchive/1998/98-95.txt.

8. Lynn Turner, Chief Accountant, U.S. Securities & Exchange Commission, from *A Roadmap for Establishing Accountability,* Washington University School of Law and the Institute for Law and Economic Policy, Scottsdale, AZ (March 10, 2001). www.sec.gov/news/speech/spch469.htm.

9. Gretchen Morgenson, "How Did So Many Get It So Wrong?" *New York Times* (December 31, 2000).

10. Michael Siconolfi, "Under Pressure: At Morgan Stanley, Analysts Were Urged to Soften Harsh Views," *Wall Street Journal* (July 14, 1992), p. A1.

11. Zacks Investment Research (December 31, 2000).

12. U.S. General Accounting Office, *Securities Markets: Actions Needed to Better Protect Investors against Unscrupulous Brokers*, GAO/GGD-94-208. www.gao.gov. See note 2 from the "Introduction" of this book on how to order a free copy.

13. *USA Today* (March 23, 2001), p. 2B. See also www.financialweb.com/skdsecshow.asp.

14. "Arrests Highlight Rise in Small-Stock Schemes," *Wall Street Journal* (October 14, 1996), p. C1.

15. Martin D. Weiss, *Safe Money Report*, no. 247 (November 7, 1994). Weiss Research, Inc., Palm Beach Gardens, FL.

16. "NASD Board of Governors Approves Proposed Rule to Strengthen Disclosures by Research Analysts" (July 2, 2001). www.nasdr.com/news/pr2001/ne_section01_033.html. Specifically, NASD President and CEO Robert R. Glauber states: "Investors need to be able to determine if they think an analyst may have a conflict of interest influencing a recommendation. Indeed, anyone who acts as an 'analyst' should fully disclose conflicts of interest."

Chapter 2

1. According to the American Bankruptcy Institute (Alexandria, VA 22314, www.abiworld.org), the number of business bankruptcy filings in the first half of 2001 was 20,335; there were 35,472 in 2000; 37,563 in 1999; 44,196 in 1998. The number of nonbusiness (or consumer) bankruptcy filings in first half of 2001 was 746,900; there were 1,217,972 in 2000; 1,290,346 in 1999; 1,398,182 in 1998. According to state insurance commissioners, 56 HMOs have failed from 1996 through 2001. Meanwhile, 78 brokerage firms have failed since 1990, according to the 2000 Securities Investor Protection Corporation (SIPC).

2. U.S. General Accounting Office, *Financial Derivatives: Actions Needed to Protect the Financial System*, GAO/GGD 94-133, May 1994. See note 2 in the "Introduction" of this book on how to order a free copy.

3. Based on a study by Weiss Ratings, Inc., Palm Beach Gardens, FL. www.weissratings.com. Data: June 30, 2001 from Wiesenberger, a Thomson Financial Company.

4. "Testimony Concerning Conflicts of Interest Faced by Brokerage Firms and Their Research Analysts by Laura S. Unger, Acting Chair, U.S. Securities & Exchange Commission, before the Subcommittee on Capital Markets, Insurance, and Government Sponsored Enterprises, Committee on Financial Services, United States House of Representatives" (July 31, 2001). See also "S.E.C. Leader Cites Conflicts of Analysts at Large Firms," *New York Times* (August 1, 2001).

5. Data collected for the first half of 2001 by Thompson Financial Data show the leading U.S. equity underwriters are Goldman Sachs, Morgan Stanley, Crédit Suisse First Boston, Citigroup-SSB, and Merrill Lynch. Collectively, they underwrote stock issuance of $48.8 billion, accounting for 70.1 percent of all underwriting activity.

6. U.S. General Accounting Office, *Securities Arbitration: Actions Needed to Address Problem of Unpaid Awards,* GAO/GGD-00-115 (June 15, 2000). See note 2 in the "Introduction" of this book on how to order a free copy.

Chapter 3

1. Kathy Bergen, "Case Puts Analysts under Scrutiny: Brokerages May Face More Claims over Conflicts," *Chicago Tribune* (July 29, 2001).

2. *Shearson/American Express v. McMahon,* 482 U.S. 220 (June 1987); *Dean Witter Reynolds, Inc., v. Byrd,* 470 U.S. 213 (1985). See also Susan Scherreik, "Your Broker Blew It. What to Do," *Business Week* (August 13, 2001).

3. U.S. General Accounting Office, *Securities Arbitration: Actions Needed to Address Problem of Unpaid Awards,* GAO/GGD-00-115 (June 15, 2000). See note 2 of the "Introduction" on how to order a free copy.

4. Nearly all of these unpaid awards were from cases decided in NASD's arbitration forum. When investors complained, NASD did take action to suspend nonpaying broker-dealers and had some success in recovering awards, but it did not monitor the payment of arbitration awards.

5. U.S. General Accounting Office, *Securities Arbitration: Actions Needed to Address Problem of Unpaid Awards,* GAO/GGD-00-115 (June 15, 2000), Executive Summary, p. 5.

6. For more details on these steps, see "How Does One Start Securities Arbitration?" at www.securitieslaw.com/arbitration.html.

Chapter 4

1. For a complete guide to bank rip-offs and how to avoid them, read Edward F. Mrkvicka, Jr., *Your Bank is Ripping You Off: From ATM Charges to Credit Card Interest to Checking Fees to Loans on Your Car and Home: How to Fight Back and Save a Fortune,* St. Martin's Griffin, New York (1997).

2. Comptroller of the Currency (OCC), *Bank Derivatives Report First Quarter 2001* (June 18, 2001), p. 1. www.occ.treas.gov/ftp/release/2001-54.doc.

3. Treasury-only money market funds themselves, like all funds, are neither sponsored nor guaranteed by the U.S. government. In addition, they are neither a deposit of nor endorsed by any bank and, therefore, are not insured under the FDIC or any other agency. However, the U.S. Treasury securities in which they invest are fully guaranteed by the U.S. Treasury Department, and the securities are held in safe-keeping at a custodian bank.

Chapter 5

1. As of December 31, 2000, the average five-year return for 2,072 no-load mutual funds is 51.7 percent. However, for 1,436 load mutual funds, it was only 48.8 percent, even without subtracting the cost of the load. If the cost of the load were subtracted, either immediately up front or distributed over many years, the returns for the load funds would be even less favorable.

2. See Weiss Ratings' *Guide to Stock Mutual Funds,* Weiss Ratings, Inc., Palm Beach Gardens, FL.

3. 1990 Nobel Prize for Economics to William Sharpe, Harry Markowitz, and Merton Miller. Go to www.nobel.se/economics/laureates/1990/press.html.

Chapter 6

1. Ruth Simon, "The Big Bad News about Fee-Only Financial Planners," *Money Magazine* (December 1995).

Chapter 7

1. "Flow of Funds for the U.S.," Federal Reserve Statistical Release, Z.1.

Chapter 8

1. The Securities Act of 1933 and subsequent case law require the disclosure of material information concerning securities offered for public sale, and it is generally agreed that any guarantees of performance, whether explicit or implicit, are in conflict with this requirement.

2. For a discussion of the amounts that each rating agency charges companies they rate, see "An Expanded Watch List of Life-Health Insurance Companies," *Insurance Forum* (November 1994), pp. 110–111. Insurance Forum, Inc., Box 245, Ellettsville, IN 47429. www.insuranceforum.com.

3. Eric Berg, "New Ratings for Insurers Are Disputed," *New York Times* (April 30, 1991).

4. In 1986, Michael Milken of Drexel Burnham Lambert, the leading proponents of junk bonds on Wall Street, persuaded several local governments around the country to issue municipal bonds for purported public purposes, raising $1.85 billion from investors. The investors, based on the disclosures furnished, thought they were buying municipal bonds for use in public projects. However, they were really buying junk bonds in disguise: Their money was invested in GICs with Executive Life Insurance Company. Executive Life, in turn, put most of the money into junk bonds. Except for one isolated transaction, none of the $1.85 billion was used for any announced public purpose. Fred Carr and Executive Life

made out like bandits, paying from 8 to 9 1/2 percent for funds and earning 15 percent from the junk bonds they bought through Milken.

5. The Securities Valuation Office established the following four bond classes: "yes," "no*," "no**," and "no." The first category, "yes," was the one considered to be investment grade, while the three "no" categories were considered junk bonds. However, the "yes" category actually included billions of dollars of bonds rated BB or lower (junk) by the leading rating agencies.

6. Based on the faulty definition of junk bonds used until 1989, the insurance commissioners reported that First Capital Life had $842 million, or 20.2 percent of its invested assets, in junk bonds at year-end 1989. However, based on the correct, standard definition of junk bonds, which the commissioners finally began using in 1990, it turned out that First Capital actually had $1.6 billion in junk bonds, or 40.7 percent of its invested assets. Fidelity Bankers Life's junk bond holdings, previously reported at $639 million or 18.3 percent of invested assets, jumped to $1.5 billion or 37.6 percent of invested assets. All told, the industry's junk bond holdings surged from $51 billion on December 31, 1988, to $84 billion on December 31, 1990, with virtually the entire increase attributable to the change in definition.

7. Eric Berg, "Insurers Forced to Report More Investments as 'Junk'," *New York Times* (April 30, 1991).

8. Martin D. Weiss, "Toward a Full Disclosure Environment in the Insurance Industry," testimony before the U.S. Senate Committee on Banking, Housing, & Urban Affairs. See especially Chart 1.

9. Ibid., Chart 2.

10. The GAO Study, *Insurance Ratings: Comparison of Private Rating Agency Ratings for Life/Health Insurers* (September 1994), states: "Weiss' ratings reflected financial vulnerability first three times more often than Best in the cases we compared. On average, Weiss' ratings reflected financial vulnerability eight months earlier than Best. The other agencies–D&P, Moody's, and S&P–rated, at most, five of the life/health insurers that became financially impaired during our comparison period. These five, among the six largest such insurers, were also rated by Best and Weiss. Weiss was the first to assign a vulnerable rating in five of the six cases; Moody's–which rated only two of the six insurers–was first in the sixth case. In no case was Best, S&P, or D&P first to reflect financial vulnerability for these six insurers. In four of these cases, Best did not assign a vulnerable rating until after the first public regulatory action." The GAO also writes: "[W]e identified 1,963 life/health insurers. Weiss rated 1,449–over 70 percent of the universe we identified, as compared to 795 rated by Best–about 40 percent. The other three raters covered 12 percent or less each."

11. For more on the failure of the guaranty association system following the large insurance company failures of the early 1990s, see "G.A.O. Finds Pension Risk in Funds Shifted to Insurers," *New York Times* (April 22, 1993), and "GAO Hits Guaranty Funds' Gaps," *National Underwriter* (May 3, 1993).

12. In a study using the same methodology as followed by the GAO in its 1994 study, *Insurance Ratings: Comparison of Private Agency Ratings for Life/Health*

Insurers (September 1994), Weiss Ratings found that, among all six rating systems, S&P's free Qualified Ratings are the most skewed to the lower end of the rating scale, while their paid-for Claims Paying Ability Ratings are among the most skewed to the high end. Further, S&P discontinues publication of the Qualified Ratings when a Claims Paying Ability Rating is purchased. Thus, whether by design or not, the net effect of the low Qualified Ratings is to blackmail companies to purchase the higher Claims Paying Ability Ratings.

13. Weiss Ratings, Inc., *At Least 49 Life and Health Insurers Have More Junk Bonds Than Capital, Increasing Vulnerability to Recent Plunge in Junk Bond Prices* (November 20, 2000). For a free copy, write to Press Releases, Weiss Ratings, 4176 Burns Road, Palm Beach Gardens, FL 33410, or go to www.weissratings .com/News/Ins_General/20001120lh.htm. Data: National Association of Insurance Commissioners (NAIC).

14. In the GAO's study, *Insurance Ratings: Comparison of Private Agency Ratings for Life/Health Insurers* (September 1994), the lowest rating category in the ratings scales of the various rating agencies is "Band 5." However, with the exception of Weiss, most of the rating agencies rarely use those bands. In 2001, although Weiss assigned a "Band 5" rating to 69 companies, S&P assigned only one, and Moody's assigned none.

Chapter 9

1. "Insurance Briefs," *Journal of Commerce* (April 20, 1994).
2. This is nothing new. Here is a quote from the insurance commissioner from New York in 1870.

As already intimated, it is believed to be a fact, now causing quite general complaint, that there are too many complicated schemes or plans of insuring, and conducting companies, as well as too many and too elaborate forms of contract or policy. Each new company announces some new feature in its business, which is to enure greatly to the advantage of the insured, and thus, with some seventy different companies, each urging their superiority over all others, he who seeks insurance, if he stops to hear all the arguments, and deliberately determine which is really the best company, is likely to die before he reaches a conclusion.

From the Eleventh Annual Report of the Superintendent of the Insurance Department of the State of New York (April 1, 1870).
3. Martin D. Weiss, "The Insurance Industry Crisis and the Benefits of Full Risk Disclosure," testimony before the U.S. House Subcommittee on Commerce, Consumer Protection, and Competitiveness (July 17, 1991). See also Martin D. Weiss, "Toward a Full Disclosure Environment in the Insurance Industry,"

testimony before the U.S. Senate Committee on Banking, Housing, and Urban Affairs (February 18, 1992); "The Crisis of Confidence in the Insurance Industry," testimony before the U.S. Senate Committee on Commerce, Science, and Transportation (May 7, 1991).

4. Eric Berg, "The Bad Boy of Insurance Ratings," *New York Times* (January 5, 1991), Business section, p. 1.

5. Joseph M. Belth, "The Disclosure Approach to the Problem of Deceptive Practices in the Life Insurance Industry," *The Insurance Forum* (August 1994), vol. 21, no. 8, pp. 81–82. See also "Deceptive Practices and the Establishment of IMSA," *The Insurance Forum* (August 1999), vol. 26, no. 8, p. 241. For copies ($5 each), write to Insurance Forum, Inc., Box 245, Ellettsville, IN 47429, or visit them on the Web at www.insuranceforum.com.

6. Major settlements were as follows: Prudential Insurance Co. of America (Newark, New Jersey)–$2.7 billion, with at least 1 million policyholders involved, settled 1996; John Hancock Financial Services, Inc. (Boston, Massachusetts)–$713 million settlement, involving 4 million policyholders, settled 1997; Metropolitan Life Insurance Co. (New York, New York)–$1.7 billion, involving 7 million policyholders, settled 1999.

7. James H. Hunt, "How to Save Money on Life Insurance," Consumer Federation of America, Washington, D.C. For more information, go to www .consumerfed.org, call 202-387-6121, or write to Consumer Federation of America, 1424 16th Street, NW, Suite 604, Washington, DC 20036.

8. One of the tacks the insurance industry developed to combat all of their bad press was to create new credentials. As of this writing, most insurance designations are awarded by The American College, an educational institution in Pennsylvania that offers college-level courses on life insurance and related matters. The college awards a handful of designations to financial services professionals, the most popular of which are the Chartered Life Underwriter (CLU), the Chartered Financial Consultant (ChFC), and the Certified Financial Planner (CFP). It also awards the Registered Health Underwriter (RHU) and the Registered Employee Benefit Consultant (REBC). At college, financial services professionals learn all about the products that they will be selling and even get sales training. And that sales training is sure to be enhanced when the merger between The American College and LUTC, Inc., is complete. What is LUTC, you ask? It's a company known for its life insurance sales training expertise. At LUTC, your insurance "advisor" can take classes like Employee Benefits. The catalog description says:

> . . . target marketing [is an] important element of this course, as are effective activities to stimulate activity within this market. The course features invaluable material on an effective preapproach, the approach, and closing techniques.

In other words, financial services professionals are furthering their education at an institution that was created to train salespeople to improve their strategies and increase their close ratio. They learn how to target (find) you, approach you, get in your door (or head), and not give up until they have sold you their product.

Chapter 11

1. For example, in the January 1990 issue of *Best's Review,* Harold Skipper, Professor of Risk Management and Insurance at Georgia State University, pointed out:

> with increasing competition from all quarters, insurers are seeking ways to operate on thinner margins, to enhance investment performance through the purchase of . . . riskier investments.

In the same issue, Earl Pomeroy, President of the National Association of Insurance Commissioners (NAIC), wrote:

> State insurance regulators are observing ominous signs of emerging solvency problems in what traditionally has been the most secure line of all–life insurance.

Similarly, in the March 1990 issue of *Best's Review,* David F. Wood, past president of the National Association of Life Underwriters, under the title "The Insolvency Chill," stated:

> It is widely acknowledged that life insurers' profit margins have declined significantly, primarily because of rapidly increasing costs, slower growth, declining interest rates in the face of long-term higher rate guarantees and stiffer competition. All these factors have severely eroded the capital base of many companies. . . ."

2. Data: Thompson Financial.

3. Yes, there were special weaknesses back then that do not exist today, such as speculative municipal bonds in Florida, based mostly on the high-risk land boom. But there are also many special weaknesses today which did not exist in the 1930s, as described later in this chapter.

4. Lynn Hume, "Disclosure: TBMA Forms Taskforce to Review Practices," *The Bond Buyer* (May 16, 2001).

5. "Milestones in Municipal Disclosure," *The Bond Buyer* (November 10, 1998).

6. Vicki Stamas, "Buchanan Sentenced to Serve Three Years and Pay $500,000 for Fraudulent Deals," *The Bond Buyer* (April 2, 1992).

7. Karen Damato, "Stock-Like Risk Is 'Ugly Secret' in Usually Safe Muni Market," *Wall Street Journal* (March 28, 2001).

8. Federal Reserve Consolidated Statement for Federal, State, and Local Governments.

9. S&P's J. J. Kenny at www.jjkenny.com/jjkenny/freepage.html.

Chapter 12

1. Weiss Ratings, Inc., "Medicare HMO Fiasco: Few Options Available for the Nearly One Million Seniors to Be Dropped from HMOs by Year-End," (November 8, 2000). See also Weiss Ratings, Inc., "Advice for the 300,000 Medicare Beneficiaries Being Dropped from Their HMOs on January 1," (November 8, 1999). For free copies, write to Press Releases, Weiss Ratings, Inc., 4176 Burns Road, Palm Beach Gardens, FL 33410, or go to www.weissratings .com/News/Ins_Medigap/20001108medigap.htm and www.weissratings.com/News/ Ins_HMO/19991108hmo.htm.

2. Weiss Ratings, Inc., "Medigap Prices Vary Dramatically Despite Standard Plans," (June 11, 2001). For a free copy, write to Press Releases, Weiss Ratings, Inc., 4176 Burns Road, Palm Beach Gardens, FL 33410, or go to www.weissratings .com/News/Ins_Medigap/20010611medigap.htm.

Chapter 13

1. Senator Charles Grassly (Iowa), Chairman of Special Committee on Aging. In addition, a 1999 GAO study shows that more than one-quarter of nursing homes had deficiencies that "caused actual harm to residents or placed them at risk of death or serious injury."

2. If you have difficulty reaching this Web site, try www.cms.hhs.gov. The Health Care Financing Administration (HCFA) has recently changed its name to the Center for Medicare and Medicaid Services (CMS).

3. Weiss Ratings, Inc., "Long-Term Care Policies Vary Drastically in Cost to Consumers," (April 5, 2000). For a free copy, write to Press Releases, Weiss Ratings, Inc., 4176 Burns Road, Palm Beach Gardens, FL 33410, or go to www .weissratings.com/News/Ins_LTC/20000405ltc.htm.

INDEX

How Many Hidden Enrons Are In YOUR Portfolio? Find out for FREE!

Author Martin D. Weiss warned investors about Enron months in advance, with a "D" rating. Now, hundreds of other large companies get Weiss's "D" rating *or worse*. Find out which ones they are — ABSOLUTELY FREE!

- **THE GENERAL ACCOUNTING OFFICE of the US CONGRESS (GAO)** heralded the fact that "Weiss beat Moody's, Standard & Poors and A.M. Best by a factor of 3 to 1 in forecasting future financial troubles at financial firms ..."

- Investigative journalist **JACK ANDERSON** reports, Weiss' financial ratings are "THREE TIMES MORE ACCURATE" than anyone else's.

- **WORTH MAGAZINE** says, "Weiss' record is so good ... compared with that of his competitors, nervous buyers need look no further."

This $45 Value Is Yours FREE!

Prudent savers and investors normally pay $45 for this valuable and timely list — but we want to give it to you absolutely FREE, as our gift. Make sure that NONE of the stocks in your 401(k) or your stock portfolio are in the companies on this list!

PLEASE SEND NO MONEY:
There's No Obligation, Nothing To Buy!

Just Dial TOLL-FREE 1-800-236-0407 NOW: We'll send you the complete list of all large companies with the worst Weiss Risk Ratings — immediately, via first class mail, or INSTANTLY, via e-mail.

— OR Send Your Request By Mail: Just complete and mail the enclosed postage-paid "FREE LIST REQUEST CARD" to: WEISS RESEARCH, 4176 Burns Road, Palm Beach Gardens, FL 33410 — today!